Driving after Class

CALIFORNIA SERIES IN PUBLIC ANTHROPOLOGY

The California Series in Public Anthropology emphasizes the anthropologist's role as an engaged intellectual. It continues anthropology's commitment to being an ethnographic witness, to describing, in human terms, how life is lived beyond the borders of many readers' experiences. But it also adds a commitment, through ethnography, to reframing the terms of public debate—transforming received, accepted understandings of social issues with new insights, new framings.

Series Editor: Robert Borofsky (Hawaii Pacific University)

Contributing Editors: Philippe Bourgois (University of Pennsylvania), Paul Farmer (Partners In Health), Alex Hinton (Rutgers University), Carolyn Nordstrom (University of Notre Dame), and Nancy Scheper-Hughes (UC Berkeley)

University of California Press Editor: Naomi Schneider

Driving after Class

ANXIOUS TIMES IN AN
AMERICAN SUBURB

Rachel Heiman

UNIVERSITY OF CALIFORNIA PRESS

University of California Press, one of the most distinguished university presses in the United States, enriches lives around the world by advancing scholarship in the humanities, social sciences, and natural sciences. Its activities are supported by the UC Press Foundation and by philanthropic contributions from individuals and institutions. For more information, visit www.ucpress.edu.

University of California Press
Oakland, California

Library of Congress Cataloging-in-Publication Data

Heiman, Rachel, author.
    Driving after class : anxious times in an American suburb / Rachel Heiman.
       pages cm
    Includes bibliographical references.
    ISBN 978-0-520-27774-8 (cloth : alk. paper) — ISBN 978-0-520-27775-5 (pbk. : alk. paper)
       1. Social classes—New Jersey.   2. Suburban life—New Jersey.
    3. Middle class—New Jersey.   4. New Jersey—Social conditions.
    I. Title.
       HN79.N53S6155 2015
       305.5′509749—dc23

                                                            2014023241

Manufactured in the United States of America

23 22 21 20 19 18 17 16 15 14
10 9 8 7 6 5 4 3 2 1

In keeping with a commitment to support environmentally responsible and sustainable printing practices, UC Press has printed this book on Natures Natural, a fiber that contains 30 percent post-consumer waste and meets the minimum requirements of ANSI/NISO Z39.48–1992 (R 1997) (Permanence of Paper).

Contents

Illustrations

TABLE

Preface

As I write this, in the winter of 2014, the United States is still reeling from the economic crash of 2008. The dramatic class inequality brought to the fore—what came to be defined through Occupy Wall Street as the problem of the 1 percent—shows no signs of diminishing. Foreclosures persist at an alarming rate, as luxury-housing markets rebound. Job growth comes in spurts and starts, while CEO compensation once again skyrockets. Banks and corporations enjoy the benefits of bailouts, with students left to shoulder the crushing debt of educational loans. Nightly newscasts about further cuts in basic social services are followed by reports on stock-market highs. Despite fomenting frustration with these conditions across the political spectrum, partisan politics repeatedly brings legislative bodies of the federal government to a standstill, compounding these problems rather than solving them. Where this will lead is still an open question, and climate change and other domestic and global concerns greatly complicate these issues. But one thing is certain: the postwar version of the American dream—the idea that suburban homeownership and its related industries would be able continually to fuel the economy, promote class mobility, and maintain a robust middle class—was dealt a severe blow.

We have spent a lot of time over the last six years looking back at what went wrong, trying to better understand how we found ourselves in a situation where the collapse of a housing bubble was able to catapult the entire economy into a downward spiral. Much of this retrospective analysis has focused, for good reason, on vulnerabilities created through "too big to fail" banking systems, the myriad of new forms of securitization and financialization, new types of speculation and computerization, and government regulations and safety nets that have been chipped away or have failed to keep pace with new market practices, decades of neoliberal policies, and new global players. Less time, however, has been spent grappling with the subjectivities produced during the lead up to the crash, which also are an important part of the story of how we have found ourselves in these conditions and with which we are still contending. Yearnings for upper-middle-class lifestyles continue to this day, as does the presumption that the only way to feel secure as a member of the middle class is to make it into the upper middle class. As we think deeply about how to create a new American dream that will be more sustainable and equitable than the last, it behooves us to take stock of the values, expectations, and longings that became deeply engrained in people's habits, sentiments, and spaces during the suburban American dream's magnified last hurrah in the late 1990s. To imagine a new future, we need to appreciate not just the material structures that have led us down a problematic path but the affective structures as well.

This book offers ethnographic insight into the production of middle-class subjectivities in the late 1990s, a profoundly contradictory time in which the lifestyle being sold was an amplified, McMansionized version of the postwar ideal, even though the structural conditions undergirding middle-class life had been incrementally undermined since the 1970s. It was the critical ascending moment before the crash, the pinnacle of feverish efforts at driving after class. Often remembered for the Internet boom, it was an extraordinarily anxious time for many members of the middle class, including those in the upper middle class. The events of 2008 simply made explicit what many had already been feeling in the late 1990s: that something was amiss. Anxieties during those years fueled classed subjectivities, spaces, and sentiments, and created a new common sense that was normalized in people's everyday lives and that continues to shape current ideas about citizenship and community—what I call in this book "rugged entitlement." In the chapters that follow, we enter the life of a suburban town during those years, feeling people's unease with class changes in their midst; viewing subtle reactions to the increasing dominance of neoliberal logics; and witnessing efforts to produce a feeling of security that often made people (and their neighbors) less secure.

There is an extraordinary amount of mythology in the United States about the generation that came of age during the Great Depression. Endless stories have been told about their scrimping and saving, even during the nation's wealthiest years. Many of us have experienced this for ourselves through our parents, grandparents, or great-grandparents. Their "normal" was produced during an insolvent and impoverished time, and their ways of being did not just go away because the times had changed. The same can be said for those whose ways of being were produced and reproduced in the late 1990s, particularly children and youth who came of age during those years. It is not that people cannot change; they can and often do. But as we continue to tackle the problems facing the country and the world, we will do well to understand the subjectivities produced during a time of *supposed* plenty for all.

Brooklyn, New York
January 2014

Acknowledgments

This book would not have been possible without the welcoming warmth, gracious honesty, and wonderful wit of so many people in the town that I call "Danboro." It is hard not to be able to thank by name each and every person, young and not as young, who were a part of this project (or whose stories are not told here, but who are connected in some way to those who must remain anonymous). You shared with me funny stories and painful moments, joyful events and frustrated aspirations, vivid memories and daily venting. I often forgot that I was doing research as we sat around your dinner tables, hung out in your dens, chitchatted at board of education meetings, or drove around town listening to music and complaining about the traffic. Thanks as well to those who graciously read and shared feedback on an earlier version of the book, or who hired me as a babysitter or to work with youth in the area when I needed to top off my research funds.

While my research for this book took place in New Jersey, the central questions that I sought to answer emerged several years earlier in Zimbabwe. During a college semester abroad through the School for International Training (and on a return visit a few years later), the Mutamukos and Rosemary Gordon became my surrogate families. It was through their everyday lives that I was able to grasp for the first time the global nature of capitalism and the far-reaching effects of American efforts at driving after class. Many years later, when I had the delight of getting to know and to work with the wonderful Cindi Katz, I realized that I had found a kindred spirit in a colleague whose analysis of class anxieties in the United States was also always already viewed through the lens of the everyday lives of children and their families in Africa.

I was extremely fortunate to develop this project at the University of Michigan during a particularly exciting intellectual moment, when new forms of interdisciplinarity were coming into being in classrooms, coffee shops, and cohort parties. I am especially grateful to Larry Hirschfeld for his unwavering commitment to the study of children and youth; to Roger Rouse for his writings—and especially his teachings—on the cultural politics of class; to Bob Fishman for guiding me through the literature on bourgeois utopias and metropolitan messes; to Val Daniel for habituating my habit of thinking about habit and for sharing my cynical optimism about the possibilities for habit-change; to Janet Finn for sharpening my thinking on discourses of adolescence in twentieth-century capitalism; to Ann Stoler for her evocative writings and passionate teachings on liberal strategies of exclusion; and to Frithjof Bergmann for his philosophical musings on what it means to be free (and *not* to be free). Whenever I needed to think through ideas or was looking for someone with whom to be mindless when I no longer wanted to think, I could always count on Adam Becker, Carla Daughtry, Todd Ettelson, Pamila Gupta, Laura Kunreuther, Charles Lord, Carole McGranahan, Janet McIntosh, Ellen Moodie, Brian Mooney, Javier Morillo-Alicea, Esra Özyürek, Penelope Papailias, John Stiles, Karen Strassler, Julie Subrin, and Gina Ulysse.

I gratefully acknowledge generous support from various foundations and institutions. The early years of this project were made possible through a training fellowship from the Spencer Foundation/American Education Research Association; National Science Foundation Graduate Student Training Fellowships through the Program in Culture and Cognition at the University of Michigan; and bountiful support from the Department of Anthropology and the Rackham Graduate School at the University of Michigan. Early revisions of the book began during a magical summer at the School for Advanced Research in Santa Fe, New Mexico, as an Ethel-Jane Westfeldt Bunting Summer Fellow. I am forever indebted to James Brooks for his early and continued support of my work and for nurturing such an extraordinary, collegial environment. My fellow fellows continue to be dear colleagues and friends, particularly Kim Christen and David Kamper. The following year, I had the honor of a Visiting Scholar position at the Russell Sage Foundation in New York, where interlocutors across a range of social science disciplines sharpened my thinking, particularly Katherine Ewing, Raquel Fernandez, José Itzigsohn, Ann Orloff, Chris Rhomberg, and David Thacher. At The New School, my academic home, I thank, in particular, my colleagues in "The City" area of study seminar for introducing me to perspectives on urbanism from a wide range of disciplines; my students in the adult Bachelor's Program for inspiring me to write a book for a broader audience; and the University for the research support to hire my wonderful research assistants, Scott Brown, Brooke Hansson, and Erick Howard, and my amazing illustrator, Brett Silvers. I also thank the Brooklyn Writers Space for being my saving-grace space when I needed a quite place during sabbatical to complete the final revisions.

A few sections in this book have appeared elsewhere. An earlier version of chapter 3 first appeared as "Gate Expectations: Discursive Displacement of the 'Old Middle Class' in an American Suburb" in *The Global Middle Classes: Theorizing through Ethnography*, edited by Rachel Heiman, Carla Freeman, and Mark Liechty (Santa Fe, NM: School for Advanced Research Press, 2012). Parts of chapter 4 appeared in "'At Risk' for Becoming Neoliberal Subjects: Rethinking the 'Normal' Middle-Class Family" in *Childhood, Youth, and Social Work in Transformation*, edited by Lynn M. Nybell, Jeffrey J. Shook, and Janet L. Finn (New York: Columbia University Press, 2001). Parts of chapter 5 appeared in "Vehicles for Rugged Entitlement: Teenagers, Sport-Utility Vehicles, and the Suburban, Upper-Middle Class" in *New Jersey History* (a scholarly journal of the New Jersey Historical Society), vol. 18, nos. 3–4 (2000), pp. 22–33. I thank the publishers for their permission to reprint these publications, and my reviewers, editors, and fellow seminar participants for helping me refine my arguments.

The University of California Press threw their support behind this book shortly after it was minted as a dissertation. I thank Rob Borofsky for his interest in the book for the Series in Public Anthropology, and Setha Low and Sherry Ortner for their invaluable early readings and recommendations. I also thank the anonymous reviewers for the press. Naomi Schneider has been an extraordinarily patient, supportive, and insightful editor. Chris Lura, Elena McAnespie, Ally Power, and Kate Warne skillfully (and swiftly!) shepherded the book through production and marketing. Carl Walesa provided meticulous copy editing, and Margie Towery brought an expert eye to the indexing.

Even though this book is about driving after class, some of the most fruitful conversations that I had while working through the material took place after subway rides to meet my writing group: Ilana Feldman, Pamila Gupta, Mani Limbert, Brian Mooney, and Karen Strassler. The camaraderie of our intellectual exchange and the intensity of our friendships were invaluable anchors throughout the writing process and continue to moor me. Many other colleagues and friends provided instrumental feedback on parts of the manuscript (and in some cases, all of it) or offered invaluable advise (or sympathy) about revising again (and again): Elsa Davidson, Dorothy Duff Brown, Kriszti Fehérváry, Carla Freeman, Dave Herbstman, Cindi Katz, Mark Liechty, Janet McIntosh, Tommy Ort, Gustav Pebbles, Lisa Rubin, Rashmi Sadana, Joe Salvatore, Rachel Sherman, Julie Subrin, Miriam Ticktin, Antina von Schnitzler, Aleksandra Wagner, and June Williamson. A special thanks to Rachel Sherman, whose close reading in the final push proved invaluable; and to Karen Strassler, whose extraordinary editorial skills and unwavering heartfelt support enabled it all come together. To the countless other colleagues and friends who are too many to name who have made their imprint on this book or who enrich my daily life in intangible ways, I cannot thank you enough.

It is hard to know where to begin to thank my family, which goes through so many twists and turns and branches and kinds of people that we have all given up caring about how it is that we are all related. What has always mattered, and what has been particularly poignant for me while finishing this book, is their love and support (and restraint in asking, "When are you going to be done?"). I have come to realize that growing up in my family, particularly as a child sitting quietly in the maelstrom, was my first foray into ethnographic exploration. Or perhaps it is simply what drew me to ethnography in the first place: knowing that it takes years of focused attention to grasp the subtleties and nuances of people and the places that matter to them, but that it is undoubtedly worth the wait.

I dedicate this book to my grandma Esther, who refused to move to New Jersey from Brooklyn, despite the waves of white-flight migration around her that had led people to towns like Danboro. As the matriarch of the family (and a stereotypical New Yorker), she loved to yell out from her seat at every family event—often interrupting whoever was giving a speech—to declare, "None of you would be here if it weren't for me!" She was right. I only wish she was still alive to come to the celebration for this book, and to meet all of my friends and colleagues without whom this book, to echo her words, would not be here if it weren't for them.

1 Introduction: Common Sense in Anxious Times

A paradoxical situation emerged in the late 1990s: the dramatic upscaling of the suburban American dream, even as the possibilities for achieving and maintaining it diminished. This book explores middle-class anxieties and suburban life during those years. It was the "dot.com boom," and the media overflowed with unbridled enthusiasm for the state of the economy, with only sparse attention paid to those who were feeling the downside of its effects, financial or otherwise. And yet, contradictory conditions of middle-class life could be seen everywhere: in suburban towns, as countless new subdivisions of ever-larger homes sprouted up while municipalities struggled to maintain their infrastructure; in people's jobs, as wages increased and stock options proliferated but job security became ever more fleeting; in aspirations for children's futures, as expectations for achievement intensified while public resources for education diminished; on credit-card statements, as credit lines expanded but were matched by new "had to have" consumer items and once-considered luxuries that had somehow become "needs"; in retirement and college funds, as balances grew dramatically on paper but were increasingly vulnerable in a volatile market. A decade later, the economy would head into a tailspin and the media would start to unpack why the middle class had come to be less secure in the late 1990s than at any time since the Great Depression. But during the 1990s, before the extraordinary amount of public discussion about the "squeeze" on the middle class, people's anxieties about transformations under way were largely dismissed amid celebrations of the generous benefits of the booming economy.

In a time before a settled narrative emerges to explain disconcerting changes in people's lives, what becomes of the anxieties produced out of this disorientation? Where do these anxieties play out in the intimacies of everyday life and the intricacies of public debate? How do they intersect with other enduring fears, hopes, and aspirations? What effects do they have on people's subjectivities, their families, and their communities? What might children and youth be learning by coming of age during a time of major class transformation? How will their new habits of everyday life shape the political-economic future and the future (or lack thereof) of a commitment to the social good? Moreover, since ways of being classed change in different historical moments, might we be able to see the friction of old and new ways of being middle class as they rub up against each other?

To explore these questions, I conducted ethnographic research in a suburban New Jersey town in the late 1990s among families who were experiencing firsthand the uneven and shifting structural conditions undergirding middle-class life and who were living in a town that embodies late-twentieth-century changes to the postwar American dream. Danboro (a pseudonym) had been a farming community until the mid-1960s, when suburbanization began with the arrival of white-flight émigrés from the outer boroughs of New York City, particularly Brooklyn. The families who flooded the town in the late 1970s and early 1980s moved to Danboro from working-class and lower-middle-class urban neighborhoods to get their piece of the suburban American dream. They were doing so, however, just as the glory days of middle-class security were coming to a close and "keeping up with the Joneses" was transforming into "keeping up with the Dow Jones."[1] The changing architectural and infrastructural landscape of the town over the years since they first moved in provided a powerful iconic expression of the shift. The houses built in the subdivisions of the 1960s and 1970s were moderately sized (by American standards) colonial-style homes, the size and style of which signified the suburban American dream in the early post-Fordist period.

During the late 1980s, a few developments of larger colonial-style homes were built. But in the late 1990s, the architectural landscape of the town began to change profoundly. Huge homes, which some disdainfully refer to as "McMansions," were built adjacent to older subdivisions. These new houses dwarfed their neighbors and produced jarring juxtapositions. When compounded with increasing concerns about overcrowding and limited public resources—whether in regard to never-ending traffic, over-flowing public schools, or diminishing open space—these architectural shifts provoked anxieties and aroused uncertainties about fiscal and discursive boundaries of inclusion and exclusion in the imagined future of the town and of the middle class itself. Like gentrification in urban areas, changes in the grandeur of suburban housing reflect a transformation of the class makeup of a town and reveal shifts in the larger class structure and the structuring of people's social locations.

To understand the manifestation of class anxieties in the intimate spaces and quotidian moments of family life and the ways they shape public discourse and municipal governance, I moved to the Danboro area in the fall of 1997. Drawing on the tools of ethnography, my research mined the habits, practices, and sentiments of everyday life for insights into the cultural politics of class in the late 1990s. Over the course of two years, I conducted participant observation and interviews in sites of public and private life, including people's homes, their town hall, and even their sport-utility vehicles. I spent time with several families and worked as an "ethnographic babysitter" to have particularly focused time in the every-day life of one family. The ethnographic sites, spaces, and situations in which I spent my days and nights included family dinners and gatherings, shopping trips to the mall and the local strip malls, workouts at the gym where stay-at-home moms gathered after kids went to school, drives around town and through neighboring areas, TV-watching parties and Nintendo-playing hangouts, after-school activities, pre-prom parties, and a host of other ordinary aspects of suburban life.[2] I also spent many evenings at public meetings in the town and the school district of which Danboro High School is a part, including those of the zoning board of adjustment, town council, planning board, and board of education.[3]

During my research I found that even as middle-class stability continued to be undermined by neoliberal policies, people's sense of entitlement to the privileges and accoutrements of the middle classes was nevertheless amplified. Anxieties emerging from these conditions played out in a nervous and somewhat aggressive struggle for the appearance and feeling of class security, rather than coalitional efforts to address structural conditions threatening middle-class life. Each chapter of the book depicts how people were trying to create for themselves "a little security in an insecure world," to borrow a tag line from a Chevy Blazer advertisement during the late 1990s. Hence I use the phrase *rugged entitlement* to capture this structure of feeling, which I witnessed in the town. The central argument of the book is that rugged entitlement—a product of neoliberalism and its limited commitment to the public good—participated in furthering conditions that intensified middle-class anxieties in the first place. This ironic state of affairs—whereby habits, practices, and purchases that temporarily appease class insecurities end up making people feel and be less secure—is what the book vividly illustrates.

Each chapter draws attention to a variety of vehicles that paved the way for the development of the sensibility of rugged entitlement. As families struggled to reorient themselves to the changing material conditions undergirding middle-class life, the ways that they were doing so produced the kinds of class-encoded habits, desires, and practices that entrench neoliberal logics: hyperconsumption and overspending that benefit corporate capital; spatial strategies that further segregation along race, class, and age lines; and privatized solutions that divert a politics of demand on the state. The economics and cultural politics of rugged entitlement, however, ended up steering many Danboro children, youth, and parents into ambivalence about the structuring and texture of their everyday lives: it is exhausting work to be strategically and persistently driving after class. But more often than not, unable to imagine the possibility of crafting another way of life, most curbed these unsettling doubts and resolutely fueled up for the ride.

A ROBUST U.S. MIDDLE CLASS: NO LONGER NEEDED AND NECESSARY?

Being middle class is inherently unsettling. As Barbara Ehrenreich has noted, "Whether the middle class looks down towards the realm of the less, or up towards the realm of more, there is the fear, always, of falling."[4] Yet in different historical moments, middle-class security can vary significantly, depending not only on the global economy and the United States' dominance within it, but also on how the state uses its power to manage and regulate capital accumulation among the bourgeoisie, or capitalist class. To put it crudely, the late 1990s was a time when the U.S. bourgeoisie no longer needed the U.S. middle class to the same extent that it had before, not unlike its decreased dependence on the U.S. working class. To better appreciate the circumstances of those years, I offer here a brief (and thus necessarily simplified) historical sketch of key moments in the development and decline of the U.S. middle class. It is a story not only of the rise and fall of the bourgeoisie's need for U.S. middle-class workers, consumers, and citizens, but also of a state that has, more often than not, aligned with bourgeois interests.

There has been a middle class in the United States since the late colonial period, whose members ranged from small producers, artisans, farmers, and shopkeepers to doctors, lawyers, clergy, and teachers to small-scale wholesalers, importers, managers, and salesmen. These "middling sorts"[5] were doing significant work for the capitalist system, but their numbers were relatively small, as was their political strength. It was not until the Progressive Era that the fortification of the middle class took place through the growth of the professional managerial sector.[6] The great expansion of production under late-nineteenth-century and early-twentieth-century monopoly capital required not only more workers for factories, more consumers for goods, and new forms of expertise in industrial engineering, but also experts to manage (and create) the "new" American worker, consumer, and citizen. The expanding workforce was heavily composed of new immigrants in a time of growing labor unrest and escalating anxieties about the possibility of socialist revolution. The role of the "middlemen" (i.e., those who not only made production more efficient but could produce hegemonic formations to contain unrest, such as Henry Ford's educators who "Americanized" his workers) became crucial, and so a portion of surplus capital went to fund the growth not only of the sciences, but also of the social sciences and social-engineering reform projects. The crucial need for these forms of expertise enabled the middle class to benefit and to grow. Yet they toiled on terms set by the bourgeoisie, and since they did not own the means of production, they were not *of* capital, and many "possessed a class outlook which was distinct from, *and often antagonistic to,* that of the capitalist class."[7] At the same time, the nature of the work of the middle class—particularly those who were psychologists, social workers, and other "helping" professionals and reform experts—placed them in an often directly antagonistic and paternalistic relationship with the working class. This small but growing middle-class workforce thus emerged in an unstable and uncomfortable position of being in-between.[8] Anxieties about securing a place for themselves fueled the expansion of this type of work, over time providing more solid ground for the class itself.

The post–World War II period was the next key moment in which the middle class proved essential for resolving the conflicts and contradictions of capital accumulation.[9] The Great Depression had tempered economic growth (and the growth of the middle class), but its unmatched severity gave rise to new forms of regulation and state-sponsored entitlements. The New Deal, combined with the wartime economy and the donation of federally funded wartime inventions and manufacturing processes to private companies, set the stage for the postwar period to be extremely lucrative for the U.S. bourgeoisie. Yet the postwar period also was an extremely anxious time. As veterans returned from war, a housing and employment crisis ensued, and ideological contention over the threat of communism escalated. It was a do-or-die moment for the future of American capitalism. The solution was a form of redistribution known as Keynesianism, enacted most notably through government funding, backing, and infrastructural support of expanded educational and small-business opportunities and mass home ownership in the form of suburban housing.[10] Financed and administered through a variety of bills (e.g., G.I. Bill, Federal Highway Act, National Defense Education Act) and agencies (e.g., Veterans Administration, Federal Housing Administration, Home Owners' Loan Corporation), these efforts sparked spectacular job growth in related industries, including "white collar" work to manage the production and circulation of commodities created through new manufacturing capabilities, ranging from cars to real estate to home goods. In turn, a vast new consumer demand for those goods was created out of the new "needs" of those workers, as they became home owners and car drivers. Yet there was a segregationist logic written into the building of the suburbs in the postwar period through the federal government's recommendation that federally backed housing loans not be granted for neighborhoods or towns with people of color. As declared in the Federal Housing Administration's *Underwriting Manual*, "If a neighborhood is to retain stability, it is necessary that properties shall continue to be occupied by the same social and racial classes."[11] So while the wealth created in the immediate postwar period was brought within reach of a newly flourishing middle class, enabled the class to grow, created new routes of class mobility through giving more Americans a piece of the pie, and tempered another moment of potential political-economic unrest, it also ripened the conditions for the civil rights and feminist movements to follow.

Equally as significant as the material achievements of Keynesianism was the ideological entrenchment of equating being in the middle class with success and with being American.[12] By the 1950s, a good portion of white (and soon-to-be white) Americans had begun to view themselves as members of the middle class. They earned decent wages, owned homes with yards, bought the latest consumer goods, drove around in cars, sent their kids off to college, and saw their lives reflected in the mass culture of the time. Middle-class suburban life came to represent what it meant to be an American. This new version of the American dream took hold, no longer a rags-to-riches story but rather class mobility that hinged on the accoutrements of the postwar middle-class ideal. It was an ideological realization of the Keynesian dream of a "revolutionary American capitalism"[13] that would get rid of economic inequality through eliminating the working class and replacing capitalists with middle-class managers. Even though that material reality was not realized, and the policies and cultural politics undergirding suburban growth directly undermined cities and attempts by people of color to acquire asset wealth through home ownership,[14] the myth that "everyone is middle class" was one its lasting legacies, as those who "made it" started to feel secure in their class positioning.

This moment of security was, however, relatively short-lived. With the onset of broad-scale, global political-economic restructuring in the 1960s, the growth and stability of the post–World War II period proved unsustainable.[15] The global dominance of the United States began to diminish as Germany, Japan, and Italy entered as key competitors in the capitalist market and as protests arose from those being exploited within the United

States and around the world. With the financial and energy crisis of 1973–1974, the capitalist system as a whole was affected.[16] Over the decades to follow, new economic theories and policies emerged to co-opt the economic situation in favor of the U.S. bourgeoisie—what now is often referred to as neoliberalism.[17] Through shifting transnational coalitional efforts, or what Gramsci refers to as "ruling blocs,"[18] the global market was expanded through new forms of speculation and privatization of various state-controlled industries and segments of the public sphere. Labor costs were reduced through offshoring and outsourcing, the increased use of subcontracting and other forms of flexible labor, and the augmented exploitation of migrant, minority, and female labor in the growing service sector. Consumption was amped up through an expanded ethos of consumerism and fine-tuned gradations of distinction matched by new means of acquiring expanded credit. These techniques of optimization were supported by new approaches to government, including applying business models to governance and reducing entitlements and safety nets for individual households while increasing support (military, security, or otherwise) for non-redistributive corporate economic growth. In short, it was a move away from the postwar liberal ideal of economic growth and government spending for the public good and the good of American capitalism and toward the neoliberal ideal of lean government that proved to be for the good of a small elite, with the rest largely left to fend for themselves.

While these efforts enabled renewed accumulation of capital among the bourgeoisie, their "faithful middlemen" did not fare quite as well, nor did the possibility for mobility into the middle class. These conditions—part of the backstory of the economic crisis to follow—placed the burdens of everyday life increasingly on the backs of individual families and local communities, amplifying the class, race, and gender inequalities produced in the postwar period. The wealth created during the economic booms of the 1980s and 1990s was acquired and distributed unequally. Some members of the middle class experienced downward mobility whereas others became more affluent. Towns like Danboro witnessed a considerable expansion of the gap separating the middle and upper middle classes (i.e., those who could afford only the moderately sized homes versus those who could afford any home in the town). In the 2000 U.S. Census, 12 percent of town residents earned more than twice the median household income in the town, with 14 percent earning over 50 percent more than the median.[19] As Sherry Ortner pointed out at the time, "The top and the bottom of the middle class began pulling away from one another . . . the upper middle class has done better and better, while the lower middle class has been slipping down into more and more difficult straits."[20]

During the 1980s, Barbara Ehrenreich wrote about sentiments that emerged among the professional middle class in the decades since its dramatic growth and affluence in the postwar period—an anxious mix of self-interest and self-loathing fueled by a "fear of falling."[21] Anthropologist Katherine Newman honed in on the immediate aftermath of the economic downturn of the 1980s, revealing how downwardly mobile members of the managerial middle class maintained their faith in meritocratic individualism, even as changing economic conditions threatened their ability to remain in their jobs, their homes, and their hometowns. Rather than feel frustration at "the system," they blamed themselves.[22] In a subsequent study in the early 1990s set in a northern New Jersey town, Newman found intense resentment among the younger members of the (white) baby boom generation, many of whom could not afford the comfortable middle-class lifestyle in which they had grown up.[23] Their frustration and anger were often directed at "illegitimate elites" (wealthy families of Asian descent) and the "parasitic underclass" (recipients of welfare), rather than at the government for no longer offering the same scale of public entitlements that enabled their parents to attain a secure middle-class positioning. Newman underscores, importantly—as I do throughout this book—that the inability to attain that which some people had always taken for granted is a product of large-scale political-economic shifts. Regardless of how people made sense of their situation, they were experiencing something that was not a "momentary glitch."[24]

This book picks up where Newman's story leaves off and joins other ethnographic efforts that explore what occurred during the late 1990s as the "widening abyss"[25] in the shrinking middle class continued to grow, though from the perspective of the less often discussed "other" boomers who did not grow up in middle-class suburbs. (The parents in Danboro whom you will meet in this book largely grew up in working-class and lower-middle-class urban neighborhoods in a city that was spiraling downward *because* of policies benefiting the suburbs. It was in part through entering into careers such as teaching, accounting, sales, law, medicine, and administration that they made their way into middle-class suburban life.) Like those in Newman's field sites, the anxious middle class in Danboro maintained frustration at themselves and at racialized and class-encoded others. But I also observed a powerful presence of anxiety and concern about people who were often ethnically similar to most long-time residents, but who were (presumed to be) higher in the hierarchy of the middle classes.

What was happening in Danboro appears to parallel some of what we see in the growing anthropological literature on the middle classes around the world, where tensions between the "old middle class" and "new middle class" are quite prevalent in many locations including India, China, Egypt, and Hungary.[26] Even though each site has dramatically different class histories, what runs through them all is that "old" and "new" refer not just to what type of work people do (e.g., civil servants versus entrepreneurs), but to people's sensibilities in regard to the state, the proper relationship between public and private, and strategies for seeking security. Class relations are produced within particular historical moments with their associated economic, cultural, political, and moral logics.[27] In the United States in the late 1990s, these tensions were a product of the shift from postwar liberal to post-1970s neoliberal political economies, class formations, and subjects.

THE RESIDUAL AND THE DOMINANT: THE POSTWAR LIBERAL SUBURB IN NEOLIBERAL TIMES

To capture the nuances of class change, we need to think *through* particular localities, for, as geographer Doreen Massey notes, "the articulation of social relations necessarily [has] a spatial form in their interactions with one another."[28] Yet as we think historically and spatially about capitalism's instantiation in novel forms, it is crucial to avoid the tendency to view a time period through the lens of its characterization, such as "the neoliberal moment." When we do, we fail to appreciate the historical variability of any moment in time and run the risk of focusing predominantly on what is "new," failing to keep in view sites and strategies that appear to come from—or only be relevant in regard to—a previous historical moment.[29] As Raymond Williams has noted, "The complexity of a culture is to be found not only in its variable processes and their social definitions—traditions, institutions, and formations—but also in the dynamic interrelations, at every point in the process, of *historically* varied and variable elements."[30]

Danboro is a particularly compelling site for exploring the "dynamic interrelations" of "historically varied and variable elements" in the United States in the late 1990s. It is a town that people moved to out of faith in the liberal promise of postwar suburbia: home ownership in a town with public schools, municipal recreation facilities, citizen-run school boards, open lawns, and no gates. Yet like most places in the neoliberal era, Danboro has seen significant changes, including increased focus on luxury markets and the interests of corporate capital, blurring of lines between public and private services and governance, and growing precarity of the professional managerial jobs held by many Danboro residents.[31] As such, it is a fruitful site for thinking about "frictions"[32] within the middle class, as residual postwar ideals confront newly dominant sensibilities associated with neoliberalism, with the "residual" (the subject of chapter 2) understood as that which "has been effectively formed in the past, but is still active in the cultural process . . . as an effective element of the present."[33]

As you drive through Danboro, some of the residual postwar elements are hard to miss. One afternoon early into my fieldwork, I toured a friend of mine—a historian from Indonesia—around town. We drove past streets of moderately sized colonial-style homes with two-car garages and fresh-cut lawns. We wound our way through housing developments differentiated from each other by coordinated street names. (Beech Drive and Cedar Way are in the "tree-names section" of the Danboro Heights subdivision; Plato Road and Homer Drive intersect in the "ancient-Greeks section" of Oak Views.) We stopped by the Danboro Municipal Complex, which includes Danboro's town hall, the Danboro Free Library, the Danboro Recreation Center, the Danboro Public Schools administrative offices, the Danboro Middle School, a vast array of well-kept soccer fields, and a host of other municipal buildings and recreation facilities. As we rode, we glimpsed (mostly white[34]) kids playing games in cul-de-sacs; strip malls that function as surrogate town centers; randomly distributed elementary schools, churches, and synagogues; and a few remaining farms and country roads reminiscent of Danboro's past as a farming community. The entire time, we drove along open roads with signs that welcome rather than with gates that exclude. At one point my friend looked over at me and exclaimed, "Whoever declared the end of suburbia has never been to Danboro!"

At first glance, Danboro does bear a striking resemblance to iconic post-war-style suburbia.[35] Its suburban development, after all, began at the tail end of the postwar period. But Danboro is also located on what was the border of the "crabgrass frontier"[36] in the late 1990s in central New Jersey, one of the fastest-growing regions in the state. If we move through Danboro with a critical geography lens tuned to signs of political-economic shifts, we can see that much has changed since the 1970s. The transformations were most vividly evident in Danboro's physical appearances. Original Levitt-built subdivisions were being dwarfed by newly built developments that some have called "luxurious Levittowns."[37] Houses in perfectly good condition were being knocked down to make room for larger, more upscale homes that awkwardly protruded in size among the originals. It seemed as if everywhere you looked, there were bulldozers clearing land that used to be farms, with signs around town directing potential buyers to the new "luxury" subdivisions under construction.

Less obvious, at least from a drive around town, were the effects of this unfettered optimization of land, particularly by development corporations allowed to maximize their profits at the expense of the municipal tax base and the wallets of local citizens. With each new subdivision of houses built, new families moved into town, adding children to school facilities that were already overcrowded and driving cars on main roads that were buckling under the weight of overdevelopment. Temporary trailers had to be added to some of the elementary schools to house overflow students, and a heated and racially charged redistricting battle was under way to address overcrowding in the high school district of which Danboro High School was a part (the subject of chapter 6). Route 2, the multilane highway that runs through Danboro and is the primary route to New York City and to most of the local malls and strip malls, was so crowded during rush hours and on weekends that everyone had their own alternative routes to avoid the frustrating traffic. With no pressure on development corporations from local or state government to provide funds to municipal coffers to address the increased infrastructural demands, the tab was picked up largely through higher property taxes, a common occurrence in New Jersey with its long history of home rule. While some after-the-fact state help addressed school needs, it did not come through requiring corporations to pay their fair share, but rather through direct funds from an already overburdened state. This, too, was the approach to alleviating congestion, although towns and regions were forced to compete for limited state funds in a dynamic that Neil Brenner calls "competitive regionalism."[38] Christine Todd Whitman, then the governor of New Jersey, supported various "open space" initiatives to curb sprawl through retaining some of New Jersey's undeveloped land. The county in which Danboro is located was fortunate to have received a "Smart Growth Planning Grant" in early 2000 to address the congestion problems along the Route 2 corridor—one of only twenty-one grants awarded throughout the state.

While the state was picking up the tab for corporate capital instead of reining it in, there also was a notable turn toward running the state "like a business,"[39] including subcontracting and privatizing some of its core functions. This blending of public governance and private enterprise manifested itself in practices such as hiring a consulting firm to manage the arduous high school redistricting process, and, on a far grander scale, closing a state psychiatric hospital located on the edge of town. In the late 1990s, the hospital was shut down along with other state-run facilities throughout New Jersey. Some patients were moved to other state hospitals, though most were sent to mental-health group homes run by nonprofit organizations (with nonunion labor) or to live on their own with a stipend and assistance in the hopes that they would learn to "self-govern"[40] their illnesses. At the same time, a nonprofit organization tried to open one of these group homes in a nearby housing development. The homeowners in the subdivision in which it was to be located fought to keep it from being built. Town officials, meanwhile, floated the idea of attracting a Fortune 500 company to the hospital land. Corporate campuses are a boon for municipal coffers; unlike housing developments, they bring in tax dollars without adding kids to the school budget.

Locally owned establishments also experienced a change of hands, in some cases via large corporations caught up in boom-time "proclamations of shareholder value."[41] Body Fitness was the most popular gym in Danboro when I began my research. It was located in a huge building with an enormous parking lot on Route 2. You couldn't miss it as you drove past. It was one of four Body Fitness gyms in the area. During my field-work, an international corporation with over a hundred gyms along the eastern seaboard and in Europe bought it out as part of a broader effort to break into the New Jersey market in advance of an IPO.[42] Like other developments hailed for their "flexibility" in the new economy, the buyout of Body Fitness did enable residents who commuted to New York City to have the option of working out at home or in the city near their office and provided the gym's employees with greater possibility for advancement. But these benefits came at an expense—literally, for those who decided to join the gym after the sale, and bureaucratically in terms of the increased hassles when the owner was no longer the guy playing basketball on Saturday mornings on the court in the back of the gym.

Gyms like Body Fitness also were part of the increasing meeting point of the privatization of public life and the growth of the service sector. This convergence made its appearance most vividly on refrigerators in homes of families with elementary school–age children, where party invitations were displayed. The "playgrounds" or "neighborhood parks" in which birthday parties were often held were located in privately owned commer-cial, full-service entertainment establishments for kids. For their teenage counterparts, where concerns about enhancing public school education loomed large, particularly as the time for college applications approached, there was a notable uptick in private tutoring and test-preparation classes.

Neoliberalism's refiguring of space and place has been on the agenda of scholars for some time now.[43] Most ethnographic research on sites of the middle class in the United States until the 2007 housing crash focused on what was new or had been exacerbated. Those studying the urban core generated a wealth of excellent work on gentrification and public–private partnerships.[44] Scholars writing about the suburbs focused largely either on communities that were architecturally new, such as New Urbanism developments, or on those that became pervasive, like gated communi-ties.[45] Towns like Danboro were relatively absent from ethnographic stud-ies exploring the cultural logics of political-economic changes in the United States.[46] This is likely because they appear at first glance to embody resid-

ual postwar middle-class ideals: open lawns, public schools, municipal recreation facilities, and town-hall politics. Yet turning our attention to communities like Danboro offers a fruitful context in which to understand how
"the familiar" came to matter differently under neoliberal conditions.

As my research in this town reveals, there is distinct resonance between
what I explore and what scholars of gated communities refer to as the
mounting penchant for "forting up."[47] Danboro may not have gated communities, which are viewed as architectural evidence of the growing "fortress mentality"[48] in the United States. In fact, an explosive zoning board
debate erupted (the subject of chapter 3) when a couple requested permission to build for their new home a six-foot-high ornamental security gate,
which would have been the first of its kind in the town. But as each chapter of this book brings to life, non-architectural mechanisms of "gating"
were also at work. They are extraordinarily powerful and operate in subtle
ways, through the everyday production of habits, desires, and sentiments;
the racialized, gendered, and class-encoded organization of space; and the
discursive and linguistic policing of borders and boundaries by means of
humor, rumor, heckling, and coded language. Although perhaps not as
glaring as gates of steel, these strategies of exclusion and inclusion—
whether through wearing high-end sports gear that neighboring towns
cannot afford (as we see in chapter 4) or driving around town in sport-
utility vehicles that place other drivers at increased risk (as we see in chapter 5) or pushing back against the idea of a regional district in which all
children, regardless of class or race, might have to be rezoned (as we see in
chapter 6)—vigorously structure the spatial relations and social milieu of
a community.

THE ETHNOGRAPHY OF COMMON SENSE
IN TIMES OF CHANGE

To think through the ways that class anxieties play out in everyday life,
how they shape people, practices, and spaces, and what new subjectivities
and spaces emerge as the dominant rubs up against the residual, we need
particular analytical frameworks to direct our ethnographic approaches
and modes of analysis. My ways of seeing, hearing, and analyzing the

middle classes in the late 1990s have been heavily influenced by theories that appreciate the dynamic workings of capitalism and class—particularly the interplay of political-economic changes and the intimacies of everyday life. Capitalist systems are always in flux. Apparent stabilities are only temporary, for there are always unresolved contradictions in the means and relations of production. When moments of crisis emerge, new regimes of accumulation are developed (i.e., new economic approaches to amassing capital); new modes of regulation come into effect (i.e., new forms of governance and politics); and new subjectivities come into being (i.e., new habits, desires, and sentiments). These practices, policies, and ways of being are (or have the potential to be) regulative—that is, adaptive to and productive of the economic, political, and social order.[49]

This emphasis on the dynamic and unstable nature of capitalist systems, which are constantly shifting and producing new tensions in everyday life, points us to look ethnographically at the ways that people are continually trying to reorient themselves amid novel conditions. They are faced with a host of contexts and conditions, including the spaces in which they live and through which they move, their position as consumers and citizens, and their location in relations of production, circulation, and reproduction (i.e., their job, be it out of the home or in the home, including childrearing). Out of these circumstances, which are infused with a range of (often contradictory) ideological discourses and disciplinary practices, emerge their subjectivities.[50] It is the way that these subjectivities are classed and how they matter (in turn, shaping practices, spaces, and others) that is the focus of this book. These ways of being and becoming are not just reflections of a particular political-economic moment; they are also an intimate part of continually shaping that moment and the moments to come.[51]

Neoliberalism was becoming the new common sense in the late 1990s. I use "common sense" here as Gramsci does, not to be confused with "good sense," but rather the uncritical, unconscious way of perceiving that is deeply ingrained and is part of how we act and feel without thinking. It is something that we experience as an "instinct" but that is in fact an "elementary historical acquisition."[52] It is the fusion of class ideologies with long-standing philosophies, religious beliefs, and other moral logics and ethical practices. Moments in time have a dominant common sense, as neoliberalism was becoming in the late 1990s, but Gramsci underscored that it is never a clear or unified common sense; it is messy, fragmented, contradictory—always intermingling with the residual, both in society and in people's "heads," with people typically having a contradictory consciousness. In other words, we often act differently from what we believe, believe differently than we act, and can suggest one belief implicitly through our behaviors yet articulate our ideology in a very different way.[53]

Common sense emerges out of what Bourdieu calls "habitus," by which he meant the dispositions that we acquire as we grow up within certain material and social conditions. It is what feels "natural" to us, what we often benignly consider to be a "life-style," but which is produced out of "the material conditions of existence characteristic of a class condition."[54] It is the meeting point of "macro" structures and "micro" qualities of everyday life; it is where material conditions and their associated ideologies and normative discourses become our selves in the most intimate and public ways: the things we desire, the words we use, who we want to hang out with, how we feel as we move through space, what makes us anxious. Habitus are, in Bourdieu's (admittedly elaborate) words, "systems of durable, transposable *dispositions,* structured structures predisposed to function as structuring structures, that is, as principles of the generation and structuring of practices and representations which can be objectively 'regulated' and 'regular' ... without being the product of the orchestrating action of a conductor."[55] They *happen* through what Peirce refers to as the "continuity of reactions"[56] in our everyday lives. This is not to say that there are no "conductors" that shape our habitus. In towns like Danboro, those who promoted Keynesianism, designed and redesigned suburban spaces, lobbied for automobility, wrote mortgage lending rules that led to highly segregated living, came up with neoliberal theories, and developed other technologies that shape people's lives continue to be influential. Yet this history is largely "forgotten" as its effects become mundane, part of our affective, embodied, and epistemological habits, no longer obviously shaping who we are. As Bourdieu remarks, the dialectic between conditions and our habitus "transforms the distribution of capital, the balance-sheet of a power relation, into a system of perceived differences ... whose objective truth is misrecognized."[57]

Despite being "misrecognized," this "balance-sheet" is very much "on view" in our habitus, making habitus useful objects of analysis for thinking about class. There are many aspects to classed subjectivities, but my focus in this book is the subtle, nonconscious habits of body and mind rather than identities or people's conscious sense of class. I never asked people directly about class. Rather, I conducted an ethnography of how class is lived, how classed subjects and spaces are made, and how class is expressed and talked about indirectly, often asking the Foucauldian question, "What was being said in what was said?"[58] This includes not only what was verbalized, but also what was revealed in people's "ordinary affects,"[59] the "unconscious patterning"[60] in their everyday lives, and the "sentimental education"[61] in their midst. As Janet Finn points out, terms such as *capitalism* and *class* may not be used in the daily lives of those with whom we spend time during our fieldwork, which was very much the case in Danboro before the 2008 crash. However, our role as ethnographers is to "think about how their stories might encode language and practices of class . . . that [mean] something to social actors as well as to cultural scholars."[62]

The "structuring structures" that compose habitus not only enable us to locate class in the intimacies of everyday life; they also provide a temporal window onto changes in class structures, class formations, and people's class positionings.[63] The ethnographic moments unpacked in this book thus reveal the tense presence of old and new, whether in regard to infrastructures, habits of affect, governmental practices, parenting desires, or space making. We see not only what is generated as the dominant rubs up against the residual, but also how the familiar comes to matter differently in a new political-economic moment with new stakes. As my analysis demonstrates, the seemingly well-known—efforts to keep new carpeting clean, concerns about hiring the right kind of babysitter, the desire to feel safe behind the wheel—have an amplified intensity and a rearticulated quality that facilitate new *effects*. There is an ever-shifting dialectic: changing historical conditions produce anxieties that shape sentiments and practices that shape spaces and policies that in turn shape other people's subjectivities that in turn shape other spaces, sentiments, practices, and policies, and so on.

Thinking about class dynamically and historically, while doing an ethnography of a contemporary moment, requires that we always be thinking about what *work* habits, desires, and sentiments might be doing, not just locally and directly, but also in regard to influencing the capitalist system. In the back of my mind was always a speculative curiosity: which aspects of people's everyday lives would prove to have lasting effects on the political economy—whether as entrenchers of the dominant common sense or as "agentive moments"[64] that shift its direction—and which were just fleeting products of a historical moment? This is, of course, a tricky task. As Alain Lipietz remarks, "It is a human practice that makes history, but not all practices are transforming."[65] I thus offer this book as an ethnographic story that "seeks to grasp the hegemonic in its active and formative but also its transformational processes."[66]

RUGGED ENTITLEMENT: A NEOLIBERAL COMMON SENSE

C. Wright Mills's classic 1951 book, *White Collar*, described the new middle-class worker in the postwar period. Mills's concern as a sociologist and public intellectual was the increasing bureaucratization of work at corporations, universities, and sites of other professions in the United States, particularly the undermining of dissent, critique, and other forms of citizenship required for genuine democracy. Mills argued that to imagine a different future we needed to understand not only the political economy of a time, but also its psychology. Just as Mills examined the dominant sensibility of his time (notably remarking that white-collar life was becoming "more typically 'American' than the frontier character probably ever was"[67]), this book focuses on the dominant common sense that emerged among the middle classes in the late 1990s. What I am calling "rugged entitlement" is an ironic descendant of that myth of rugged individualism—a contradictory offspring of decreasing state entitlements and an amplified sense of entitlement to the privileges and accoutrements of the middle class. It emerged among those who were invested in (and felt entitled to) the postwar version of middle-class suburban life, and who struggled to make that dream a reality for themselves and their children as it was becoming increasing fragile—with an anxious sense that they must vigilantly pursue their own interests to maintain and further their class position.

Rugged entitlement may best be described as a "structure of feeling." Raymond Williams describes a structure of feeling as "a particular quality of social experience and relationship, historically distinct from other particular qualities, which gives the sense of a generation or period."[68] This "change of presence," Williams explains, does not have to have a "definition, classification, or rationalization before [it] exert[s] palpable pressures and set[s] effective limits on experience and action."[69] As Williams points out, new structures of feeling not only emerge with the rise of a new class; they also result from "contradiction, fracture, or mutation *within* a class."[70] The growing chasm within the shrinking middle class, combined with emerging neoliberal sensibilities and a sense of entitlement to an upscaled postwar American dream, is what created the conditions of possibility for the emergence of rugged entitlement in towns like Danboro. At the time it was, as Williams would describe it, "a kind of feeling and thinking which is indeed social and material, but [exists] . . . in an embryonic phase before it can become fully articulate and defined."[71]

Rugged entitlement captures some aspects of what it means to be a "neoliberal subject"—shorthand for the type of person produced during this political-economic formation. There is not *one* neoliberal subject; there are particularly located neoliberal subjects. In the United States, new subjectivities reveal a contemporary working out of the long-standing tension between the founding ideals of liberalism (a government that protects life, liberty, and property, with property and the market considered the ideal sites for cultivating human potential) and republicanism (a polity of independent citizens, considered equal regardless of their rank, with the polity itself as the ideal site for cultivation).[72] This ever-present tension lies at the heart of the constant contention over the role of the state in liberal democracies.[73] In the United States the protean nature of liberal democracy is evidenced in its history, with different time periods revealing different takes on whether the individual citizen (or groups of citizens) is the main concern of the state, or whether it is property owners or the owners of capital. As Jeffrey Lustig has remarked, since the dawn of the modern corporation, the scales have tipped in favor of "corporate liberalism."[74]

My choice of phrase—*rugged entitlement*—is a play on the myth of rugged individualism. As historian Stephanie Coontz points out, the figure of the "rugged individualist" (and its close counterpart, the "self-sufficient family") are fundamental American ideals of self-reliance and enterprise, despite the fact that "depending on support beyond the family has been the *rule* rather than the *exception* in American history."[75] The early American West is a case in point: frontier individuals and families undoubtedly worked very hard, but they would not have existed and survived had the government not relocated and killed scores of Native Americans, passed on cultivated Indian land to colonial settlers far below cost, and provided robust military protection and public subsidies, among other things. Individuals, families, and local businesses were able to stay afloat only because of a combination of federal support and local mutual-aid societies, churches, associations, and other close-knit communities of "obligation, debt, and dependence."[76] There was no such thing as a rugged "individual." In fact, as Coontz emphasizes, anti-government sentiments in the Old West emerged not in reaction to government intervention but rather out of disgruntlement when the government did *not* provide certain funds or aid; in the realm of land, for example, the government provided far more support to railroad and logging companies than it did to settlers and small enterprise.

The phrase (and myth of) rugged individualism, however, was not created during the frontier days but rather during the boom years of the 1920s, when the professional-managerial class was fortifying itself. During those years, great trepidation about socialist revolutions sweeping across Europe led not only to the need for professional-managerial workers to hegemonically create "class harmony," but also to a renewed celebration of the so-called American spirit. In tacit opposition to the socialist model, this dominant ideology was articulated most notably in Herbert Hoover's 1922 address titled "American Individualism," in which he stated his faith in a "social Force" that is "far higher" and "springs from something infinitely more enduring; it springs from the *one* source of human progress—that each individual shall be given the chance and stimulation for development of the best with which he has been endowed in heart and mind; it is the sole source of progress; it is American individualism."[77] The phrase for this ideological claim transformed over the years from *American individualism* into *rugged individualism*, ultimately invoking the mythic history of the rugged pioneer in its celebration of individual effort and initiative.

Yet, as historian Charles Beard passionately argued in his 1931 polemic, *The Myth of Rugged American Individualism*, the federal government's efforts in the early years of the Great Depression, as in all decades past,

were largely in service of stimulating big business and helping the bourgeoisie. It was not the socialists, he facetiously clarified, who pushed the
U.S. government into the business of railways, waterways, roadways,
farming, aviation, commerce, and various forms of trade; rather, it was
bankers and businessmen, both small and large, including farmers. As
Beard pointed out, the same businessmen who incessantly lobbied government for their own ends were also the biggest proponents of the idea
of rugged individualism. "From day to day," Beard remarked, "it becomes
increasingly evident that some of our economic leaders (by no means all of
them) are using the phrase as an excuse for avoiding responsibility. . . . If
a smoke screen big enough can be laid on the land, our commercial pres-
tidigitators may work wonders—for themselves."[78]

The "smoke screen" of rugged individualism masks not only the reality
exposed starkly in the Depression: that capitalism works best with state support and regulation, and that the government had long been undergirding
corporate growth. But as the history of middle-class growth in the United
States demonstrates, the state's role in capitalist regulation also involves
supporting particular groups of individuals. Decades after the growth of the
middle class in the postwar period, the smoke screen had come to include
the myth of the "self-sufficient" white suburban family who pulled themselves out of the working class and into their new homes through sheer hard
work. Yet like the frontier family, that hard work was matched by an equal
amount of hard work on the part of the state, and on the part of industries
receiving heavy support from the state. Despite massive middle-class entitlements, benefits, and tax breaks, a discourse emerged in the late 1970s and
1980s on the "welfare queen," suggesting that it was only the racialized poor
who received state support, "ignoring the historical dependence of pioneer
and suburban families on public support."[79] As Katherine Newman
remarked in her ethnography of a New Jersey suburb in the 1980s, "What
was an achievement to be proud of for [their parents'] generation became
an expectation, a norm, an entitlement in [the baby boom] generation."[80]
This was the case not just for those who grew up in the suburbs, but also for
those, like many in Danboro, who longed for that dream ideal. My term thus
calls the "American spirit" what it really is: rugged entitlement.

"Rugged entitlement" in the late 1990s was a response to growing trepidation and conflict within the middle class, as the liberal-democracy pen-

dulum swung back more toward corporate welfare by the state. Those on the downwardly mobile side were angst-ridden about the growing insecurity of a class position that they had spent their lives trying to achieve or maintain. The lucky ones experiencing the benefits of the booming-economy moment often felt a sense of vertigo as they continued to amass wealth. The stock prices in their portfolios were moving upward, just like the height of their new sport-utility vehicles. But the farther one is from the ground, the more anxious and dizzying the view from above. Add to this people's collapsing confidence in public services and safety nets ranging from public education to Social Security. And sprinkle in the fact that those who transformed Danboro into a suburban community twenty years after the postwar boom, unlike an earlier generation of suburban pioneers, bought their piece of the American dream with less help from government-sponsored housing programs, and were confronting a changing landscape in their town that reflected the chasm in the middle class. You have the perfect ingredients for a new kind of wary entitlement.

Small wonder that many people in Danboro, as you will see, indulged in a bit of pastoral nostalgia (often for farms that were being transformed into housing developments) and were increasingly adopting a kind of "rugged" persona, including driving SUVs. It was as if they felt that they had better be tough and strong and drive their stakes in. People's anxieties frequently played out in regard to objects of display and often manifested in struggles over borders and boundaries. Many of these efforts revealed means of seeking security that do not necessarily make you more secure— an affective structure resonant with what Lauren Berlant has termed "cruel optimism"[81]—or that secure your own "community"[82] at the expense of neighbors. Whatever form rugged entitlement took, it helped mask the reality that Charles Beard wrote against almost seventy years before: the state is often more focused on the concerns of corporate capital than on the everyday lives of its citizens.

FROM ZIMBABWE TO NEW JERSEY

Although my research for this book took place in New Jersey, the central questions I sought to answer emerged several years earlier in Zimbabwe.

I had been studying anthropology and critical pedagogy in college, and I decided to spend a semester abroad in Zimbabwe during the spring of 1991. Zimbabwe's independence was still quite new, and intense public discussions were under way on the nation's progress and regress in the decade since independence in 1980. With Zimbabwe's nation-state formation occurring at the dawn of a transformative decade in the workings of global capitalism, its post-settler state concerns about capital, labor, and land were infused with the pressures of new International Monetary Fund policies. My time in Zimbabwe thus proved to be a crash course in the paradoxical situation facing many nations in the Global South during those years: a strong commitment to the reform of problematic colonial legacies while at the same time increasing pressure to embark on economic structural adjustment. For many, efforts to open up the nation to foreign investment looked like economic imperialism, or colonialism in new clothes.

I continued to be compelled by this tension when I began my graduate studies in anthropology, particularly debates over how much "colonial" there might still be in the postcolonial subject. I spent my first two years developing a dissertation project to explore what it was like, particularly for upwardly mobile Zimbabwean youth, to come of age during a time of great debate about the ideal national subject. I wondered: how was this tension playing out in their everyday lives? And how might I ethnographically view quotidian moments of subject formation? I made plans to go back to Zimbabwe during the summer of 1995 to do preliminary research in an Anglican boarding school attended by one of the children from my semester-abroad homestay family. The school was part of what enabled her parents to transition from humble village childhoods to modest urban lower-middle-class adult lives.

When I got off the plane in Harare that summer, I had my first encounter with changing economic conditions from structural adjustment when I exchanged money. During my semester abroad, the value of the U.S. dollar in relation to the Zimbabwe dollar was one to three. In just over four years, it had become one to eight. Granted, the hyperinflation and humanitarian crisis to hit Zimbabwe in the years to follow makes the devaluation in 1995 pale in comparison. But at the time, it was a striking object lesson in concerns that had been raised in 1991 when the nation first started to feel the effects of structural adjustment. The next day, I came across a literal sign of those anticipated changes: "Deloitte & Touche," the name of a prominent multinational accounting-services firm, emblazoned across the top of an office building.

These changes were the topic of conversation the following Sunday with a young man who was a cousin of my homestay family. We were at the family's weekly post-church gathering, and he was venting frustration over rising unemployment and the depressed standard of living. He balked at those who had faith in structural adjustment and who had believed that the booming tourism and economic growth in Zimbabwe in 1991 would eventually come to benefit the majority of Zimbabweans. He then asked a poignant question: Why did Americans feel the need to "suck up the world's wealth" and claim that free-trade agreements would benefit everyone, when clearly they were in the best interest of Americans? He asked a good question. I at first (albeit somewhat defensively) remarked that not all Americans agreed with the practices of U.S. corporations and politicians. And yet, I acknowledged, most Americans do not think about the global effects of their everyday ways of being.

When I left Zimbabwe that summer, this conversation weighed heavily on my mind. On the one hand, the United States was indeed sucking up a lot of the world's wealth, and had been for quite some time. Yet the economic power of the United States was diminishing, and its bourgeoisie was anxiously scrambling to retool how it did business, including attempts to create new markets in places like Zimbabwe. But these efforts—what are often referred to under the rubric of "globalization" or "liberalization"— also involved the implementation of new policies and practices within the United States, leading to growing inequality and diminishing economic mobility in the United States as well, albeit on a different scale. It was clear in the fine print that amid the emerging Internet boom in the United States, the rich were becoming filthy rich, the poor were getting poorer, and many people previously positioned in the middle class were experiencing downward mobility or witnessing a growing expanse separating the middle and the upper middle classes. So while free-trade agreements and other political-economic policies were indeed in the interests of some Americans, there was an increasingly smaller number who were benefitting, and an alarmingly larger number being left behind.

My experiences in Zimbabwe and my studies in graduate school helped me realize that the economic theories behind structural adjustment in places like Zimbabwe came from the same roots as those propelling change in the United States, though in distinct ways. While it is now common in academic circles to refer to these logics under the rubric of *neoliberalism*, at the time a host of terms were used to encapsulate that moment in capitalism: *global, postmodern, post-industrial, post-Fordist, transnational, advanced liberal,* or simply *the new economy.* I always was drawn to the phrase *late capitalism,* because it encompassed the expectation of a crash.[83] An extensive body of literature had emerged on how the changing global economic order was affecting the poor and the working class, both abroad and in the United States.[84] There also was a growing research focus on the new global elite (i.e., those most benefitting from neoliberal policies, including free trade).[85] Yet less well studied was how the U.S. bourgeoisie's "faithful middlemen" were faring as middle-class security eroded.

What would it mean to bring the U.S. middle classes into global class theorizing? What might be the best approach in a place like the United States with a long history of discomfort with talking explicitly and realistically about class? How might studying "at home" answer my Zimbabwean friend's haunting question about Americans' sense of entitlement to their disproportionate share of the world's wealth? How might the anxious "longing to secure"[86] that characterizes the middle class play a role in shaping conditions that affect the present and future not only of people in Zimbabwe and the working class and poor worldwide, but also of the middle classes themselves?

When I decided to switch my research to the United States, I realized that the site for my new project was right in front of my eyes. I had been working for years with youth as a counselor and then as a group leader at a sleepaway summer camp in upstate New York. Each summer over the course of nine years (1989–97) I had several campers who were from Danboro.[87] Through the stories they told, the people they described, the moments they celebrated, and the frustrations they vented, I was consistently struck by the competitive intensity that permeated their depictions of life in Danboro, particularly when it came to objects of class display and the policing of social boundaries. As more and more kids from Danboro started attending the camp over the years, "Danboro" turned into a sign. When uttered, it indexed a sense of entitlement. I did know a few kids from Danboro whose privilege and sense of entitlement were a pervasive part of their "common sense," so naturalized that they were not aware of how present it was. Yet all of the campers from Danboro whom I got to know quite well over the years belied such simple castings. I knew their hurts and their hopes, their humor and their warmth, as well as how they struggled with what it meant to be from Danboro. Being relatively privileged within the middle class, of course, does not mean that one does not experience pain or loss, nor that one cannot be sympathetic and generous. But at the same time, I was curious about how this penchant for class display and social gatekeeping was formed and what effects it might have on Danboro's youth and on the larger society in which they would live their lives.

From what I knew about Danboro youth, I was interested in how their parents' trajectories were a part of this story, playing a role in organizing the spaces through which their children moved; fueling the normative discourses that their children encountered; and thereby setting the conditions of possibility for their children's habitus. I had come to know many of their parents over the years. Most were from Brooklyn and had moved out of the city to suburban Danboro in the late 1970s and early 1980s to raise their children in a house with a lawn (rather than in cramped Brooklyn apartments) and to be in Danboro schools (as opposed to the struggling ones in their old urban neighborhoods). I got a sense from them of their awe over what their children had. They often joked about how they were "spoiling" their kids, which—they freely admitted—was exactly what they wanted for them: to have all the things they never had while growing up in working-class and lower-middle-class families. But I also knew that it was not easy for many parents to sustain their lifestyle, or to keep up with the increasing escalation of the suburban American dream that surrounded them in their town. There was often a hint of anxiousness as they spoke about the new things that they wanted, and the old things they took for granted like public schools and job security. In what ways did it matter that they got their piece of the American dream just as it was becoming harder to attain and maintain amid the rise of neoliberal approaches to governance and social welfare? How do parents' anxieties and insecurities (which get projected and passed on to their children) fuel the regulation of naturalized class values and dispositions? This is, of course, a local story, specific to the articulation of the global economic system in a particular New Jersey suburb at the tail end of "white flight." Yet I would argue that by looking closer at a town like Danboro, we can not only understand how a transitional moment played out locally, but also gain a better understanding of its global effects.

"AT RISK" FOR ENTRENCHING RUGGED ENTITLEMENT

The Columbine massacre, in which two high school seniors went on an hourlong school-shooting spree before committing suicide, occurred almost a year and a half into my fieldwork. During casual conversations with many parents during the media-blitz aftermath of the incident, I often was asked to draw upon my knowledge of youth. People wanted to hear psychological theories about alienation and rage, popular-culture readings of the Goth scene, media studies on the effects of violent video games and Internet access, or anthropological understandings of peer culture. I had enough knowledge to comment peripherally on these issues, yet I always felt uncomfortable during these discussions. These were not the kinds of issues consuming my thoughts during the time I was spending in their town and in their daily lives. How could I justify dedicating several years of my life trying to figure out what makes white, middle- to upper-middle-class suburban teenagers (and their parents) "at risk" for entrenching rugged entitlement when people were trying to figure out which boy in their town might be "at risk" for going on a shooting rampage? I felt this uneasiness at other times when local crises arose, such as when a teenager ended up in the hospital after a heroin overdose or another from a suicide attempt, or when a girl had extreme anorexia or a boy had severe fits of anger during his parents' messy divorce. During all of these moments, I couldn't help but worry that my work on the development of classed subjectivities and spaces might seem frivolous in light of more tangible and pressing problems.

These incidents were exceptional moments. But there were many other instances throughout my fieldwork that raised more mundane concerns that nevertheless were significant to people and also were not the focus of my work. One afternoon, for example, I was at the home of the Degen family (a pseudonym, as are all names throughout the book) to get official permission to be in my study, for which they had all agreed. Before they signed the permission forms, I reiterated that my research involved exploring what it was like to grow up during the boom economy in a town like Danboro. As Diane, seventeen-year-old Erika's mother, grabbed a pen to sign the forms, she patted Erika on the head, began to laugh, and teased that she looked forward to hearing more about "kids who grow up in good homes and amount to nothing!" Ken, Erika's father, was laughing at Diane's joke as he went to sign, but then he became more serious as he asked, "Why don't kids read anymore? If the book wasn't made into a movie, Erika doesn't know the story." It was then Erika's turn to sign, and she did so in awkward silence as her mother told me that she hoped I would be able to explain "why these kids still smoke cigarettes with all that we know about what it does to you." She understood why they sometimes smoked "the other stuff." "That's fun," she acknowledged, "but smoking cigarettes is just plain dumb." Needless to say, Erika began to squirm, particularly as her mother looked her straight in the eye and suggested that maybe they should go on a field trip to the cancer ward.

The questions that I explore in this book address concerns about youth that are rarely identified as "problems," big or small. I am not looking at the dysfunctional or even the slight dysfunctions among the functional. Rather, I am exploring how the functional function and how that way of being functional is produced, is a reflection of class shifts, and participates in regulating the capitalist system in increasingly neoliberal ways. I always had a hard time explaining what I meant by this when describing my work to families like the Degens, and why I relied on the Bourdieu-like wording in the previous sentence. I knew that there was a powerful connection between what I was studying and a variety of stressful aspects of their lives, even if the questions I pursued were not those that consumed them.

I came to see that one way to view the connection was to politically invert our use of "at risk" categories. "At risk" categories often reveal more about the problems of our society than the problems of the youth so categorized.[88] When there are so many young people growing up in communities with limited resources and discriminatory practices, are they "at risk," or is our society putting them at risk? Are they a threat to a healthy social order, or is it the lack of equity in regard to standard-of-living jobs, quality and affordable education and health care, and possibilities for mobility?[89] If the larger problem is the normative social order, what would it mean to transform "at risk" categories and focus on youth who represent supposed success stories, who are becoming "good" neoliberal subjects, and thus (if unwittingly) participating in exacerbating class and racial inequalities? Might that very "success" be the threat to a healthy social order?

The youth that you will meet in this book are all developing in line with the social order. When my fieldwork was over, they were heading off to college and were en route to achieving their own successes. In towns like Danboro, a determined drive to secure one's own place would—for the most part—be seen as evidence of a child's ability to make it in the world. No media, school, or state would worry, and no parents would seek to find the best treatment, the finest therapists, and the right medication.[90] And yet, as I argue, their seemingly harmless—even admirable—habits, desires, and practices put "at risk" the possibility that a new, more equitable social order might come into being. In not challenging the structural conditions that created financial pressures and related stressors in their lives, they, along with their parents, were digging themselves in deeper and limiting the possibility for imagining a society that would benefit all classes, races, and ages, including their own.

I say "their own" because middle-class youth no longer necessarily benefit from the social order, as class security becomes a privilege of the privileged few. More and more members of the middle class are experiencing downward mobility, and not coincidently, middle-class youth are being increasingly labeled "at risk," albeit in different ways than those suggested above.[91] These concerns are capitalized upon by industries ranging from pharmaceutical companies to mental-health providers.[92] White middle-class youth escape some of the more extreme effects of this discourse.[93] But they, too, are increasingly considered "at risk," particularly when they are believed not to be doing their part in regulating the capitalist order of things; or when they are not becoming the type of subject who can handle the volatility of the new global economic order; or when there is simply no longer a place for them in it. The explosion of medications for and categories of attention deficit disorder, depression, and anxiety is a case in point.[94]

It is therefore not only for the good of the less privileged classes to scrutinize the development of habits, desires, and sentiments among "relatively privileged"[95] youth on track to success. It also is in their own interest, I would argue. Yet I do not focus exclusively on the experiences of youth in this book.[96] Their worlds cannot be understood without equal attention to the larger context of tensions in their town, intimate moments in their homes, normative discourses in their midst, their parents' class trajectories, and the state of the political economy. The existing system gets naturalized, taken for granted, and regulated in their everyday lives, despite moments of ambivalence, questioning, and doubt.

THE PREDICAMENT OF BLAME IN A LIBERAL DEMOCRACY

I end this introduction with a caveat on the predicament of using people's lives as "evidence" in a story about the state of liberal democracy in the United States. The form of "critique" in which I engage in this book should not be confused with "criticism" in which individual *people* are considered "bad" or "wrong." Rather, it is, as Foucault has described it, a "historical analysis of the *limits* that are imposed on us."[97] Because of those limits, we tend to become what the common sense of our historical moment leads us to be. Yet the public discourse in the United States—profoundly shaped by the tenets of liberal ideology, which emphasizes personal responsibility over structural constraints—leads us to err on the side of locating blame in people rather than on the limited conditions of possibility in which they are continually becoming.[98] This has become even more pronounced amid the neoliberal ideological touting of self-governance.

The challenge of critiquing without criticizing plagued me while conducting fieldwork.[99] When having casual dinners at people's houses, driving around town with them to visit their friends or to run an errand, or doing one-on-one interviews that often broached topics that were quite personal and intimate in nature, I constantly worried about the prospect of a misreading of my book as a condemnation of the people of Danboro. I knew that everyone would remain anonymous in the text through my use of pseudonyms and altered identifying details. But it still made me uncomfortable to turn their lives into a text for public discussion. I agonized over the possibility that those whose stories I tell—all warm and welcoming people—might be judged or blamed for their ways of being and for their small part in the entrenchment of neoliberalism, when my ultimate goal was to understand the limits of what people (and the world) were becoming in a pivotal historical moment.[100]

I realized that I had to either abandon the project or figure out how to try to write the book in a way that highlights this reminder from Marx, which Gramsci underscored: people tend to take on the common sense of their time, more often than not. The people in this book, like all people regardless of their class positioning, are just trying to live their lives within the limits of what is possible, or at least what seems possible. It makes sense that rugged entitlement was pervasive in a town like Danboro during the late 1990s, as the postwar American dream was further chipped away through a wave of sentiment in the nation against government-sponsored entitlements and policies for individual people and local communities (as opposed to corporate entities). Rather than blame *people* for participating in the emergence and exaggeration of this structure of feeling, our efforts are best served by trying to figure out how to switch its direction in the many sites in which it still endures. This book is an attempt to explore a bit of what we are up against.

2 Being Post-Brooklyn

It was a miserably hot afternoon during the summer of 1997, just before I was about to begin my fieldwork in Danboro. I was walking along a tree-covered dirt path on visiting day at the summer camp, holding a cold water bottle to my forehead to find relief from the oppressive heat. When I emerged from the path, I spotted a crowd of parents from Danboro under the shade of a nearby tree. Their contagious laughter filled the air, as did the flurry of their hands, which alternated between animating their conversation and wiping beads of sweat from their brows. They waved me over with welcoming smiles on their faces, subduing their heat-exhaustion giggles long enough to warn me that they all were a bit delirious from the heat. Steve, the father of one of my campers, introduced me to a couple whom I had never met before. They also were from Danboro, but their children were in younger age groups in the camp. Steve explained to them that I was working on my Ph.D., and that when the summer was over I would be doing research in Danboro. They all laughed in a startled kind of way, suggesting surprise that their town might provide anything fruitful for someone looking at it through a scrutinous lens. One of the fathers then humorously asked, "Are you studying Post-Brooklyn Stress Disorder?" We all laughed at his joke, for it is well known that a good portion of the people who live in Danboro were born and raised and even had their first child in Brooklyn before moving out of the city to Danboro when it was time for child number two.

It may have been a heat-induced occasion for the display of wit when this man joked about "Post-Brooklyn Stress Disorder." However, jokes often reveal "the inadequacy of the [available] categories of thought for expressing the nature of [one's] existence."[1] This man's humorous articulation of the ontological struggles facing many residents of Danboro speaks to the fact that there has been little sustained effort to tease apart the multifaceted nature of people's way of being in communities such as this one. The flow of migration over the Verrazano Bridge and the Outerbridge Crossing may not seem as significant as the changes that most residents' forebearers experienced when they crossed the Atlantic from Minsk or Naples.[2] Nevertheless, the move from the urban to the suburban brought on a profound rearticulation of the class aspirations, racial anxieties, and spatial orientations that had been a part of their everyday lives in Brooklyn. Despite the fact that it had been over fifteen to twenty years since many of the families in this book moved out to Danboro,[3] habits and dispositions that were formed in Brooklyn were continually shaping their community and infusing much of what people found stressful and (dis)ordering in their lives. Brooklyn—particularly all that was supposedly left behind *and* all that was hoped for through the migration itself—was always already very much a part of everyday life in the town.

In order to understand how structural transformations entailed in neoliberalism are being filtered and responded to, we need to appreciate the specificity of place, and as such, the local habitus and the historical production of it. For this town and this particular account of tensions over the shift to neoliberalism, the habitus was shaped by the experience of Brooklyn and the move away from it. Danboro residents are not just suburban American, but ethnic white, post-urban suburban American. The majority of residents in Danboro on whom I focused in my study got their piece of the American dream via a move from a city disinvested in during the postwar liberal era to a suburb on the brink of experiencing the changes of the neoliberal era.

This chapter provides an introduction to a few of the families I spent time with during my research and provides a first glimpse of significant widespread sentiments and sensibilities in Danboro. Through formal interviews, sidebar conversations, and the random moments that make up so much of ethnographic fieldwork, each section portrays different aspects of post-Brooklynness and conveys the trepidations, frustrations, and longings that were a part of so many people's lives. Although the decision to move out of Brooklyn for most of these families was motivated by a mix of urban fears, racial anxieties, pastoral yearnings, and class desires for attaining a piece of the suburban American dream, you will see that the ideal life that so many people fantasized about eluded them—if not right away, then in the years after they moved into Danboro. By the time of my research, worries about overcrowded schools, unbearable traffic, diminishing open space, and racial encroachments were making many people wonder if much of what was so appealing about Danboro was disappearing and if some of what was intentionally left behind in Brooklyn was creeping back into their lives.

In addition to these concerns—or rather, intensified by them—were the excessive levels to which some people in town were taking their cravings for success and security (financial and otherwise). Undue emphasis on appearances and extraordinary pressure to participate in the pervasive aesthetics of class display were leading to new regimes of visibility and generating intense anxieties about the future. Given the silent presence of the material transformation of the middle class during those years, along with the visible changing landscape of the town, it was no surprise that most remaining glimmers of hope that utopian dreams would one day be realized in Danboro were transformed into foreboding visions of an ominous future and nostalgic longings for old Brooklyn neighborhoods and the early years of Danboro.

THE RESIDUAL URBAN

The Danboro residents who had moved into the moderately sized homes in the 1970s and early 1980s described to me their feelings of awe upon moving in their mid to late twenties into their new homes, which at the time they considered to be enormous. They had grown up in modest apartments and two-family homes in working-class and lower-middle-class urban neighborhoods and spent their childhoods playing on stoops and sidewalks and in neighborhood parks. Their everyday lives resembled little of the version of white middle-class suburban life that permeated popular culture in the post–World War II period. During their childhoods, when many of their white baby boom generation peers moved to the suburbs, their less affluent families moved to the edges of Brooklyn, part of the white-flight migration within the city. They spent their early adult years in the neighborhoods in which they had grown up, but by the time they were ready to raise their own children in the late 1970s, New York City had spiraled into a fiscal and racial crisis fueled by "urban renewal"[4] policies of slum clearance and redlining that compounded, racialized, and spatialized the effects of industrial decline. Despite having adored their urban childhoods, the desire to attain a piece of the suburban American dream prompted them to take a financial leap and leave the city behind. They struggled to make that dream a reality for themselves and their children, and they were doing so at the start of the post-Fordist period and the rise of neoliberal approaches to social welfare.

This book picks up where many stories in Brooklyn from the 1970s leave off, like those portrayed in Jonathan Rieder's *Canarsie: The Jews and Italians of Brooklyn against Liberalism*. Rieder's ethnographic account illustrates the beliefs, actions, and sentiments of working-class and lower-middle-class Italians and Jews in the Brooklyn neighborhood of Canarsie during the 1970s. Many people in Canarsie had moved there from other neighborhoods in Brooklyn and were "watching white Brooklyn shrink down to a thin sliver along its south shore."[5] When a proposal was made to bus African-American children to Canarsie schools from one of the neighborhoods that many residents of Canarsie had fled, an "antibusing insurgency" occurred, which included a white boycott of the schools; rocks being thrown at school buses; and marchers raising banners that read, "Canarsie Schools for Canarsie Children." Rieder's story focuses on those who stayed and defended their turf. But many residents in that "thin sliver" along the south shore of Brooklyn (e.g., Bensonhurst, Sheepshead Bay, lower Flatbush, Canarsie) left the city and moved to suburbs like Danboro.[6]

This wave of crabgrass pioneers, like so many before them, were following their desire for the American dream, the dark side of which implies that good schools, nice homes, and peaceful neighborhoods depend on the *absence* of the lower classes and particularly of people of color. Yet little ethnographic work has explored the articulation of urban-renewal logics with the experience of moving to suburbia from a city that was undermined by that rationality. While some might question the value of exploring the implications of white flight long after its heyday, this "post-urban"[7] sensibility continues to be a powerful force structuring the everyday lives of people and their community. Their histories as white ethnics who fled a "darkening" Brooklyn inextricably color the racial politics through which they maneuver class relations. Moreover, their class shift "up," which "sealed" their whiteness, coincided with their migration to the suburbs—the last piece of attaining the American dream.[8]

Those migrating from Brooklyn to Danboro during the late 1970s and early 1980s were largely people of Jewish, Italian, and, to a lesser extent, Irish descent. Because of my focus on families who moved to Danboro at the dawn of the neoliberal era, the families whom you will meet in this book are largely from these groups.[9] I do not, however, mark the ethnicity of specific individuals. Their geographic move was a racial shift into whiteness that eclipsed some aspects of the earlier divide between Jews and Italians. Differences, of course, still remain, and ethnicity does matter in people's lives. But my hope in foregrounding post-Brooklynness is to underscore an aspect of the geographic and historic particularity of people's lives that is less studied yet is critical to understanding the development of classed subjectivities in this town.[10]

The people in Danboro have a profound (and proud) sense of being from Brooklyn. There is great nostalgia—not for the "old country," but for Brooklyn (i.e., the "old" Brooklyn before its decline and subsequent gentrification). A deli in one of the original strip malls in town has a series of old pictures in its front window: one of Ebbets Field, another of the Brooklyn Bridge, and two from the turn of the last century when Brooklyn's streets were filled with horse-drawn carriages. Brooklyn, like faith in the postwar suburban liberal ideal, is part of the residual in this town, the "experiences, meanings, and values which cannot be expressed . . . in terms of the dominant culture, [but] are nevertheless lived and practiced on the basis of the residue . . . of some previous social and cultural institution or formation."[11] The fact that Danboro is a "post-Brooklyn" community, therefore, does not mean that the "post" is of the "past"; rather, that which is "post" continues to be lived, practiced, and engaged in the present, with children as a prime engine through which the "post" remains "present." As Raymond Williams underscores, while "a residual cultural element is usually at some distance from the effective dominant culture, . . . some version of it . . . will in most cases have to be incorporated if the effective dominant culture is to make sense in these areas."[12] As this book reveals, the newly dominant neoliberal sensibilities of the late 1990s rearticulated class anxieties, which were infused with and exacerbated by the racial fears and ambivalences of white flight. This dynamic played a role in firing up the conditions of possibility for the development and entrenchment of rugged entitlement.

An investigation of the residual, however, is often tricky, for its active manifestations (e.g., race and class anxieties, spatial longings, and liberal tendencies) tend to pose a threat to the dominant social order (e.g., neoliberal tendencies and upscaling of the American dream) in one way or another. Consequently, they are often diluted or reinterpreted or incorporated through some form of inclusion or exclusion.[13] An inquiry into the residual thus requires the kind of "collateral experience"[14] that goes beyond "thick description."[15] It demands a historicized understanding of the present that is attuned to the local habitus. This chapter offers an introduction to the filter through which so much is experienced, understood, seen, felt, and heard in Danboro. It is the context for making sense of the subtext at work in a wide range of ethnographic moments that I explore in the book as a whole, since much of my analysis is a discourse analysis in the Foucauldian sense, which is to say that it is not solely about what is said explicitly, but also about what Foucault so gracefully describes as "what was being said in what was said."[16]

The poignancy of the man's quip about Post-Brooklyn Stress Disorder thus serves as an apt starting point for this chapter's ethnographic exploration of Danboro's Brooklyn "diaspora" community. The considerable presence of humor in Danboro attests to the fact that many people felt overwhelmed by the forces shaping their lives, particularly those that appeared beyond their control. Throughout the book, as in this chapter, there is much laughter and giggling that is often coupled with pauses and silences. They were part of a larger continuous effort (albeit largely not a conscious one) to mask (and at times, reveal) anxieties about class positioning and whiteness that were hidden behind facades of confidence in people's everyday lives. They speak quite powerfully to the discomfort, embarrassment, and anxiety that parents and youth in town feel about many things in their lives, particularly when confessing that which they considered politically incorrect or likely to seem unbelievable or weird.[17] This was often the case when their admission let on that their ostensibly ideal life in Danboro—a town whose address is quite coveted and is an object of class display in itself—was not all that it was imagined or assumed to be, highlighting the intimate relationship between laughter and acknowledgment of the residual.

"THAT'S WHY GOD CREATED NEW JERSEY"

One night I was talking with Stu, who worked as a sales representative. I had spent a lot of time with his seventeen-year-old daughter, Lauren, during my fieldwork, and I had come to know the family quite well. We were sitting on a black wrap-around leather couch in their den, and beside us was a mantel full of pictures of Lauren and her older sister, Katie. There were snapshots from schools and proms, on soccer fields and at family affairs. Stu was telling me about the reasons that he and his wife, Linda, decided to leave Brooklyn in the late 1970s, when Katie was a newborn. They had been living in an apartment in Sheepshead Bay, part of that "thin sliver" along the south shore of Brooklyn. There were constant problems with their apartment and with the owner of their building. Stu joked that the decisive moment came when Linda saw a roach in the apartment. But the more we talked, he allowed their array of fears, desires, and concerns to come to light: "You know . . . I had enough money to buy a house. . . . [I] was tired of playing ball in a schoolyard. . . . I wanted some grass. . . . We weren't thrilled, you know, with the city, with the potential of having [Katie] go to a city school."

As Stu continued discussing those years, he acknowledged that they also left because of how their neighborhood was changing. When he was around nine or ten years old, his family moved to Sheepshead Bay from one of the "darkening" neighborhoods in northern Brooklyn. Linda's family had done the same around that time. "I am not going to say that I am bigoted," he remarked with an adamant look, after which he chuckled and admitted with a sheepish smile that his kids sometimes call him Archie Bunker. He continued, "I just . . . I saw how our neighborhood changed. . . . Russians moved in . . . blacks moved in. You found that there were, um . . ." He paused for a moment, and said that when he was a kid, he and his friends used to take the subway on their own to Yankee Stadium. By the time Katie was born, he never would have let his kids do the same. "I would be afraid," he admitted. Sure, when he was a kid, there were always "people that you [would] hang out with [and] other people that you would not hang out with." But during the years around when Katie was born, Stu underscored, "there started to be a lot more people that you wouldn't hang out with." It was not so much that Sheepshead Bay was "turf land." But still, you knew "where you would go. That area started getting smaller." The neighborhood was still "okay," but regardless, they decided they were leaving: "I think we just got to the point one day where we said, 'Let's get out of here.'" Stu offered a bit of his quick-witted brand of irreverent humor as he proclaimed, "That's why God created New Jersey!" In a self-mocking tone, he confessed that he and Linda were declaring to themselves, "Let's go to the suburbs! Let's breathe fresh air!" Scoffing at what now felt naive to him, he added, "You know, that typical bullshit stuff."

While Stu tends to mock the way his life's trajectory has been bound up in the standard narratives associated with the American dream, his wife, Linda, can still muster the sense of awe and wonder with which she first encountered the Danboro area. While sitting in their formal living room one afternoon so that we could have some privacy, since no one in their family ever really hung out in there (the couches were a bit too firm, and there was no TV), Linda told me about a summer when she was teenager. One of her older cousins, who had three kids, had asked her if she wanted to be her mother's helper. Her cousin at that time was living a few miles from Danboro. Linda described the rural nature of the Danboro area during those years with a sense of amazement in her voice, as she remarked that her cousin was "like a pioneer!" Linda and I both giggled when she uttered this phrase, during which Linda paused her laughter long enough to emphasize that it *really was* like being a pioneer, for most of the area was still farms.[18] As she continued, she leaned toward me and emphasized: "This was *1967*."

Figure 1. Levitt development home, built in the late 1960s.

The year 1967 has come to signify a time in the United States when white suburban baby boomers danced in the streets of San Francisco and lashed out against consumer capitalism, while their black urban counterparts rose up in city streets to protest disinvestment in their neighborhoods. But for many working-class and lower-middle-class teenagers like Linda, who did not grow up in the iconic suburbs and who found the unrest in their cities unsettling, viewing a still-largely rural place slated as the next suburban frontier was their version of a mind-expanding trip. Linda had never seen the kind of life that her cousin was living. (See figure 1 for the type of house being built during those years.) "I was brought up in an apartment in Brooklyn and [that] is what I was used to," she explained. When she came home to Brooklyn after that summer, she was effusive when she described the place to her mother: "This was like heaven. There was land. There was grass. There were trees. We went to a swim club." Linda brought me back in time with her as she embodied her teen-age sense of wonder, underscoring that it was simply "unbelievable."

Linda had often shared stories with Stu about those weeks with her cousin, gushing the first time she told Stu, "There's this place in Jersey. It's

Figure 2. Moderately sized colonial-style home, built in the late 1970s.

beautiful!" When Linda and Stu decided to look for a house in 1977, not surprisingly, the first place they came to was where she had spent that summer. During their house-hunting trips, Stu also fell in love with the area, and he really loved Five Oaks, the first housing development that they saw and one of only three subdivisions in Danboro at the time. "He loved the land and the houses," Linda explained. They were the biggest houses in Danboro at the time, and they had basements. (See figure 2.) Every time they saw those homes, Stu's astonishment (which he does not acknowledge much anymore without sarcasm) came through in stunned expressions of "Oh my God." But Linda kept telling him with a disappointed yet practical cadence in her voice, "We can't do it. There's just no way." The houses in Five Oaks were above their budget. Even getting a house in the more affordable development in which Linda and Stu ended up buying was a financial risk, but they "went for it." People back in Brooklyn told them, "My God! You're crazy!. . . . What are you getting into?" For nights, Linda didn't sleep. "[Katie] was only a year old . . . . We knew nobody here. Nobody." Her cousin was no longer living in the area.

The first people that Linda and Stu met when they moved into their new house were their next-door neighbors. Their neighbors had not learned about the Danboro area through family; they just knew what had become commonplace wisdom in Brooklyn at the time: if you wanted to buy a house in the suburbs, you should look in New Jersey—and *not* on Long Island. Long Island was considered too congested, and this area of New Jersey was more affordable and had lower property taxes and a faster commute into the city than comparable towns on Long Island. "So," as Linda portrayed it, "they went over the bridge[s] and they came to Jersey and this was the place they liked." For people like Linda and Stu's neighbors, who wanted what Linda described as *"real* country," Danboro was what they fantasized about while sitting on their stoops in Brooklyn. "They liked the idea that it was so barren, that it was so quiet. . . . And they loved the open air." They had moved to Danboro in 1969, when the subdivision was first being built. "I mean, they told me that when they moved in there were still cows on my property." With amazement in her voice, Linda added, "They were still grazing!" Linda then encapsulated what people were craving during those years: "Most of the people here are from Brooklyn, Queens. They're, you know, people that wanted to escape."

The fantasy of living the pastoral life has been a key element in shaping understandings of the "city" and the "country."[19] It has long been a part of the lure of the sub-urban, particularly for those who long for nature or who feel overrun, overwhelmed, or trapped in some way by the conditions of the city. Yet the yearning to be amid the pastoral is often more about the fact that it is not the city and is accessible to nature, rather than a desire for the full realities of the rural.[20] As most people in Danboro remarked, they like the idea of driving past farms, getting their fruit from a nearby orchard, and seeing tractors and other symbols of rugged existence. But at the end of the day, they want to come home to their own little piece of (unproductive) land with a modern home, preferably one with a basement and a nice-sized backyard. And they want certain amenities. When I asked Linda about what was available to them when they first moved to Danboro in the late 1970s, she had a sense of revulsion in her voice and her body shuddered in disgust as she described the options at the time: "I used to do my food shopping down at [the neighboring town of] Milldale. . . . There was no, um, I mean, it was horrible. A&P was . . . up here, but it was like this fleabag, disgusting store and that was it. . . . [A] little shopping center . . . was here, but I don't even remember what was [in it]. . . . The nearest mall was [about forty minutes away] . . . and it was like one store."

The abundance of amenities was not the only aspect of urban life that post-urban residents of Danboro were sad to leave behind. They also missed walking. Danboro, like most American suburbs built in the post-war period, is geared almost entirely toward automobility. It spans over thirty square miles with no public transportation developed for travel within the community.[21] Sidewalks were built within many housing developments and on a few of the small main roads that crosscut town, which is nice for walking to a neighbor's house or biking to see a friend in a neighboring development. But for most activities in people's everyday lives, the distances are too far, require a stint on a dangerous road, or are simply traveled by car because car culture dominates. This was particularly a problem for children and teenagers not old enough to drive or without access to a car, and for day laborers unable to afford a car or whose legal status made it impossible for them to get a driver's license.

Nancy, a teacher in one of the local high schools, whose seventeen-year-old daughter I also spent time with during my fieldwork, spoke to me about the spatial disorientation that she and Danielle felt when they first moved from Brooklyn when Danielle was three years old. "I won't forget," Nancy recalled. "We were out here about a week or two, and Danielle looked at me, because we were getting in the car *again*." Nancy said "again" in a whiny tone often attributed to teenagers, but which we all employ now and then when we have had enough of something. Danielle had looked up at her with curious, perceptive eyes and asked, "We're never going to walk anywhere again, are we?" Nancy laughed as she shared Danielle's words with me, emphasizing their cuteness despite the sad and poignant truth in her question. Nancy responded to her daughter by sorrowfully acknowledging, "I don't think so." She then explained to Danielle that they might walk next door to a friend's house or maybe down the street, but that would be about it. Danielle had rarely been in the car as a baby. Nancy and her husband, Eric, did have a car in the city, but they rarely used it. "We walked everywhere," Nancy recalled. "We walked to the playground. We walked to the bakery. We walked to the supermarket.

I mean, you know, and all of a sudden it was over. . . . And I don't think she liked the car as much."

While Danielle's reaction to the suburbs was infused with a mourning for the loss of walking, Nancy was most struck by the different ways that relationships were formed. She and Eric, like many people in Danboro, had family living in town before they moved in. The "pioneer" in their family created a snowball effect, with other family members and friends from Brooklyn following suit, one by one. Despite this close-knit network, Nancy missed the "spontaneous" ways of meeting other people that she loved in the city: "You would go to the playground, you would see the same lady every day and you just sit down next to her, and all of a sudden, you know. . . . I'm still friendly with some of the women I bumped into at the playground with [Danielle] . . . you don't have that here." When Nancy tried to think of the ways that she met people once they moved to Danboro, she paused for a minute, and then recounted, "We met a lot of people through business. . . . Some families that we're friendly with [our son] went to nursery school [with]. . . . You start getting friendly . . . you have . . . [play] groups and stuff. . . . It's different. It's a different way of meeting people." While Nancy appreciates what you get in suburban spaces, such as "being able to walk out and being in your own backyard and that kind of thing," she still longs for "the sort of place that you could . . . run into people you knew." For many people in town, cul-de-sacs, with their semi-protected nook of public space filled with children playing, were reminiscent of this aspect of urban neighborhood parks and a nostalgic reminder of the streets and stoops of their old Brooklyn neighborhoods. For others, streets within a development that were not throughways to other streets and thus were less trafficked created a similar feel, particularly among first-wave owners, who nostalgically recall the close-knit community created on those types of blocks, with last-minute watching of each other's kids and helping out amid sicknesses and deaths in the family.

I then asked Nancy how she felt about the loss of so much open space in the area and the congestion that has followed. She proceeded to tell me about a conversation that she and Eric had: "We must have been out here two years, and I said to him, 'I can't stand it! . . . They're building everywhere.'" Eric looked at her with a smirk on his face, laughing as he playfully made fun of her by asking, "Do you remember the farm that was here?!" Realizing that Eric was referring to the farm that used to be where their house was now standing, she acknowledged, "Of course I do. But that's okay. I'm here now. They can stop building!" As she continued lamenting, her associations brought together many of the concerns that I heard from people in Danboro:

> It's just that I don't want to see them . . . squishing a lot of houses into a small area. . . . If we had enough open space and we had enough room in the schools, it wouldn't bother me how big Danboro was, as long as we had the facilities, that we have enough policemen, . . . that there are going to be enough playgrounds. . . . I don't want it to become where it's so crowded that all the things I came out here for aren't here anymore. You know, and the schools predominantly. I mean . . . you leave the city, where there are classes [with around] thirty kids, and you don't want to see your kids in a room that has thirty kids.

Linda, too, lamented the overcrowding, particularly the traffic. The drive to where she used to shop in Milldale took seven or eight minutes when they first moved to Danboro; by 1999, it took twice as long—sometimes three times depending on the traffic. Linda managed to evade some of the traffic by avoiding Route 2 on Saturdays and Sundays when the mall traffic was really bad. Like Nancy, she was a teacher, so she could do her errands in the afternoons during the week. If she *had* to go on Route 2 during the weekend, she went in the late afternoon. Linda was thankful, though, for all the new supermarkets and strip malls that were built over the years. She concluded with resolve, "I guess with expansion of homes comes everything else that goes with it. I mean, it's fine with me." Plus, she added, "it's great for the kids and, you know . . . it's available to them. But, um, . . . I don't know. . . . It doesn't bother me. . . . I guess I'm used to this style now."

Although Linda may be used to the traffic and has found a way of avoiding frustration with it in her daily life, she told me that she does feel a bit crestfallen when she reflects on what it was that attracted her to Danboro in the first place. She waxed nostalgic about those years. It was almost as if she no longer believed it herself anymore as she recalled with astonishment, "There was no traffic. Nobody was living here. . . . That's the reason we didn't go look to Long Island—because it was congested already.

Whoever knew that [here] would be as congested . . . , you know?" Yet she acknowledged that there was an intuitive feeling that Danboro was up-and-coming: "There was always a sense that, because the land, the value of . . . for what you got for your house." But notice that this "sense" of Danboro's future was, in part, in regard to its return on one's investment, the eventual payback for the risk of buying a home that might have been a bit of a stretch at the start in a town that was early in its suburban development. Therein lies the rub of the American dream in towns like Danboro, which are so appealing in their early years because of their pastoral presence, minimal traffic, affordable homes, and good schools. But much of what increases property values, particularly when done without a concerted effort to focus on regional planning, puts most people at risk for insecure access to much of what they came for and for increasing aggravation and discontent in their everyday lives.[22]

In light of her complaints about Danboro and nostalgia for Brooklyn, I asked Nancy if she was happy with her decision to move to Danboro. "Oh, yes. Absolutely," she replied. "I think it was a great place to raise the kids and everything like that. I don't think I would have wanted to stay [in Brooklyn]." Nancy and Eric, like Stu and Linda, were not happy with the idea of their children going to the city schools. The elementary school in their neighborhood was fine, but, as Nancy explained, "by the time they got to the high school and all, um, they were mixing the neighborhoods. . . . It wasn't that it was black or. . . . It was, you know, you worried about who was getting shot." Nancy, unlike Stu, would never have been called an Archie Bunker. She was very progressive in her racial politics, and she and Eric almost did stay in the city, for they could have afforded to send Danielle to a private school. But they did not want Danielle to have that experience. They still had faith in the liberal ideal, including public schooling.

For those whose racial anxieties were central to their move, however, the time of my fieldwork brought forth hints of the racial concerns that they had had when they left their old neighborhoods in Brooklyn. People would sometimes comment about the recent immigrants from Mexico, who could be seen throughout the day waiting for buses along Route 2. Stu most noticed the changes while riding the bus into Manhattan every morning for work. When he and Linda first moved to Danboro, most of the people getting onto the bus from the neighboring towns were white. Now, Stu explained, there were "a very diverse group of people on the bus as opposed to twenty years ago." By the time the bus made its last stop in the area before getting onto the Garden State Parkway, there were a considerable number of people on it who were, in Stu's terms, "black," "Indian," and "Oriental."[23] Stu spoke about these shifts with a sense of resignation: "So, I mean, every area changes and there is good and there is bad and, you know, we roll with it." But many people were not okay to just "roll with it." Their racial anxieties were transformed into particularly active manifestations of the residual during those years.

BORDERING THE RESIDUAL

My move to the Danboro area was infused with my own, quite different, set of idealizations, expectations, disorientations, and frustrations. In the fall of 1997, I spent a couple of months searching for an apartment in Danboro. I was looking for a cheap place to rent, for, like most ethnographers doing place-based research, I planned to live in my field site. Before I began to look, I imagined that my fieldwork wouldn't begin until I was unpacked and settled into the community itself. But it immediately became clear that my exploration of Danboro began the minute I opened the classified pages in the local newspaper. Weeks would go by without any listings for rentals in Danboro. And when there were, they were for either an entire detached house or a three-bedroom townhouse, neither of which my soon-to-be roommate, an elementary school teacher, and I could afford. I did notice, however, that there were always several listings for rentals in Milldale, which shares a border with Danboro on the southern end of town. Quite ironic, I thought: I was going to Danboro to study class, and I couldn't afford to live in town. After getting over my initial frustration, I resigned myself to the idea of living in Milldale. Since the public high school that Danboro students attend is part of the Milldale Regional High School District, I at least would be living within Danboro's high school district.

Most of the apartments for rent in Milldale are located in the downtown areas that flank commercial Main Street. In just a few minutes of driving up and down these side streets, which contain many historic homes and buildings, you move through quite diverse neighborhoods. Some blocks are comprised of working-class families who recently emigrated from Mexico, whereas others are made up of working-class and middle-class African-American families who have long been part of the community. Still others consist of white working-class and white middle- to upper-middle-class families. However, when people from Danboro envision those who live in the downtown area of Milldale, they "see" only working-class people of color. As John Berger has pointed out, "The way we see things is affected by what we know or what we believe. . . . Our vision is continually . . . constituting what is present to us *as we are*."[24] The intersection of enduring white-flight anxieties and the lingering lore of suburban downtown decay was quite potent; it created a sensibility among many residents of Danboro such that they noticed primarily racialized and assumed-to-be-poor others, despite the class and race diversity of Milldale's downtown community.[25]

It quickly became clear to me in conversations with people from Danboro during our apartment hunt that it was outside the normative discourse even to consider living in downtown Milldale. The one time that I mentioned it as a possibility, the young adults whom I was with laughed; they assumed that I was joking. The apartments in Milldale that were "acceptable," I soon learned, were predominantly places marked in the classifieds as being a part of Greenhedge, a gated community to the west of downtown Milldale. Despite the fact that Greenhedge was a bit above my budget, I got the sense that living there was a sacrifice I had to make in order to explore class sensibilities from a standpoint that Laura Nader refers to as studying "sideways"[26]—that is, among one's class peers. If people like me and my roommate (i.e., white and raised in the middle to upper middle class) were going to rent in the area, and in Milldale in particular, the solution that made the most "sense" to many people in Danboro was to find a place in Greenhedge. So sure enough, after another month of searching, we signed a lease for a two-bedroom apartment in Greenhedge.

Most people in towns like Danboro are fond of the fact that there are specific municipal ordinances written primarily to ensure that renters, for the most part, are zoned out of their town. Zoning laws, like those minimizing rentals in Danboro, have long been particularly useful strategies for exclusion. Zoning out people deemed "undesirable" because of their positioning in the economic order of things has always been a way, in light of the racial politics of class in the United States, also to keep out people of color, like those living in downtown Milldale.[27] But zoning laws can only go so far, particularly as they come under fire.[28] So people who want to seal themselves off increasingly do so within gated communities, the architectural twin of zoning regulations.[29] Hence developments like Greenhedge.

It is not just the residual presence of white-flight sensibilities that affects how people "see" the downtown area of Milldale. There also are other conditions that provoke and exacerbate these anxieties. Take, for example, the ways that "Milldale" is semiotically represented in the newspapers. Milldale is the county seat, and so it houses a courthouse, jails, and other state and county offices and facilities. Whenever an article is written about a trial that is taking place in the courthouse or is about someone who is being held in a jail, the location that is listed below the byline for the article is always "Milldale." It does not matter where the crime took place or where the people who are on trial are from; Milldale is the place that is listed. Although they are perhaps subtle, powerful semiotic effects arise every time crime events are linked to Milldale through site locators in the newspaper. I saw evidence of this when I was at a party in Manhattan during my fieldwork. I ran into someone whom I had not seen in a while. When I mentioned that I was living in Milldale, she had a curious look in her eye and asked me if Milldale was a really dangerous place. I knew that she had little sense of any of the places in New Jersey, so I was quite curious as to where she had gotten this image of Milldale. She said that she had been reading all of the articles in the *New York Times* about a sensational trial that was taking place involving a teenage murderer and a pedophile. At first I was confused because the murder had taken place in a town located fifteen minutes from Milldale. But the next time I saw an article written about the case in the paper, I noticed that "Milldale" was listed below the byline because the trial was taking place in the superior court in Milldale, and the pedophile was being held on separate charges in a jail in Milldale. Unable to keep track of all the locations associated with this case, she just remembered "Milldale."

People who were from Danboro often reacted with clumsy apprehension when they heard that I lived in Milldale. One instance occurred while

I was at the Body Fitness gym on Route 2 in Danboro. Body Fitness was a rich fieldwork site: full of moms after their kids had been sent off to school in the morning, and loaded with other adults and teenagers in the afternoon and evening. Since these kinds of private spaces are the town centers in suburbs like Danboro, they enable great opportunities for engaging in conversations with (and overhearing conversations of) people with whom I was not spending focused time. On this particular morning, I was getting onto an elliptical machine next to a woman whose trainer had just walked away for a minute. She turned to me and began idle gym chitchat when a man came over to us and asked if he could change the channel on the television. Assuming that he wanted to watch basketball since it was during March Madness, she told him that she was waiting for tonight's game. She pointed to her T-shirt—which had "Michigan" written on it— and said "Michigan!" in a patriotic kind of way, with her arm raised high in the air and her fist clenched tight.

Seeing this as a great opening for talking with this woman more in depth, I asked her if she had gone to the University of Michigan. "No," she replied; she had gone to Brooklyn College, but both of her kids were attending Michigan. I then asked her if she was from Danboro, to which she responded "Yes!" in a tone quite similar to her pledge of allegiance to Michigan. She asked where I was from, and in the same tone I replied, "Milldale." Her face instantly transformed into the kind of look that is not actually a specific look, but rather as if someone doesn't know how to respond. After a few seconds of awkward silence, which felt like an eternity, I explained that I was asking because I was a Ph.D. student from Michigan doing research in Danboro. I noted that I had worked with kids from Danboro, which is why I had moved into the area. Her body language completely transformed once I shared my connections and cultural capital, and our conversation resumed its previous ease.

My Milldale positioning actually ended up being a handy device in terms of my research methodology. Throughout the nineteen months that I lived in Greenhedge, I never grew tired of observing how my neighbors answered the question, "Where do you live?" I noticed that when they were asked this question by someone from Danboro, they almost always said that they lived in "Greenhedge" rather than in "Milldale." I soon began to play this classification game. When I wanted to draw on my class privilege in order to make sure people would feel like I was "one of them," I'd say that I was from Greenhedge. When I didn't want people to think that I was "one of those people" (i.e., a Danboro-type person), I'd say that I was from Milldale. In many ways, being zoned out of Danboro and living in this interstitial, ambiguous location enabled me to move in and out of conversations and spaces in a way that I might not have been able to do if I had been a resident of Danboro. With just a switch of a name, I was able to shift the set of essentializing assumptions that were likely to be projected onto me by people I was just meeting.

MY PROJECT AND *THE* PROJECTS

Residual white-flight sensibilities in Danboro were not only rearticulated and provoked by Milldale. They were also actively present in conversational moments, embodied forms, and material objects having to do with a variety of other places and personal traces. One such instance occurred while I was getting official permission to be in my study from Shari and her daughter, Stephanie, who was seventeen years old at the time. We had arranged to meet at their house one early afternoon while Stephanie was home from school recuperating from minor surgery. I drove over to their house, walked past a Lexus and a Jeep Grand Cherokee parked in the driveway, and rang the doorbell of their moderately sized colonial-style home. Stephanie opened the door and invited me to follow her upstairs to her bedroom, where we all could sit and talk comfortably. Stephanie sat down on her bed, while her mother sat on the floor leaning up against Stephanie's closet doors. I, too, found a spot on the floor. I started to describe my study, explaining that "my project will explore what it is like to grow up during the economic boom years" and that "through my project I hope to understand how class shifts are experienced in everyday life." Both Shari and Stephanie listened intently, jumping in at times to offer their thoughts on what I might find as I dug further into people's daily lives in Danboro. But at one point, I noticed Shari giggling and smirking, and as I was asking, "What do you think about my project?" she waved at me to stop. She apologized for laughing and explained that it was bizarre for her to hear me keep talking about "my project" because every time I said "project" she thought that I was referring to housing projects in the city. She said that she knew that was not what I was talking about, but that every time I said it, it threw her. I had not mentioned anything about the city in my project description, yet the word *project* was so overloaded with the significance of project-as-public-housing that it obscured other meanings of the word. This moment powerfully indexed how present the city was in people's minds, particularly those aspects of the city they had intentionally left behind.

Shari then asked us to come into her bedroom so she could fold laundry while we continued to chat. Stephanie's younger brother, Jake, joined us. Usually kicked out of his sister's room, he could hang out with us now that we were in neutral territory. We continued talking about my project, which I thereafter called my "research." Despite this shift in nomenclature, I decided to ask Shari about her relationship with the city. She immediately launched into a story about a recent trip she and a friend had taken to see a show in the East Village. They took the train into the city and then took the subway to get to the theater. When Shari uttered the word *subway*, her accentuated intonation suggested that it was a *really big deal* that she was on the subway. She explained that she *never* goes on the subway and was really uncomfortable the whole time. There had been two men staring at her, so she pulled her sleeves down over her hands in order to cover her rings. One of those rings, I could see, was a sizeable diamond. Whether or not the two men were threateningly staring at her or just people-watching, as many people do on the subway, it was her objects of class display that made her feel vulnerably visible. Many families in Danboro "rediscovered" the city and began to enjoy it again as gentrification began to take hold in the 1990s. But for some people like Shari, the city continued to be imagined and experienced as if trapped in time during the moment when they fled, with their discomfort perhaps exacerbated by being newly upper-middle-classed people in the urban spaces they had left behind.

Since Shari, like Stu, often waxed nostalgic to me about the years when she was growing up in the city (before its "decline"), I asked her if she rode the subway back then. "Oh, yes," she exuberantly exclaimed. She and her friends used to take the subway to Greenwich Village. But, she continued, "it was different then." Recently, she shared, her husband, Jay, had the kids with him in the city, and he took them on the subway. When she found out that he did this, she yelled at him for "doing that to her kids." As Shari uttered those words, I looked at the kids. Jake was playing with the dog, so I couldn't tell if he was listening. Stephanie was clearly attentive, but without comment. I knew from the time I had spent with her family that Stephanie was not shy about letting her mom know when she disagreed with her. I took her silence to be an implicit agreement, suggesting that there was nothing particularly disagreeable about what her mother had said.

Another sign of the urban residual was the bandage across Stephanie's nose. Stephanie was home from school that day because she was recuperating from rhinoplasty (i.e., a nose job). Nose jobs—a way of ridding oneself of a protruding sign of ethnicity—represent an aesthetic desire shaped by (and in turn, shaping) normative notions of white, middle-class beauty.[30] The tape across Stephanie's nose was a powerful marker of broader efforts to transcend old urban "ethnic" neighborhoods. Nose jobs were quite common among the Jews and Italians in Danboro, whose class shift "up" coincided with their migration to a "white" suburban town.

Suntans also could be a site for the expression of embodied post-ethnic white anxieties. One morning I was waiting in line at a bagel store on Route 2. There were two people in line behind me, and their conversation suggested that they had not seen each other in a while. They looked to be in their late fifties or early sixties, and their accents gave away that they had grown up in Brooklyn. The woman told the man that she was very excited about her daughter's upcoming wedding, and confessed to him that she had been taking days off from work to go to the beach to get a suntan so that she would look beautiful by the weekend. The man jokingly warned her not to get too tan or she might look Puerto Rican in the pictures.

Lauren, Linda and Stu's seventeen-year-old daughter, raised the flip side of these anxieties about being not quite white. She had grown concerned about how few black people there were in Danboro.[31] She had had one black friend when she was younger, but her friend's family moved when they were in eighth grade, and they lost touch: "[She] . . . was like the only black person that *ever* entered my life. . . . And . . . the *only* black person I've ever been friends with in my *whole entire life*. . . . I don't think there's one black family . . . in my whole development or at least that I know of. Like that, that blows me away . . . like it's weird. . . . And [it] scares the shit out of me." I asked Lauren why it scared her so much. She explained, "Because what's going to happen to me when I'm in the real [world]—not to say that I'm inexperienced with people, but like, thinking about where I grew up. . . . What happens if for the rest of my life I only work with black people?"

Lauren began to reflect on two moments that had brought this problem to the fore for her. The first was when she made an offhand comment about a black person while speaking with a white friend who had grown up in Brooklyn. Her friend got really mad at her, as Lauren explained:

> To her, she's always had black people in her life . . . she lives around black people. To me . . . if I said a word about a black person, no one would know. No one would care because nobody is friends with one, you know. And it's really a dick thing to say, but it's true. . . . And I just feel like in the real world—not that I would ever say something mean in public about a black person—but I don't know, like if I heard a joke about a black person, I wouldn't know whether to laugh in public because . . . you know, you don't know who's around. But I've never had to face that because a black person's never been around.[32]

Lauren did face this situation when she and her friend Erika were visiting colleges. "[Erika] said something about a black person and then like you turn around and there were like twelve black people . . . standing behind [us]." Lauren felt incredibly uncomfortable when this happened: "It's very hard to not understand people and then have to be with them every day. . . . I feel like that's going to affect me a lot. And it affects a lot of people, like especially where we live."

Yet despite these concerns, Lauren felt conflicted. She is really happy that she grew up in Danboro because, as she put it, "Everything's so safe here. . . . Like I have such security here and that's what I love about it." She added with an uneasy appreciation in her voice, "It really sucks that I—like I'm happy where I grew up. I'm happy that we didn't have conflicts, you know. Like there [wasn't] racism because there weren't really any black people to be racist against." It is interesting to think back to her father Stu's comments about the reasons that he and Linda decided to move to Danboro to raise Lauren and her sister. He had hoped to raise them in a

town where they would be far from the racial tensions and other conditions they had experienced during their last few years in Brooklyn. Hearing
Lauren suggest that there was no racism in Danboro because no one was
black, juxtaposed with her comments about feeling safe in her (white)
town, reveals just how powerfully active manifestations of residual white-
flight sensibilities have been incorporated. Lauren may feel like Danboro
is not the "real world" and that her father, Stu, is an "Archie" relic from the
1970s. But her comments reveal how very real the racial politics in Danboro
were and how sedimented long-standing logics written into the landscape
through redlining and other exclusionary practices have become.

The ways that racialized, class-encoded anxieties and white-flight resid-
uals conjoined with child-rearing predicaments were materially apparent
one Saturday night several months into my fieldwork. Lauren, Erika, and
I had different plans for the evening, but we decided to meet up afterward
at Erika's house. When I arrived, Erika was sitting out front on the steps
that lead up a hill from her driveway to the front door. The steps are somewhat concealed amid heavily landscaped shrubbery and trees, making it a
perfect spot for her to sneak a quick smoke while waiting for a friend to
arrive: outside in the fresh air away from parents and yet somewhat hidden from the gaze of neighbors across the cul-de-sac. I sat down next to
Erika and joined the wait for Lauren. Lauren had been at the T. G. I.
Friday's on Route 2, a frequent hangout for teenagers. Erika and I soon
started to get cold, so we went inside, where she put on the television so we
could catch the last few minutes of *Saturday Night Live*. When it ended,
we decided to watch the show that came on after, *Showtime at the Apollo*.
As we watched African-American men and women perform onstage at the
famous Apollo Theater in Harlem, Erika commented that she's "fascinated
with black people." Just as I was about to ask her about her curiosity,
Lauren stormed through the door and apologized for being late. The next
thing I knew, we were standing around the island in Erika's kitchen, swap-
ping tales from our evenings.

As the wee hours of the night wore on, we decided it was time to crash.
Erika showed me to the downstairs guest room. The room felt cozy in
comparison with the grandness of some of the other rooms in the house, a
few of which were made to feel larger with mirrors lining the walls. While
I was looking around for an extra blanket after Erika had gone upstairs,

my eye caught sight of a book that was resting on the nightstand. It was Anthony E. Wolf's *Get Out of My Life, but First Could You Drive Me and Cheryl to the Mall?: A Parent's Guide to the New Teenager*. I chuckled as I picked up the book, wondering if her parents actually used it for child-rearing advice or if one of their friends bought it for them as a gag gift. Still holding the Wolf book in my hand, I looked down at the nightstand and realized that it had been resting on top of another book, entitled *When Brooklyn Was the World, 1920–1957*. As I picked up that book, I saw that beneath it was yet another nostalgia picture book about Brooklyn. These three books offered a poetic juxtaposition. The layering of today's dilemmas on top of yesterday's existence was a glaring representation of how so many of Danboro parents' concerns for their kids are enmeshed in their post-Brooklyn sensibilities. Brooklyn—as represented in images reminiscent of the pictures in the window of the local deli—was right there in double force, just underneath the surface of concerns about their kids. These types of nostalgia books create a dreamlike utopian past, as if Brooklyn was "innocent" when there were white working-class people in the neighborhoods represented, but turned "bad" as people of color moved in.[33] They articulate and generate a conflicted relationship to urban life, whiteness, and class positioning, and mirror back longings and anxieties still present many years after Brooklyn was left behind. As with jokes, unarticulated sentiments and poignant memories often break to the surface or make themselves known in objects—memory objects that are the materiality of history, where the past is continuously rearticulated in the conditions of the present.[34] Sure, these books were not on display in the living room; they were in the guest room. But they were still out there for someone to come across and see. Like Erika smoking her cigarettes: her parents know she smokes, everyone on the block knows she smokes, and yet she still sits in that little spot off to the side.

MIRRORS AT DANBORO HIGH: FACADES, APPEARANCES, AND DISPLAY

Not long after I had moved into the area, I was at a party with several people who had attended Danboro High School during the late 1980s and early 1990s. A couple of people asked me questions about the nature of my research and the types of issues that concerned me. In turn, they began to nostalgically recall their experiences growing up in Danboro. Amid the flood of memories, Mike, a guy in his mid-twenties, made a comment about the full-length mirrors in the halls of Danboro High School. These mirrors are not just randomly placed; they are indented into the wall, just like mirrors in dressing rooms in department stores. Mike said that while he was in high school, he had never thought twice about the presence or the placement of these mirrors. It had never struck him as bizarre that a high school would have demarcated spaces—in halls and not just in bathrooms—in which to quickly check out one's appearance or to take an elongated look at oneself on the way to class. It wasn't until he was in college that he realized how bizarre it was. He had been sitting around with a bunch of his fraternity brothers, telling a story in which one of these mirrors figured merely as a location. It had nothing to do with the point of the story itself. Nonetheless, he ended up being unable to finish the story because his friends were so shocked by the fact that his high school had dressing-room mirrors in the hallways. They couldn't believe it, and couldn't get past it in order to let Mike finish his story. While Mike was telling this anecdote, Jessica, who was a couple of years older than Mike and who also had gone to Danboro High School, had a look of shocked revelation on her face. She was clearly stunned as she admitted that she had never realized how bizarre it was that they had mirrors like that in their school. It wasn't until just then, when Mike pointed this out, that she realized how peculiar it actually was. She had figured that every school was like that. Well, actually, come to think of it, she acknowledged, she never really gave it a second thought. Almost simultaneously, all the people in the room from Danboro and from neighboring towns knowingly laughed and then commented—practically in unison—that it's "SOOOooo . . . Danboro" to have mirrors like that in the hallways of their school.

To refer to something as being "SOOOooo . . . Danboro" is a way of proclaiming that it forms a part of the Danboro habitus. It is everyday language for the utterly familiar. In the context of our discussion that night, the mirrors pointed to the extraordinary pressure in Danboro on children, youth, and adults to constantly monitor their appearance and to relentlessly view themselves as others might see them. There is constant pressure in Danboro—as a town in which to live and as a site for the development of habits, desires, and sensibilities—to reflect one's class privilege in houses, yards, cars, clothes, bodies, desires, politics, and even kids. For some families, these accoutrements and ways of being mirror that which has been newly acquired; for others, they index tenuous attainments and anxious yearnings. This "concern for 'seeming,'"[35] is thus much more than evidence of what Thorstein Veblen called a human penchant for "invidious comparison."[36] Rather, it should be understood as indexical of anxieties about the growing class divide and the shrinking middle class and generative in regard to habits, desires, sentiments, and structures of feeling. The fixation on display marks a Hegelian dialectic of seeking recognition as a certain classed person *because* the conditions of one's class positioning are far from secure.[37]

When I asked Linda how she would describe Danboro to someone who knew nothing about it, she at first grasped at adjectives and descriptive phrases, including "hardworking," "strivers," and people who "want the best, only the best." She then offered an example of what she was trying to describe: "I mean, I've walked into people's houses where there must have been about fifty thousand dollars' worth of landscaping in the front. They have a pool, magnificent pool with a gazebo in the back. And no furniture. . . . Maybe their . . . kitchen is done . . . but there's nothing in their living room, there's nothing in their dining room." Linda paused for a moment, and then commented, "It blows your mind!" When I asked her why she thought people chose to live like that, she explained, "It's for *show* . . . because you could *see* that, you can invite [people] to go to your backyard, swim in your pool." Linda continued, adding that many families also often mortgaged out their homes to be able to afford nice clothes, to drive fancy cars, to have full-time maids, and to go on expensive cruises from which they could return and "brag."

Nancy also referred to this type of "show" when we were discussing her perception of Danboro:

> It's a lovely community—don't, you know, don't get me wrong. And I think
> that it's . . . a very cohesive community. I think you'd find help if you needed
> it and that whole kind of thing. But . . . I think sometimes the values are in
> the wrong place. One of the things that gets me about Danboro is the *facade*.
> And there really is a big one. A lot of the houses you'll walk into will be just

magnificent on the outside and the most gorgeous landscaping and the nicest cars out front. And you walk in and the homes are empty . . . . I mean, it's always *to impress*.[38]

Nancy said that she felt like many of these people never outgrew their adolescent pining to be with the "in crowd" and thus to have the biggest and the best to "show off." And yet, she added, there also is a "socioeconomic" dynamic going on, for a lot of people think that it's very nice to be from town and to have a Danboro address. "It's like, you know, a 'moving on up' kind of thing," she added.[39]

When I asked Linda her thoughts on this showiness, she said she thought it came from the fact that so many people in Danboro grew up in Brooklyn. "I think maybe they want better than they had," she mused. "A lot of the people around here grew up . . . in apartment houses. Most of us went to city schools and didn't have a choice. I mean, all the people that I know went to Brooklyn College." In the course of uttering those last few phrases, Linda shifted her frame of reference from "they" to "us," including herself among those she was talking about, transforming her tone from disparaging to empathic. She returned to the sense of awe with which she described her first glimpse of the Danboro area when she was fifteen: "I think this was a dream. And people, I mean, I never thought that *I* would ever live in a house like this. I mean, it was a dream." She acknowledged that she, like so many people in town, wanted for her children what she didn't have, and yet she felt that people took those desires to an extreme level. She offered an example from the young kids in her classes. "They come in in Polo," Linda described. "I mean, these little [kids]. And then when they rip their jeans, these parents get crazy because the pants were forty dollars. . . . When my kids went to school . . . they were very clean and neat, but I did not send them in expensive clothes."

Even once kids grow into young adults, parents continue to be concerned with how their children reflect their class positioning. One afternoon, I was in the apartment of a young couple who were about to get married. Jennifer had grown up in Danboro and was a friend of Linda's family; her fiancée, Bobby, was from another town. That day, Jennifer and Bobby had driven an hour each way to an upscale department store in northern New Jersey to register for engagement and wedding gifts.

Neither of them had been particularly thrilled about going through the drudgery of this particular nuptial ritual, although each one came back excited about particular items that they hoped would one day become theirs. When you register at this kind of store, they give you a bar-code reader in the form of a hand-held gun to zap all of the items that you like directly onto a computer list. Both Jennifer and Bobby spoke about the whimsy they felt while so easily being able to beam items onto their list. After hours of picking out items, they both had turned giddy and started to imagine that they were playing laser tag, ducking and hiding behind glass displays before shooting another item onto their list. It was during this moment of near delirium that Bobby decided to add a cool-looking humidor to their list, and that Jennifer, who loves funky cooking gadgets, threw in an antique-looking toaster that caught her eye.

It had been a long day, but they were both feeling quite content now that the task was done and they could blissfully rest on their couch. Jennifer was really excited about what they had picked out, and so decided to call her parents to tell them about everything. Jennifer's mother answered the phone, and Jennifer immediately and enthusiastically began to read her the list. Jennifer provided extraordinarily animated details about each of the items: what it looked like, what it could do, whether or not both she and Bobby fell in love with it, which ones they could not agree upon. Bobby, on the other hand, had had enough of it all for the day, so he went into another room to watch television, while Jennifer continued her descriptions without pause. That is, until she got to the crystal. Just after she mentioned the brand of crystal wine glasses for which they had registered, there was an unsettling pause in her voice, and then the conversation turned contentious. When Jennifer hung up the phone, she immediately bolted out to their back patio, dragging me and a pack of cigarettes along with her. Flustered and aggravated, she puffed away as she told me about the end of the conversation. Her mother did not like the brand of crystal that she and Bobby had chosen. It was too "cheap." Her mother couldn't understand why they had picked out thirteen-dollar glasses and not something on the level of Waterford crystal. She suggested to Jennifer that they drive back to the store the next day and reregister. Jennifer tried to explain to her that she and Bobby liked the glasses they had chosen. Plus, she told her mother, it made more sense to buy something affordable since crystal breaks and eventually needs to be replaced.

Jennifer decided not to tell Bobby about the conversation, figuring that it would blow over. Bobby was always frustrated with such concern for objects of display, which he often half-jokingly commented was part of the deal when marrying a Danboro girl. But it did not blow over. Jennifer's father called back a little while later to let her know that he agreed with her mother about the crystal. He also told her that he didn't understand why they registered for so many little things and not just big, expensive items. Despite Jennifer's attempt to explain to her parents that they had registered for what *they* wanted—which she thought was the point— Jennifer ceded to her parents' will. She went into the other room to break the news to Bobby that their original Sunday plans would have to be canceled in order to make another trip to the store.

Such concern for display was also found in intimate spaces that very few people outside of one's close circle were likely to see. Shari and her husband, Jay, had renovated their bathroom, and one afternoon Shari excitedly showed me her favorite part: the shower. It was made of glass, which enabled all the exquisite tile work to be on display. As she enthusiastically described the design process, I noticed a pile of neatly folded towels and artistically displayed soaps resting on a sitting ledge inside of the shower. I was impressed that she took such care after showering each day to return the shower to its pristine form. But as I learned a few minutes later, the shower was so nice that they did not want to use it. Since the glass fogs up when you shower, it takes a while to make it look nice again. She and Jay continued to shower in the kids' bathroom, where they had been showering throughout the construction. Much like the mirrors at Danboro High, which allow people to see a reflection of who they are, these private spaces—when not fogged up—enable people to feel like the people they aspire to be.

Nancy told me that she would never forget the first time she encountered in Danboro the sensibility of choosing display over practicality. It was about a month after she and her husband, Eric, had moved out from Brooklyn. She had been chatting with a few women she had just met, all of whom lived in her development. At one point during the conversation, it came up that Nancy's husband was a doctor. One of the women in the

Figure 3. Larger colonial-style home, built in the 1980s.

group stopped in her tracks and in a somewhat congratulatory tone said to Nancy, "Oh, he's a doctor! You won't be living *here* long!" Surprised by this woman's comment, Nancy asked her in a perplexed tone, "Why? I just moved in." Practically in unison, with smirks of jealousy on their faces, all of the other women replied, "Because you'll be buying one of the *bigger* houses!" (See figure 3 for an example of the bigger houses being built at the time.) Nancy still was feeling confused and explained to them, "I have one kid. What do I need a bigger house for?" The women were taken aback by what they perceived as Nancy's naïveté. Nancy had yet to learn the logic of Danboro, which she clarified for me as she joked, "It wouldn't be, you know, *statusy* enough to live in this little house. I'd have to have a house with four more rooms that were empty!" I could see that her smile was tinged with a hint of despair. Nancy acknowledged how painful that time was for her: "Yeah, that was what was said to me. I was here a month. I was not happy. . . . I wanted to go back. I really did."

Nancy never moved out of her original house. Linda, however, admitted that when she and Stu first moved into their home in Danboro, they expected one day to move "up" and out of their "starter house" into something larger. But when it was time for them to think about moving, it was during the housing boom of the mid-1980s. Property taxes had gone up considerably, and interest rates were almost twice as high as they were for their original home loan. They took a moment to really consider it and realized that they were comfortable in their house, so why fall prey to the pressure to move? They aren't "fancy" people, Linda remarked, and they like living financially within their means. So they stayed put and added a room onto their house. Sure, Linda, Stu, and their children often joke about how they live in the "poor section of town" because there are no basements in the homes and you never spot a Mercedes in a driveway in their development. But, as Linda noted, they are able "to sleep at night" because they have created a lifestyle they can afford.

A few days after I had these separate conversations, I ran into Nancy and Linda at pre-prom parties that their daughters were attending. It was a spectacular early evening in June. Not a cloud in the sky. Warm enough for young women in strapless gowns to go without shawls and yet crisp enough for young men in tuxedos to have sweatless brows. Picture-perfect, literally. Three houses on the same block—in one of the more upscale developments—were all having parties. A fitting context for performing this coming-of-age ritual for culturally bourgeois adulthoods.[40] As parents in casual wear finished taking pictures—or rather, when kids in formal attire grew tired of having their picture taken—the 150 or so guests from all of the parties began spilling onto the perfectly manicured front lawns. The crowds blended together as everyone walked toward the limousine-jammed cul-de-sac at the end of the block.

I spotted Nancy in the crowd and walked toward her to say hello. As I approached, she waved her hand and pointed in a direction toward which she wanted me to look. As I glanced up the driveway on which we were standing, I saw what she wanted me to notice: a garage door left open so that everyone approaching the cul-de-sac would be sure to see that family's new white Porsche. As I turned my head back in Nancy's direction, I grinned and nodded my head, acknowledging to her that I understood that this was an example of what she had been talking about during our conversation a few days before. A few minutes later, I ran into Linda. We ended up standing side by side, giggling as we watched a traffic gridlock ensue as all of the limousines and all of the parents in their cars tried to leave at the same time. Watching over this "scene," which is how all of the parents around me were referring to it, Linda raised both of her hands high in the air and proclaimed, "Welcome to Danboro!"

Despite the fact that so much significance was accorded to appearances, both Linda and Nancy, in tandem with their husbands—like so many other parents in town—consciously tried to work against this penchant for display in how they were raising their children. However, the pressure to flaunt wealth—*because* people were watching—was "out there." There may have been only one person in town who was like this for every twenty-five people who were down-to-earth, as many people suggested to me and as I experienced for myself during my fieldwork. But as Foucault has pointed out, a sense of "permanent visibility" does not require anyone to be actually looking. The internalization of the gaze (real *or* imagined) creates a "generalized surveillance" that leads to self-monitoring.[41]

During a conversation with Nancy and Eric's seventeen-year-old daughter, Danielle, the internalization of this see-and-be-seen sensibility emerged in a most unexpected way. Danielle had just seen *The Truman Show,* a movie about man who thinks his life is real when in fact it is a TV show being filmed in a tightly controlled set designed to depict the picture-perfect life. She told me that she really liked the movie, even though a lot of her friends thought Jim Carrey was too funny to play a dramatic role. When I asked her what she liked about it, she started to speak very slowly, with lots of "umm"s and "I don't know"s and pauses, and then offered, "It's just like it was a different kind of plot, you know. It wasn't like your everyday movie." There was something in Danielle's pauses that made me feel there was something more. I asked, "What else about it?" With a giggle in her voice, as if embarrassed about what she was about to say, she shared, "When I was little [in elementary school] . . . I used to think there were . . . video cameras everywhere. . . . I was like paranoid about this." As she spoke, she burst into overwhelming laughter, the kind that produces tears. I could feel that this had been very scary for her at the time, despite the fact that she could now laugh about it. Curious as to what led to this, I asked, "Did your parents . . . videotape you a lot when you were a baby?" She said, "No, no. I don't know. I just, I was paranoid about it. . . . You know how [in stores] there are video cameras sometimes? . . . I wouldn't want to go into dressing rooms 'cause I thought there'd be a video camera there." I asked her what her parents thought about this. She said they thought it was funny because she was really little. Danielle added that she was anxious about this even when she was at home: "I would think there were video cameras watching me. I don't know why." She laughed again, commenting on how "weird" it was.

Equally strange for Danielle was finding out that she was not alone in having this "paranoia." The friend with whom she had gone to see *The Truman Show* had the same fears: "It was weird. I told my friend, and she's like, 'I went through a phase like that, too!'" I wondered how many more kids in Danboro went through this "phase"—particularly girls, considering the gendered politics of visibility. Monitoring appearances and viewing oneself through the lens of how others see you is "SOOOooo . . . Danboro," as the people at the party that night suggested to me. Anxieties about constantly being seen were already palpable for Danielle in elementary school. She hadn't even gotten to her high school years; she hadn't yet encountered the mirrors at Danboro High.

BEING SEEN, BEING TAKEN, BEING CROWDED OUT

Erika also spoke to me about one of her childhood fears, which further complicates the predicament of persistent display and visibility, compounded with the residual effects of growing up amid post-Brooklynness, as embodied in the nostalgia picture books in the guest bedroom in her house. It was Erika's dad who had left their garage door open during the pre-prom parties, giving everyone no choice but to see his new white Porsche. Like the Porsche, the upscale house that Erika's family moved into when she was nine years old from a smaller house in town is also an emblem of newly acquired class privilege—of "moving on up," as Nancy referred to it. So, too, is the development in which Erika's house is located—the type of subdivision that Nancy's neighbors assumed she would move to because her husband was a doctor. But this regime of visibility, combined with changing fiscal conditions and overdevelopment in

Danboro, created the conditions of possibility for many people, like Erika, to feel vulnerable.

I asked Erika about what it was like when she first moved from her old house to her new one. She remembered being really excited about her new house, the enthusiasm for which has never faded. "I love it!" she passionately proclaimed. "I'm so proud of it. I love when people see it and say, 'Oh, it's so beautiful.' It just makes me proud. Because some people are, 'Oh, whatever. My house.' I don't know. I'm very proud of it. Like I could say it's mine. And most kids definitely don't feel that way." Erika told me that she had been thinking about this a lot because her parents were discussing the possibility of selling the house and moving into something smaller after Erika went to college. Erika said that this possibility made her sad because she thought that one day she might raise her kids in the house, although she wasn't sure if she would want to live in Danboro, per se, but definitely in a town like it. "You'd want to live in . . . a suburb?" I inquired. Erika replied, "Yeah. Well, at least . . . when I have a family, I do . . . . I don't want to have them grow up anywhere else . . . . I want them to have like a *backyaaard* and like a *playyyygrouuund*." Erika elongated her pronunciation of *backyard* and *playground* in a cutesy, childlike fashion, as if to emphasize their fantastical, dreamlike quality.

It felt to me as if Erika answered that last question through the standard American-dream narrative about raising kids in the suburbs. I wanted to hear more about what specifically she loved about Danboro and why she wanted one day to raise her own kids in a town like it. When I asked her to elaborate, Erika explained, "Okay. Well being that, when . . . I was a kid, my one fear in life was getting kidnapped." She giggled as she continued, "Even now, I'll still think about it. . . . I remember my nightmares that I used to have so perfectly." Curious that my question about her love of Danboro brought forth a fear that she had while growing up in it, I asked, "Was there some . . . event or was it like on the news all the time?" She replied, "No. It was just like my fear." She then guessed, "Maybe like getting those things in the mailbox, like 'Have you seen?'" Erika took another moment to think, after which she gave up and declared while laughing, "I don't know. . . . Nothing like that's ever happened here . . . the crime's not that bad. It's like stupid crime, nothing like murders or anything like that."

She then added with a matter-of-fact chuckle, "That's why I don't think I'd be such a good city person."

Erika's laughter felt somewhat different than that which accompanied Danielle's admission of her "weird" fears. Erika laughed in a way that was more contained and not as full of embarrassment as Danielle's giggles were. It was as if Erika did not think that her fear was so unfounded, though she remained visibly perplexed and curious about her fear of being kidnapped. Perhaps this was because her sensibilities were in sync with the post-urban, white-flight narrative so prevalent in her community, embedded in the landscape of her town, and embodied in the books that her parents had on display in their guest bedroom. This came across most poignantly as our conversation resumed. A few seconds after saying that she would not be such a good city person, she began to talk about how much she loved the aesthetics of order in Danboro: "It's, it's very pretty. It's, it's just like very, everything's like taken care of and everything looks like so . . . nice. Like well cut." She then added, with a sense of disappointment in her voice, "They keep building, though. Like there's no room anymore. . . . [But] it doesn't affect me, except like when the roads are just closed. . . . That's annoying."

But perhaps it did affect her in ways that she had not yet articulated. Her continued stream of associations was quite striking. Erika is proud of her house and likes the fact that it is viewed by others as beautiful, as if it were a reflection of who she is and who she hopes she always will be. She loves the neatness in Danboro that Lauren also mentioned; her fear of being taken is eased by the controlled order represented in those well-cut lawns. But if the landscape of Danboro really made her feel safe, why did she have this fear in the first place? Is it simply because no controlled environment is truly safe from intruders? Or could it also be that the regime of visibility in Danboro made her, like Danielle in her childhood, feel continuously in view of a disembodied, unverifiable gaze, in her house atop its hill and with its wide-open Porsche-filled garage? It is poignantly paradoxical that Erika was unable to feel secure: the same aesthetic of display that provides people in Danboro with an illusory sense of security and momentary relief from class anxieties and urban fears ended up creating a disciplinary community with unnerving surveillance and exposure. Erika's fear of being kidnapped was perhaps made newly available to her as her parents discussed selling her house; as roads were closed due to traffic; and as people were crowded out of her town. I don't mean to suggest a psychoanalytical projection of class anxieties onto the way she was seeing her town and experiencing her fears. Nonetheless, if there is "no room anymore," as she pointed out, maybe she won't be able to raise her children in a town like Danboro. Is that what she might be taken away from?

While Danboro has always been a town that has attended to various forms of class passing (with all its racial implications), display came to matter differently during the economic boom years of the 1990s. Increasing anxieties about the changes in the town and the areas surrounding it intersected with the chasm growing in the shrinking middle class. The playing field in Danboro may never have actually been level, as forms of nostalgia might suggest. Yet the influx of new families moving into huge homes with grand facades and the increasing penchant for the display of wealth (both real and desired) set the stage for a pervasive sense of insecurity among many people, even those in the new homes. As the following chapter reveals through a debate at a zoning board meeting over a new homeowner's request for a six-foot-high security gate, some people were starting to feel like "sightseers" in their own town. While the aesthetics of security are always predicated on an Other—an outside threat that must be kept out—in the late 1990s it was becoming evident that the outside threat involved not only kinds of people but also sensibilities about suburban life.

3 Gate Expectations

Tarragon Hills, a brand-new upscale subdivision of twenty-three custom homes ("No Two Homes Alike!" proclaimed the sales billboard) was constructed in Danboro during the time of my fieldwork. (See figure 4.) Tarragon Hills was typical of the influx during those years of huge homes, which some disdainfully refer to as "McMansions."[1] As one father described it at the time, "Houses looked like they were dropping from the sky!" Often built adjacent to older subdivisions of moderately sized colonial-style homes, like those in which Stu, Linda, and Lauren, and Nancy, Eric, and Danielle live, these new houses dwarfed their neighbors and produced jarring juxtapositions, mirroring the upscaling of the suburban American dream across the country.[2] When compounded with increasing concerns about overcrowding—triggered by never-ending traffic, overflowing public schools, and diminishing open space—these architectural shifts provoked class anxieties and roused uncertainties about the fiscal and discursive boundaries of inclusion and exclusion in the imagined future of the town. Like gentrification in urban areas, changes in the grandeur of suburban housing reflect a transformation of the class makeup of a town and reveal shifts in the larger class structure, the structuring of people's social locations, and moral discourses on private property.

Figure 4. Completed homes in Tarragon Hills, built in the late 1990s.

By the late 1990s, Danboro real estate had seen many years of inflation because the town was part of a metropolitan region experiencing pressure from new flows of capital and the people that came with it. Danboro is on the edge of commuting distance to New York City and has highly desired public schools. Most of the town's remaining farmland had been developed into subdivisions of huge homes like those in Tarragon Hills, further raising property values in the town. For some residents, especially retirees, it was a nice opportunity to cash out.[3] For other residents who moved unwillingly to more affordable towns at that time, their move was a form of displacement—an inflationary form of gentrification.[4] They had found that they no longer could afford their taxes, which in New Jersey are based heavily on property values. Those residents who could afford to stay and who wanted to do so, who are the focus of my discussion in this book, witnessed in their town the escalation of a new development in the spatialization of class in the United States. Spatial segregation was no longer mapped simply according to where the working class, middle class, and elites live. The middle class and the upper

Figure 5. Proposed six-foot-high gate.

middle class came to be increasingly segregated into different spatial locations.[5]

It was in this context that a couple buying a home in Tarragon Hills sought to build a large security gate across their driveway. (See figure 5.) The couple designed the gate to both correspond to the style of their home and be consistent with the scale of the house. Accordingly, it was a big gate: the stanchions were sketched at eight feet long, and the gate was drawn to run twenty feet across the driveway and reach six feet in height at its maximum points. However, a zoning ordinance in Danboro states that a gate in the front yard of a property can be no more than three feet high at its maximum point.[6] So the developers of Tarragon Hills had to submit an application to the Danboro Zoning Board of Adjustment to request a variance to build the couple their six-foot-high security gate,[7] which would have been the first of its kind in Danboro—a town with no gated communities and only a few individual gates.[8]

As Constance Perin has pointed out, "Developers and, often enough, their requests for variances and zoning amendments, light up for old-timers the early warning system of social shifts to come."[9] The request for this gate was one such cautionary moment. An ordinance that sets a maximum height of three feet for a gate or a fence in the front of one's property implies hope on the part of the authors of the zoning code to preserve a bit of the pastoral amid suburban growth. Three feet of height is typically enough to keep small children and dogs *in,* while staying within the spirit of community signified in the shared democratic lawn promulgated by Frederick Law Olmsted.[10] But a six-foot-high gate like the one designed by the Tarragon Hills couple is much more about keeping people *out,* with an "aesthetics of security"[11] that emulates the regal. Granted, there were already a few developments of large, ornate homes built during the housing boom of the 1980s. That was when Erika's family moved from their smaller house to their larger house on the cul-de-sac where the pre-prom parties had merged on that warm spring night. And the style of the gate was to some degree in keeping with ornate aesthetics of display ordinarily considered "SOOOooo Danboro"; Danboro is certainly not an "old money" town where people are modest in their display of wealth. But no one— until this request—had ever come to the zoning board seeking to build a six-foot-high ornamental security gate to go along with their huge home.

The public hearing for this gate request, which is the focus of my discussion in this chapter, became quite contentious and turned into a heated dispute that took people in the room by surprise.[12] Gate requests are usually quick and easy, since most people who submit an application to build an oversized gate or fence in the front of their property do so because they live on a main road and are concerned that their young children might climb over a three-foot-high fence and get into harm's way; they are usually asking to build a modest fence around their property. It rarely takes more than twenty minutes for the board to confirm that there really is a safety issue at stake and to determine the additional height that it will allow. Yet this gate request took far longer to resolve than anyone had expected, though I use the word *resolve* extremely loosely here. There was a vote among the board members that ultimately finalized the variance that the board would allow. However, the highly antagonistic debate that night over the need for such a gate and its ornamental design unearthed critical tensions that are illustrative of the shifting moral logics of property ownership in Danboro and other comparable suburban communities during the late 1990s. Amid significant changes in the class structure, the proposed six-foot-high gate—at once a mechanism for security and an object of class distinction—acquired considerable semiotic force.[13] Its style and, particularly, its scale blurred the boundaries between security concerns, aesthetic desires, and social dividing lines, leading the variance request to become a request for far more than relief of the township's three-foot-high ordinance. It became a challenge to the type of middle-class town long promoted and encouraged in Danboro and a sign for longer-term residents of the possibility of being locked outside the discursive and/or financial gates of their own town. This debate proved to be a diagnostic of the shift under way in both class structure and ideology, crystallizing the tension between those who hold a liberal democratic understanding of land use and those who have given up on those ideals in favor of unabashed claims to private property.

It is important to keep in mind the limited public discourse on the conditions of middle-class life in the United States in the late 1990s, when this debate took place. The media was largely celebrating the real estate and economic boom, with little attention to its downside. It was still several years before the burst of the housing bubble and a few more before the economic crisis—well before the media would begin to be flooded with a resounding critique of the "squeeze" on the middle class, the dramatic class divide, the overmortgaging of daily lives, the freewheeling movement of capital into real estate and securities, and the threat that these conditions placed on people's abilities to remain in their homes and their hometowns. As such, the reactions in the debate that night were, in Gramsci's terms, "commonsense," "spontaneous" responses to the spatialization of class shifts under way in that moment, rather than "the result of any systematic educational activity on the part of an already conscious leading group. [They were] . . . formed through everyday experience illuminated by 'common sense,' i.e., by the traditional popular conception of the world."[14] People's reactions that night were based on a "popular conception" of their town during a time when local spatial, moral, and class changes were challenging their sense of their community and its boundaries of inclusion, but there was not yet a narrative in the public discourse that articulated these conditions in structural terms.

It is because of the unexpected and spontaneous nature of the reaction to the gate proposal that I bring fine-grained attention to the debate it prompted. The board's final decision was not shaped simply by the semiotics of the proposed gate; it was the process of the debate itself—through narratives of legal argumentation, utterances of particular terms, and meaning making in the room in regard to publics—that shaped the outcome. My close reading will demonstrate *how* this occurred by animating the microprocesses often erased in more macrolevel accounts of "what happened" in legal and policy decisions.[15] Class anxieties hovering at the edges of everyday life in the town produced the "arena for the encounter,"[16] to use Bakhtin's phrasing. The tectonic shifts in the middle class affecting many residents in Danboro shaped how those on the zoning board and in the audience interpreted what was said. As Bakhtin's work reminds us, each word and phrase employed (and, at times, hurled as an epithet) during the debate could not "fail to brush up against thousands of living dialogic threads, woven by socio-ideological consciousness around the given object of an utterance."[17] Attention to microprocesses that shaped the outcome of the debate helps disentangle the "dialogic threads" woven into the zoning board meeting and reveals how class anxieties became a powerful subtext in the discussion and had a material effect on the built environment of the town.[18]

Through a close discursive and linguistic analysis of the zoning board debate that night, this chapter addresses a series of questions: What insights can be gained about shifting middle-class configurations and social dividing lines in the United States through examining struggles over the built environment in suburbs like Danboro? What can we learn about middle-class space making by paying close attention to class anxieties, which hover at the edges of everyday life and shape discursive possibilities at often unexpected moments? Under what conditions—and through what processes—are racialized urban fears disentangled from trepidation about the security of postwar American-dream aspirations, including its associated moral expectations with regard to community and property? And what is the historical significance of an effort to forestall the construction of this type of gate during a time when gates and gated communities were being built in record numbers across the United States, as well as in other countries with expanding middle classes?

FROM LIBERAL STRATEGIES OF EXCLUSION TO UNABASHED CLAIMS TO PRIVATE PROPERTY

To appreciate the ideological and historical significance of this debate, I offer here some brief useful historical context on gates and zoning debates in the United States, beginning with the first planned suburb. Frederick Law Olmsted, America's most influential landscape architect, is famous for his design of New York City's Central Park, but his most profound influence on the American landscape was arguably his vision for suburban land use. The landscape in the United States, he believed, should not be carved up with stone walls—aristocratic relics—to mark the edges of private property, as was prevalent in the English countryside that he visited in the mid–nineteenth century. Rather, he felt that the American landscape ought to exemplify the democratic ideal, with people living in houses with lawns that flowed together seamlessly, as if everyone lived together in one big park.[19] When Olmsted designed Riverside, Illinois, one of the first planned suburban communities in the United States, the nation was just a few years from the end of the Civil War, and in much need of unifying ideals to create and build the "imagined community"[20] of an American public.

During the late nineteenth century, Olmsted continued his efforts to limit walls, gates, and fences in the United States, but during the early years of private restrictive covenants, he conceded that if a property owner felt the need for a gate or fence, it should be limited to a maximum height of three feet; people could see over this height, and so the spirit of the democratic ideal of the shared lawn could remain.[21] It was still several decades before the first municipal zoning codes came into effect, and almost a century before the mass production of suburbs in the post–World War II period, but the idea of setting a maximum height of three feet for gates and fences along the front of one's property became a land-use habit and the starting point for land-use master plans in many suburban municipalities across the country.[22] It is important to keep in mind, however, that the United States was founded on a strong commitment to liberal democracy and its core Lockean ideals; this approach to the suburban landscape may promote an *ideal* of shared community, but it masks the reality and exclusions of private property. It is this moral logic of property that I refer to as the residual, since this ideal dictated the shape of Danboro during the early years of its suburbanization but was by the 1990s in tension with a new dominant logic.

Many municipalities in the United States over the years altered their zoning ordinances to allow gates and fences higher than three feet. There are several of these in New Jersey, though certain regions, most notably California, the Southwest, and the Southeast have been at the forefront in the growth of gates and gated communities, sometimes within municipalities, but often on unincorporated land.[23] This dramatic move away from the ideal of the liberal democratic landscape—and toward an unapologetic claim to and marking of private property that I refer to as the newly dominant moral logic of property—can be viewed as part of the larger trend of "neoliberalizing space"[24] in the United States since the late 1970s, which includes the intensification of gentrification, the expansion of private homeowner associations, the militarization of urban space, and the incursion of public-private partnerships into public domains of governance.[25] Evan McKenzie calls this neoliberalizing space in suburbia "privatopia,"[26] characterized by the privatization of policies and services that used to be enforced and provided by municipal governments. But despite the trend of moving away from municipal town halls and toward private homeowner associations and gated communities, town halls and other sites of public governance continue to be key sites for struggles over land use and the built environment.[27] Debates within them provide a window onto local articulations of larger political-economic shifts and their associated cultural and moral logics.

Zoning debates are particularly fruitful sites in which to explore tensions over the spatialization of class shifts; they offer a nexus through which to view the concerns of a particular historical moment, revealing the ways that public and private desires and anxieties merge and intersect with processes of space making.[28] When zoning began in the United States in the late 1880s, the first ordinances were requested on behalf of wealthy merchants who wanted to keep immigrant workers and businesses out of their neighborhoods.[29] Since zoning is a means of demarcating boundaries of inclusion and exclusion, in each historical moment we need to again ask the question: *What* land uses (and therefore *what kinds* of people and/or practices) are being excluded, and for what ends? Considering that it has long been apartment buildings and low-income housing that have provoked anxieties in suburbia, concerns about an accoutrement of high-income housing reveal a new chapter in the history of contention over zoning ordinances.

Despite the democratic ideal that the shared lawn in America was meant to evoke, the building of much of the suburbs was intentionally exclusionary. In the early 1900s, when municipalities began to devise large-scale zoning plans, many suburbs created residential districts (or

entire towns) that prohibited property owners from constructing multid-
welling apartments and small lots (i.e., what the working class and poor
could afford). Given the racial politics of class in the United States, this
enabled the exclusion of racialized others.[30] "Large-lot zoning"[31] was first
challenged in the New Jersey State Supreme Court in the 1952 landmark
case *Lionshead Lake, Inc. v. Township of Wayne.* The judges proved sympathetic to the argument that "the tide of suburban development" would
"engulf the rustic character" of these small towns. They argued that since
township officials were supposed to advance the "community as a social,
economic and political unit,"[32] it was within their charge to set these land
rules. As noted by Kirp, Dwyer, and Rosenthal, "community" within this
decision became defined as "those already living there and financially able
to stay put; anyone else is perceived as a stranger outside the gates."[33]
Often referred to as "snob zoning,"[34] these strategies to assuage white,
middle-class fears of property-value decline enabled race and class exclusions long after racial discrimination in housing deeds was deemed
unconstitutional and racial bias in federal housing loans had officially
ceased. This approach to negotiating social borders, which Richard
Babcock refers to as the "zoning game,"[35] is an exemplary "liberal strategy
of exclusion,"[36] whereby inclusionary claims enable exclusionary practices. It took until the mid-1980s in New Jersey for snob zoning to be
effectively challenged, though it still very much exists.[37] It is part of the
reason I was unable to live in Danboro while conducting my fieldwork.
There were no apartment buildings in town (and thus minimal affordable
housing). It is striking that a mere fifteen years after extensive battles for
fair housing regulations in New Jersey had finally succeeded, the influx of
high-income housing and a six-foot-high ornamental security gate started
to cause concern.

Legal battles over zoning rules have always exposed the fundamental
tension between private property and the public good, particularly who
counts as the "public" and what "good" is at stake. This is not surprising
given the long-term, uneasy relationship between private property and
the public good in a liberal democracy. John Locke's writings remind us
that "[t]he only way whereby any one . . . puts on the *bonds of civil society,*
is by agreeing with other men to join and unite into a community for their
comfortable, safe, and peaceable living one amongst another, in a secure

enjoyment of their properties, and a greater security against any, that are not of it."[38] Exclusionary zoning laws, a twentieth-century addition to the "bonds of civil society," clearly exhibit this spirit of dealing with those who are "not of it," who are kept outside the community in order to ensure its "security." Yet what is often left out of commentaries on exclusionary possibilities enabled through ordinances is that zoning—like civil society itself—is also deemed necessary to curb the desires of fellow property owners. As Gerald Frug points out, "While zoning limits property-owners' ability to do what they want with their own property, it also assures them that their investment in a home will not be undermined by the actions of their neighbors."[39] In the late 1990s, neighbors from developments like Tarragon Hills risked pricing people out of their own town and taking away the "secure enjoyment of their properties." Suburban zoning laws in the late 1990s thus began to be used as a technology—through limiting the height of gates, for example—to restrain excessive optimization of property. This means of reining in the architectural extravagances of neighbors was a zoning game for the late 1990s neoliberal moment. It sheds light on cracks in processes of neoliberalizing space as residual ideologies fought to survive as neoliberal logics were becoming materially and discursively dominant.

FROM PROTECTING THE PASTORAL IDEAL TO KEEPING OUT THE "REGAL"

Danboro's town hall provides a fitting setting for this debate and its struggle over the limits of rugged entitlement. The building had been a working barn, and the exterior still reflects that. It is practically twice the height of the two adjoining modern buildings, which contain the offices of the township administration, the police department, and the courts. The town hall building, a symbol of Danboro's rural past, creates quite a commanding vision as you glimpse it from the main road that leads to the municipal center. During my fieldwork, I learned to appreciate these moments of pastoral nostalgia that so many people spoke to me about. Usually brief but still powerful, there can be much beauty as you glimpse a farm tucked away behind two strip malls or as you drive up to Danboro's retrofitted barn town hall after taking a shortcut through interconnected subdivisions of postwar colonial-style homes. As is the nature of these short-lived escapes, there is always that jarring moment that snaps you out of it. On the night of this zoning board meeting, that moment came when I walked from the calmly lit darkness of the parking lot into the buzzing glare of the bright lighting of the town hall itself.

Despite its barn exterior, the interior had been retrofitted to resemble a typical town hall. There is seating on a raised, semicircular platform in the front for board members, two tables nearby for lawyers and applicants, a podium for members of the public to share their thoughts, and rows of benches for the audience. On the night of this hearing, the clusters of conversation in the room among the fifty or so people in attendance were typical of most meetings that I had attended. The smokers were checking their watches to see if they had enough time to step outside to grab one last cigarette before the meeting began. A few people were complaining about the traffic on Route 2 during their commute home from the city. Others were talking about how their kids were driving them nuts. There also were a few quiet exchanges among those who were hoping that the meeting would not run too late so that they could make it home in time for their favorite 10 P.M. television shows. These meetings do not begin until 8 P.M., since board members are appointed volunteers who typically have day jobs.

The majority of town residents at the meeting of the zoning board that night were from a subdivision of moderately sized homes that backs up against a commercial park containing a four-thousand-square-foot sports-focused entertainment complex—one of the many commercial play spaces for kids in the area. The owners of the complex wanted to offer teen dances in their facility, and their request for a variance to do so was on the agenda that night. It was no surprise that many residents from the development were in attendance, for it was rumored that these dances might attract teenagers from downtown Milldale. I took a seat near these residents, since I, too, thought that this would be the most contested item on the agenda, sure to throw into relief the racial politics of class anxieties. I had no idea that the gate request would prove to be so significant.

As I took out my tape recorder, an elderly man sitting next to me asked if I was a reporter. I explained to him that I was an anthropologist doing research in the town. After we chatted for a bit about my project, I inquired about why he was attending the meeting. He explained that he was a volunteer for the Danboro Township Historic Commission, which sends a representative to all zoning meetings to keep a watchful eye on what needs to be protected, particularly the remaining buildings from Danboro's pastoral past. As he was speaking, he pointed to a banner hanging on the wall that depicted the Danboro Township logo, which consists of sketches of the town's historic properties surrounding a historic tree in the town. With resigned humor, he commented that the insignia of Danboro should instead have a bulldozer in the center of it. Indeed, the Danboro area, once known for being plowed, was constantly being bulldozed to make way for new developments.

In the early 1960s, William Dobriner wrote about class tensions in what he called "reluctant suburbs"—small towns that became suburbanized—reluctantly—during the postwar period.[40] It is interesting to consider the rearticulation of those tensions in places like Danboro, which once were reluctant suburbs and may still be experienced as such by oldtimers like the man from the historic commission; yet in the late 1990s, a new type of reluctance emerged in regard to the new huge homes, one that created common ground between old-timers and first-wave suburbanites. As this debate reveals, protecting pastoral remnants and excluding outsiders were no longer the only pressing concerns in towns like Danboro. Apprehension about the influx of the "regal" took center stage, and led to curious instances of bonding by the end of the night between this man and those from the development behind Grand Slam, one of the many subdivisions that original residents like him had long bemoaned.[41]

"UNDUE HARDSHIP" VERSUS "THE PUBLIC GOOD"

The agenda for this meeting was—as usual—overburdened. The inexhaustible construction in Danboro during the late 1990s inundated the zoning board with requests of all kinds. In the spirit of moving as quickly as possible through the agenda, Joan,[42] the chairperson of the zoning board, decided to move the gate request up on the agenda. It was thought best to get the gate application out of the way before tackling other items,

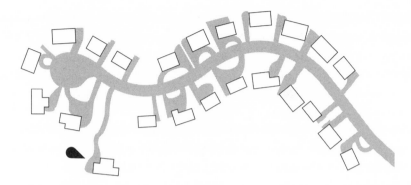

Figure 6. Flag lot. Illustration by Brett Silvers.

like the teen dances, that were expected to require lengthier discussion. When their gate case was called earlier than expected, the lawyer and the developer from the real estate development corporation building Tarragon Hills began to smile and approached the front of the room to present their case with a slight skip in their step, perhaps imagining that they might make it home earlier than anticipated. In a confident and matter-of-fact tone, David, the lawyer, explained to the board that the lot in question is an "anomaly." All of the other houses in the subdivision are set back from the road at distances ranging from 40 to 90 feet, whereas this particular home—on a "flag lot"[43]—is set back over 250 feet from the road, tucked away in the woods. (See figure 6.) The driveway—approximately 400 feet long—winds its way around trees before reaching the house in the rear of the lot. David explained that the gate being requested was for "security," the reasons for which the developer standing by his side would express to the board in a moment. He then emphasized, "There are certain circumstances being *unique* to the *shape* of the property that would warrant a relief." He also highlighted that they all (i.e., he, the developer, and the prospective purchaser) "feel that it can be done without any *detriment* to any of the neighbors."

These last two statements, sprinkled with legal language, are particularly important when it comes to the zoning regulations at stake in this case. The Danboro Township Land Use Development Code states that the zoning board may grant a variance only "where, by reason of *exceptional* narrowness, shallowness or *shape of such property,* or by reason of exceptional topographic conditions, or by reason of other extraordinary and exceptional situation or condition of such piece of property, the strict application of any regulation . . . would result in peculiar and exceptional practical difficulties to, or exceptional and *undue hardship* upon, the developer of such property."[44] At the same time, however, the code also states, "No variance or other relief may be granted under the provisions of this section unless such variance or other relief can be granted without *substantial detriment* to the *public good.*"[45]

In light of the ambiguous meanings and protean implications of words and phrases like *hardship, substantial detriment,* and *public good,* which depend heavily on the idiosyncrasies of local towns and the larger historical context, it is imperative that legal teams understand the particularities of place (in both space and time) when pleading their cases. It was at this point (and perhaps in this spirit) that David turned the microphone over to Jay, the developer. David explained to the board that Jay was best able to represent the prospective purchaser's concerns since he had been working directly with him on the concept plans for the property. But Jay was also a resident of the town, which was made known to all when he was sworn in and had to state his address.[46] It is a beneficial strategy for development corporations to have as their representative a hometown resident—someone who is both in the know and also known.

The atmosphere in the room shifted to a more relaxed and familiar tenor when Jay began his testimony. After restating the unique dimensions of the lot, he pointed out that as you drive through the development, the driveway is easily mistaken for another road. Although the driveway is "obviously narrower than a roadway," he acknowledged, "it's certainly striking as *not consistent* with the other homes." He explained that the lot needed to be created in this fashion because of wetlands requirements.[47] During construction, he explained, the prospective purchaser came to him with security concerns. He frequently travels abroad for work, leaving his wife and children home alone for lengthy periods of time, and he was worried, Jay explained, that "somebody could—unannounced—come up the driveway." Since the house "sits on its own away from all the other homes, it's really hard to see what's going on [back] there." The man wanted to find a way to enable his wife and children to control who came up to the house while he was away. The gate would have an electronic mechanism with a bell and an intercom system built into it. Jay explained that they all felt that this solution was "reasonable."

Jay then elaborated the prospective purchaser's concerns, particularly the possibility that some drivers might confuse the driveway with a roadway "if they are *not familiar* with the neighborhood and they're *sightseeing* or they get lost or they make a turn—and there they are pulling up in the front of this house, *who knows when or what time of night.*" Jay underscored that this made the man very uncomfortable. As Jay was saying this, a woman on the board nodded in agreement and murmured a quiet "yeah" under her breath. Perhaps it was her sympathetic body language and utterance that led Jay to feel that he could stop articulating his argument, or maybe he had planned to end his comments on that point. Regardless, he wrapped up his portion by pointing out that the six-foot-high gate that they were requesting was only for the width of the driveway, plus stanchions supporting it on either side. "Other than that," Jay added, "we're not seeking any other assistance with any heights for the rest of the property at this point."

David returned to the microphone, concluding their opening arguments by pointing out how the gate would accommodate necessary provisions, the first being the need for the fire and police departments to be able to get onto the property in the event of an emergency. He explained to the board that the motor of the gate would have a mechanism linking it to the alarm system in the house. Should the alarm go off, the gate would automatically open, thus providing for "the reverse side of the security, being able to gain access to the property." As a result, David emphasized, their request for this gate would not have any "negative impact"—his language for what the zoning code refers to as a "detriment to the public good." He then addressed another potential negative impact on the community: the aesthetics of the gate. (Danboro's land-use code grants the zoning board the power to "promote a desirable visual environment"[48] and to "encourage good aesthetics."[49]) He assured the board that the gate would not be an "eyesore," for it would be set back approximately twenty-five to thirty feet from the curb line.

David seemed quite confident as he closed, casually remarking that this was all he had. His tone and comportment implied that he expected the board to move to a vote right away, or at most to briefly ask a few clarifying questions. His apparent assurance was not surprising. Joan had moved their request up on the agenda because she thought that it would be quick. He and Jay had addressed the fundamental provisions in the zoning code, particularly the need for there to be something "unique" about the property that was creating an "undue hardship," and noted that the unique shape of the lot was in accommodation with environmentally friendly wetlands delineations. Jay's description of the prospective purchaser's worries was met with a sign of approval by a woman on the board, and they had acknowledged the limits of private property and the need to tend to local governance when they spoke to the accommodation of municipal services and policies, including police and fire department access and the zoning laws themselves. Additionally, they had tended to the aesthetic aspects of a "detriment to the public good," noting that the gate would not create an eyesore.

Despite their seemingly tight argument and the rapport that Jay apparently had with the board, the case that they constructed was resting on the shaky ground of class anxieties. Once the question-and-answer period began, the foundation of their case was unearthed, its retaining walls were chipped away, and the very structure of their claims caved in. Their real estate development corporation may technically be in the business of constructing custom homes, but they also are reconstructing towns that have a "sense" about who they are and what they do not want to become. A commonsense reaction emerged from members of the board as the hearing continued, unexpectedly extending the debate and shifting its tone from cordial to contentious.

SIGHTSEERS, TRESPASSERS, AND SECURITY CONCERNS

As Joan began the inquiry, it immediately became clear that she was not convinced by their argument regarding security concerns. She asked, "Now, is this . . . gate connecting to any other fencing on the property?" Jay shook his head no as he responded, "It's strictly just to preclude anybody from coming up the driveway. . . . On one side of the property, at this point, it's heavily wooded and people would not be able to get around. On the other side . . . there's another neighbor who has some landscaping and you would not be able to get around that way either." Joan had a look in her eye that indicated she was skeptical about something Jay was saying. "Let's, let's just talk about this," she proposed. "You mentioned that . . . [with this] long driveway . . . [the purchaser is] concerned that maybe somebody would have thought this was a road [to] outside the development or into another area?" Jay nodded in agreement and added, "Somebody that wasn't familiar with it, looking at this long straight alleyway/roadway/driveway . . . would think that this was another road . . . to another section of the development, when in actuality, it leads directly to this gentleman's house." David jumped in: "If I can elaborate on that as well. . . . You get quite a few sightseers who like to drive around and just see homes. . . . The concern was that a sightseer will actually find his way down the driveway to see the home maybe a little bit better . . . and . . . that will be a *trespass*." The gate would help "avoid any confusion that that was *private property* starting from the depression in the roadway where it meets the driveway." He then underscored, "That was *one* of his concerns, in addition to the security concern for his family."

It may have been the added tidbit thrown in about a "trespass" onto "private property," or maybe it was just general doubt, but Joan and other members of the board seemed to become more suspicious of the security claim. In a tone that revealed impatience, Joan reasoned, "Well, let's go on to the concern with safety. If the gate was attached to a fence that surrounded the property, we could talk about *security* because now we have a lock-in gate that's . . . surrounding the property." Becoming sarcastic, she added, "So you have a security compound, *if that's what you need in Danboro*. But what we have here is an *ornamental* gate to preclude somebody from driving up the driveway." Acting as if she were merely confused by their request, Joan asked in a coy, albeit reproachful tone, "Um, a sign at the bottom of the driveway wouldn't work the same . . . 'No Road,' 'No Legal Access'? I mean, why . . . a large ornamental gate just to block the driveway?"

David calmly responded, "Clearly, if somebody wants to climb their way into the property, he can climb over a six-foot-high or a four-foot-high [gate], for that matter. So, it's not . . . the township does have a good police department." But, he added, "the concern would be to preclude cars from being able to come through." Jay then jumped in: "The house itself is a very large home and it does get a lot of *looks*. . . . People are driving up to it on a regular basis. People *we* don't know. And that's under construction. And they have *no problem* driving down a dirt driveway to go look at the house a little closer. . . . [The homeowner] feels that people [are] going to be continuously doing that, notwithstanding the fact that it's *private property*." As Jay uttered these words, people in the audience shifted in their seats and turned to catch their neighbors' eyes. There had already been skepticism on Joan's part about the need for extra height when Jay and David first mapped out their case. But at this point in the hearing, a rupture occurred. When they were pressed to clarify their request, the concerns that had been foregrounded in their opening arguments gave way. No longer was the main fear a scenario in which a unique and incon- sistent driveway confused drivers who *inadvertently* found themselves at the secluded home. The issue was now trepidation about sightseers who *intentionally* committed a trespass, and whose desire to look showed dis- regard for the nature of private property.

Jay, however, had made a strategic move when he emphatically pointed out that the sightseers were "people *we* don't know." Like all members of the zoning board and most audience members that night, he, too, was a resident of Danboro. This underscoring was perhaps an attempt to clarify for everyone in the room that "sightseers" was meant to index a collective outsider; whether cars ended up on the doorstep of the prospective pur- chaser's home by way of intention or mishap, the sightseers were implied to be those outside the cozy comfort zone of Danboro's town hall. At that moment, I presumed that Jay was referring to people who live in the neighboring downtown area of Milldale. Coded language—in which racialized, class-encoded others are the referents—features prominently in the normative discourse in this white-flight town.[50] Lawyers inevitably draw on ambiguous terms and phrases like these to plead their cases since biased racial sentiments cannot explicitly be articulated in public munici- pal forums. But utilizing the term *sightseers* ended up being a colossal miscalculation. For one thing, there was an awkward juxtaposition between the term *sightseers* and descriptions of when they were doing their looking; it is quite difficult to sightsee at night. But more significant, there are many people in Danboro who like to go see new houses under construction and even get out of their cars to walk through the homes. It would not have seemed strange to any of the kids with whom I spent time during my fieldwork if their parents decided to stop and check out a new development while on their way home from the mall on a Saturday afternoon. The lawyer's and developer's use of *sightseers* was thus a bit too close to home. There was a palpable feeling in the room, which remained tangible throughout the hearing, that it was not a common Other who would be excluded if the variance were granted for this gate. It was as if *they* (that is, current town residents) were the sightseers being indexed, as if the prospective purchaser was proposing a gate to keep *them* out. Was it possible that they were no longer part of the meaningful "we" in the town, and that newcomers like the couple buying this house—with their moral logic of neoliberal privatopia—were a sign of what their town was becoming?

Objects being indexed by an utterance such as "sightseers" are, in Bakhtin's words, "overlain with qualifications, open to dispute, charged with value, already enveloped in an obscuring mist—or, on the contrary, by the 'light' of alien words that have already been spoken about it."[51] The "obscuring mist" of class anxieties, combined with the alienating words being used to describe those who were looking, made it extremely difficult for the lawyer and the developer to appropriate *sightseer* for their own uses. "Many words stubbornly resist . . . ; it is as if they put themselves in quotation marks against the will of the speaker. Language is not a neutral medium that passes freely and easily into the private property of the speaker's intentions; it is populated—overpopulated—with the intentions of others."[52] Once *sightseers* was in quotation marks that night, the lawyer's and the developer's efforts to control its referent were futile. And when Jay said that it was "people *we* don't know," maybe he *was* referring to other residents of Danboro who were strangers to him, David, and the prospective purchaser. Was it possible that those who had moved to Danboro during the early years of suburbanization, with their postwar liberal democratic understanding of private property, were now not unlike those targeted as undesirable in postwar exclusionary zoning practices, albeit now under the guise of sightseers who have no qualms about committing a trespass on private property and who thereby require gates to be kept out?

The subtextual anxiety about the possibility of becoming "stranger[s] outside the gates"[53] in their own town—both for people and for the local government—was illuminated as the conversation continued and Joan questioned Jay and David about the township's ability to access the property in an emergency. Joan asked, "Should the alarm system go off, the gate will automatically open?" David replied, "That's correct." Joan then inquired, "Should the power go out, what happens with the gate?" He explained that the system would be equipped with a battery backup. He was about to add something else, but Joan cut him off, calling attention to the fact that it is a *"very small* battery." In a skeptical, caustic voice, she pondered out loud, *"That* battery is going to open *this* gate *and* maintain the alarm system?" Jay jumped in and pointed out that there also would be a manual override to open the gate when the electricity was not working. David then added, "If the board was so inclined to grant the relief, we would certainly propose that the resolution meet the satisfaction of the township's police department [and] fire department, in terms of the ability to gain access and any overrides or backups as well." He conceded that if they could not come up with a system that was to the board's satisfaction, they understood that they would not be entitled to whatever relief was granted. It is the zoning board's duty to ensure—should a variance be granted—municipal access to a property in the event of an emergency. This particular line of questioning (i.e., about the "reverse side of security") was thus standard procedure in this regard. Nonetheless, the discussion suggested a subtext of defensive anxieties about what *else* it would mean if local government services were locked outside a gate within its municipal borders.

BARRICADES, STOCKADES, AND EXCLUSIONARY ORNAMENTALS

The tenor of the conversation continued to imply that there was something acutely troubling about this variance request, as if the appeal for a six-foot-high gate was asking far too much. This became particularly vivid during a linguistic tug-of-war regarding the ornamentation and aesthetics of the gate. As the discussion ensued, one of the board members interjected, with an annoyed look on his face, "Let me, um, . . . ask a question that will hopefully cut to the chase. . . . You testified that the purpose of erecting this *ornamental* fence is to [avoid] the cars driving down the driveway. Why do you need a six-foot fence?. . . . You're doubling [the height allowed by the ordinance] because you have an *ornamental* light on both sides and you have a very ornate ornamental on it in the center. If you cut those two lights out and you cut off the ornamental, you would be at four feet, which is one foot above the ordinance." The term *ornamental* can connote simple aesthetic additions, but also can suggest superfluous embellishments. By foregrounding the excessive ornamental aspects of the gate, the board member challenged the claim of functionality for the extra height sought.

David responded by first acknowledging that the "ability to stop people from driving down the road would be accomplished even within the township's ordinance." However, he explained, the prospective purchaser came up with a design that would also "fit the home." He does have a "legitimate concern . . . [about] the ability of people to traverse on the property," but he also is concerned that the design of the gate be "consistent" with the home. David continued:

> If we were to build it at three feet, the *impact* would be the same, I would feel, as six feet. . . . It's just his way of beautifying the entrance to this home in addition to providing his security concerns. . . . Whether we can stop the traffic with a three-foot fence? I think clearly that's obvious we could. But . . . he wants to do more than just simply put up a, you know, a *simple* gate that's gonna just look as, as a *barricade*. He wants to do something that will also beautify and be consistent with what he is doing on the property and in the development itself.

What David was implying, whether intentionally or not, was that the maximum height that the township allows—which has long been deemed appropriate for the town—imposes and maintains an unbecoming simplicity on par with no-nonsense military structures.

Joan quickly seized upon David's choice of words, deftly inverting his claims: "I understand that he wants to stop people from going into his driveway. But I think that the ultimate height of six feet is rather, um, *obtrusive* to the development when *nobody else* has something of this nature. It's gonna . . . almost appear as if there's a six-foot *stockade* across his driveway." By suggesting that the proposed six-foot-high gate would look like a "stockade," or a defensive fortification, Joan trumped David's claim that Danboro's three-foot zoning code was promoting simple-looking barricades. But more important, her remarks underscored the key tension in the case. David said that the prospective purchaser wanted his gate to be "consistent" with their home and with the development. But the proposed six-foot-high gate would not only be inconsistent with the development since, as Joan pointed out, "*nobody else* has something of this nature." It would also be incompatible with the town, since there were no other gates of its kind.

As the conversation continued, however, it seemed as if Jay and David were not clued in to these implications of their request. When David readied himself to reply to Joan's allegation, he took a deep breath, as if trying to control himself. After saying that he was going to "phrase this as intelligently" as he could (thus implying that the board was not getting his point), he tried to refute Joan's claim that "*nobody else* has something of this nature" by pointing out that there were quite a few people in the development who had stanchions that supported mailboxes, which "beautify their home" and were built in a way that was "consistent with the style of the home." (See figure 7 for typical stanchions.) But when he started his next sentence, Joan interrupted forcefully: "*No.* There are *no* mailboxes six feet high," after which she looked him squarely in the eye with a combat smile, as if to let him know that he was not getting away with such a claim. With a confident laugh, he acknowledged, "No, no, they're all about three feet high." He then explained that he was just trying to remind the board that the height of six feet represents the "tallest part of the ornamental section." Jay jumped into the conversation and in a semiannoyed tone reminded the board that the gate would be barely visible: "If I can just make one comment. This is not being built right at the edge of the driveway where the roadway is. It's inset quite a bit. . . . If you drove straight through the neighborhood, this would not pop out at you. It's twenty-five to thirty feet in and off of the road." He then told the board that they would be "more than willing" to push the gate back even farther into the vegetation.

Joan then said that she was wondering "how it's going to look aesthetically in the cul-de-sac." The driveway is located near a cul-de-sac at the end of the street. Cul-de-sacs are significantly distinct from other parts of

Figure 7. Typical stanchions.

subdivisions. Because of the limited presence of cars, children flock there to ride bikes and to play street games. They are semiotically powerful sites, indexing "community" and "neighborhood" through being a shared, public gathering place. In an extremely frustrated and hasty tone, Jay pointed out, "First of all, actually, the house is not even in the cul-de-sac. It's just before you get there. So it's actually part of the straight run of the road." He then underscored that they set the gate back so that it would not be at the curb line and "stand out."

Joan snapped back, "*Again*, the fence doesn't have to be six feet high." She then voiced what was clearly on most people's minds, for there was a lot of head nodding when she said, "It just appears that there isn't a valid reason other than they *like* it to be six feet high." David responded by asking her, "Is there a particular height that you would feel comfortable with, Madame Chairperson?" Before she had a chance to answer, another board member said, "I'm six-six, and I'm considered a pretty tall guy. This is a *tall* fence. Even though it's set back twenty to thirty feet, it's a mammoth-looking fence." He then said that he would recommend that it be no more than four feet at the highest point: "I think it would fit in nicer to the surrounding area."

Jay and David conferred for a moment, after which Jay returned to the stanchions issue. As he was reminding the board that stanchions are built on many properties, Joan stopped him in the middle of his comments, speaking over him as she said, "So, we really don't want to talk about this." Joan never explicitly stated what the "this" was that they did not want to talk about. Perhaps it was the fact that once the indexicality of the sightseers had shifted, it no longer mattered whether other people had stanchions; whether the gate would be seen or how far back it was located; whether it was on the cul-de-sac or on the straight run of the road; or whether it was the ornamentals or the gate itself that was causing the extra height. The bottom line was that "nobody else" in town had a six-foot-high, regal-style gate to keep people *out*.

This important distinction—which matters deeply when powerful anxieties about exclusion and discursive displacement are at play—seemed to be lost on Jay and David. This was most evident when Jay retook the floor. In a conciliatory tone he pointed out, "It's not a question of trying to negotiate with the board. At three feet, the concern is that it would be about waist high. It wouldn't accomplish any kind of grand entrance." When Jay uttered the words *grand entrance,* many in the audience looked shocked. He was still trying to make that point? Apparently not sensing the sentiment in the room, Jay *did* negotiate: "Maybe the board would be inclined at five feet, to allow—" But before he had a chance to finish, Joan jumped in, sounding extremely irritated and tired, albeit willing to negotiate: "Personally, I would feel a lot better if it was no greater than five feet high. . . . And I think that's a compromise . . . that maybe we could live with." Jay tried to interject a comment, but Joan forcefully continued, "Personally, other than stopping somebody from going up the driveway, I see *no* security from this fence whatsoever. I can understand that the . . . purchaser is concerned with them thinking it's an access road. . . . But it's definitely not offering any security when you can just walk around it." Perhaps trying to cut their losses, David concluded, "With that, Madame Chairperson, we would like to amend our application before the board to . . . five feet."

OPENING THE DOOR TO FUTURE FENCING

Joan paused for a moment, took a deep breath, and looked around the room. It was time to give the public an opportunity to share their thoughts. The one person who spoke lived right next door to the property in the same development and raised an issue that brought the predicament of exclusionary possibilities to another level. He explained that he was worried "that we might be talking about a fence around the property after this is constructed. . . . I wouldn't want to see even a five-foot fence across the entire property to match a five-foot gate." The board attorney pointed out to the man, "For your information, the application here is just for the gate that has been discussed here. If they wanted to then put [up] a five-foot fence, they would have to come back in front of the board." The neighbor cut him off at the end, nervously explaining, "I understand that. However, if you allow construction of a five-foot gate, I feel that it would open the door possibly to a fence that would match it, at the same height." The board attorney reiterated, "They would need to return to this board."

The attorney's comment clearly sidestepped the neighbor's fear of soon living next to a "security compound," as Joan had remarked earlier in the meeting—the possibility of which was insinuated at the start of the hearing when Jay ended his opening statements by declaring, "We're not seeking any other assistance with any heights for the rest of the property *at this point*." And the likelihood was made even more pronounced when David joined the discussion. He pointed out to the board that he and the neighbor, whom he referred to by name, "know each other well enough, and I think we still have a very good rapport." He then looked the man in the eye, said that he understood his concerns, but acknowledged: "Regrettably, the township's ordinance, as it's drafted now, would allow a fence in the front yard, a fence on the side yard, with restrictions as to height. And this relief, granted or not, would not preclude this particular resident, when he moves in, from making an application and fencing in his entire property. This particular section of the property, rather than having a three-foot-high [fence], would have a five-foot-high [fence]." While claiming to understand the neighbor's concerns, David seemed not to appreciate the exclusionary semiotic effects of a five-foot-high fence and what one property owner's approach to neoliberal self-optimization means to his neighbors.[54] This obliviousness was acutely evident when he added, "The extent of the impact, as I indicated earlier . . . is no negative impact on the community itself, *at all*. Whether he is going to actually [add] additional fencing, I can't intelligently comment."

Sounding increasingly frustrated with the direction of the conversation, David tried to bring the discussion back to security concerns and aesthetic possibilities. His approach, however, was strikingly confrontational: "I concur with your comments, Madame Chairperson, that if somebody wants to get in, a three-foot-high fence is not going to stop them. Maybe the *dogs* on the other side of a three-foot fence might. . . . The purpose here is just, in part, to beautify the entrance; to provide some security to preclude the cars from coming in; and we're hoping with some compromise, we can accomplish both of those without having just a simple three-foot-high stockade fence." There was a flabbergasted pause in the room when David finished speaking. As if an image of dogs being used to keep sightseers at bay was not provocation enough, he had uttered the words *simple* and *stockade* in a matter-of-fact tone, as if there were nothing divisive about them. Within this context, those words felt as hostile as the dogs, and the chasm in understanding in the debate felt as wide as the rift growing between residual and dominant moral logics of private property in the United States.

DESIRE, HARDSHIP, AND A "FEELING" OF SECURITY

After an awkward silence, Joan asked the board members to offer their thoughts in preparation for taking a vote. The first to speak proposed that the prospective purchaser get rid of "the lights and the swoop in the middle that's ornamental and just keep it to a *plain*, four-foot fence." He explained that this would still accomplish what the purchaser wanted to do, which was to prevent cars from entering the property. The next board member spoke in a sympathetic tone, acknowledging that he understood "the prospective owner's desire to have this [gate] kind of be ornamental to go along with the type of house that he wants." He agreed that the main part of the fence should be four feet, but he felt that there should also be allowed a bit more height for some design. "We could probably make some sort of a design or something that's maybe a half a foot higher, or something in the middle to swoop it down that way." It is striking that the second board member used *we* in his statement. This inclusive pronoun was an implicit acknowledgment—despite all the concerns raised during the meeting—of the legitimacy of the couple's desire for a gate that was aesthetically and dimensionally consistent with their home. The proposed gate's style embodied an aesthetic that could be considered "SOOOooo . . . Danboro," and the board member even offered design recommendations. But since the couple's home—like other new houses built in Danboro during those years—was out of scale with the moderately sized homes in town, the normative desire for consistency *within* properties competes with the desire for consistency *across* properties. The proposed gate semiotically teetered on this style-scale tension and, by default, on the tension between private property and the public good, which can include the feeling of being part of the meaningful, dominant "we" of the town.

The next board member's comments threw this predicament into relief: "I've heard *desire* on the part of the applicant to beautify the property, to present a fence that's consistent with the scale of the house. And I can understand that." But, he reminded everyone, "I think the charge we have is to try and find reasons consistent with the law to grant variances." The next board member underscored this point: "I think it's the obligation of this board to hear applicants who have a valid reason for *hardship*. I think you've come in and made a security statement at the beginning, but we've relented on that and it is an ornamental, decorative thing. . . . I don't feel that any *hardship* has been established, and I'm not in favor of anything higher than three feet, as the code so states." The final board member agreed that there were "limited reasons" to justify six feet or five feet. However, she was willing to compromise and grant a variance for four feet, with extra height for the "decorations."

Joan took another deep breath, looked around the room, and said that she had been listening carefully to everyone's comments. While she agreed "as far as there being no proof to grant a variance," she thought that the applicant "offered somewhat his concern for people driving up what would appear to be a roadway . . . [or] an access road out . . . since the house is set back so much further than everybody else's house." Joan proposed that the gate be three feet high across, with an allowable extra foot for the lights and the decorative effect. "It'll give the contract purchaser of the house some *feeling* of security so that somebody's not driving up."

Joan's appreciation for the prospective purchaser's need for a *"feeling* of security" was also a significant acknowledgment—particularly right after the other board members' recognition of the couple's desire for the gate to be consistent with the house—that aesthetic desires do not necessarily trump security concerns. It is quite common for people to have aesthetic desires enmeshed with tangible fears and elusive anxieties, which are complicated and compounded by the predicament of visibility and those who "look." As Erika's stream of associations about her well-cut lawn in the previous chapter revealed, it is fully within the normative sentiments in Danboro, and the United States more broadly, that the proposed gate could make the couple feel safer *because* of its grand aesthetics, even if it was not truly secure. The mounting penchant for gated communities, sport-utility vehicles, and other efforts to consume a *feeling* of class security in the United States are cases in point. So while "aesthetic desires" and "hardship" may have been opposed throughout the debate, their relationship, as this part of the meeting recognized, is clearly far more complex. This moment of empathy, however, was short-lived—and quickly eroded as the debate entered the final wrap-up and people in the audience started to get punchy.

MOCKING REGAL PRETENSIONS

Joan began to contemplate out loud the predicament that the couple would face if they had to stay within the limits of the ordinance: "There's no way to construct a fence . . . in any ornamental fashion . . . at three feet straight across. . . . If we give 'em an extra foot to put the lights on and to put that ornamental . . . *crown* . . . [it] might allow for what they want the fence to look like." The instant that *crown* came out of her mouth, several people in the audience began to laugh, and then a smirk formed on Joan's face. Wit—with the "lively current of unease powering [it]"[55]—grants people another medium through which to critique, deflate, and defend against perceived threats.[56] This type of humor enabled a more pointed criticism of the exclusionary implications of the request through mocking its regal pretensions.

There were still a few board members, however, who—regardless of the humorous tone in the room—continued to directly oppose the request, reiterating concerns that had been raised all evening: they had not heard any reason "under the law" for the gate to be higher than three feet; the application did not "meet the hardship [requirement] clearly set forth in the statute"; the request was "more of an aesthetic application"; and there was no other fencing like it in the neighborhood, so the gate would be a "detriment." And one board member reminded everyone that Danboro was "trying to avoid gates like in Roseburg"—an affluent town that borders Danboro and allows six-foot-high gates. This abrupt loss of appreciation for the couple's desire for aesthetic consistency underscored that while consistency (in general) was a commonsense desire in the town, a stronger desire was for consistency *across* the town.

Joan then stated what everyone in the room was probably thinking: "On something that was very simple, it has turned into something that is not so simple!" She reminded everyone, "Let's keep in mind that three feet would be allowed anyway. So what we're talking about . . . is one foot for some ornamental crown on the top and two lights." She noted that she had been out to the property, and that there is "somewhat of an unusual circumstance" since the driveway does look like a street. She then remarked in a serious tone, albeit with emphasis of her Brooklyn accent, "I wouldn't want to have to plow that driveway when it snows." There were some chuckles from the crowd, after which she smiled and added with flair, "Because it's very big!" She then asked for consensus from the board for three feet with one extra foot allowed for the ornamentals, "keeping in mind that he could have a three-foot stockade fence straight across the property, if he desired to do so." She then quickly rephrased her words, pointing out that it would be "a three-foot *fence* across the property. *Not stockade.* I'm sorry. I didn't mean that. But it could *resemble* something that looks like that, if he wanted to do so!" There was more laughter in the room, during which a woman sitting near me, a resident of one of the moderately sized homes behind the commercial park, joked that it could be a "picket fence!"

Joan then asked David, "Is this something you would compromise to . . . or is the applicant gonna just say, 'Forget it'?" He replied that "the applicant'll seek to get as much relief as I can from this board." He then turned and spoke in the direction of the board attorney, seemingly still not getting it:

> I believe our burden is not just a matter of establishing positive criteria that we have a special hardship, which I think has been established by the unique shape of the property and the concerns that are associated with the long driveway, which is *inconsistent* with everything else. More importantly . . . I don't think that there would be any impact on the community. . . . Quite the contrary, I think that the . . . three-foot-high straight run of the gate . . . would probably have a worse impact on the area than allowing them to do something a little more *elaborate,* that would allow them to *beautify the general area.*

The whole time he was speaking, most audience members seemed no longer to be listening. He may have continued to imagine that an "elaborate" gate would "beautify the general area," but most people in the room had long before agreed—through explicit statements, sidebar jokes, and knowing glances—that "beautifying" can be taken too far. If the proposed gate were allowed, it would modify the boundaries of what is "SOOOooo . . . Danboro" and require a redefinition of what is consistent and inconsistent in the town. While developers attract buyers to subdivisions like Tarragon Hills by proclaiming that there are "No Two Homes Alike!" and operate under the principle that the optimization of a property necessarily benefits neighboring properties, there is only so far that uniqueness can be taken until it becomes a detriment. The proposed gate would further upscale the town, possibly price more people out, and create a relentless reminder for those who hold residual middle-class sensibilities of the radically altered middle-class playing field and its norms in regard to private property.

It was now time for Joan's final statement for the record in preparation for the board vote. She was particularly careful with her wording: "Taking into consideration the applicant's desire . . . to protect the driveway, which appears as a roadway because of the unusual shape of the property, the applicant has asked for a fence to be placed across the driveway. The fence is to be no more than three feet high with an extra foot allowed for lights on either end and an ornamental crown-shaped design in the middle. The lights will serve as, um, additional protection." When Joan mentioned the "ornamental crown-shaped design," there were bursts of giggles in the audience, and the woman who had made the "picket fence" comment murmured under her breath, "coat of arms." Several people in the audience laughed at her comment, during which the man from the historic commission leaned in her direction and joined the "collusive sideplay"[57] by asking, "Did they pick a color yet?" The woman turned her head in his direction, chuckling in confirmation as she caught his eye. People like this elderly man, who have been living in Danboro since it was a farming community, have long lamented the presence of suburbanites like this woman, who index the loss of Danboro's pastoral past. But in the face of encroaching privatopia and through newly dominant middle-class sensibilities being articulated in bourgeois terms, these two groups appreciated their commonalities in this historical moment. With their shared concerns about the influx of the regal, a feeling of communitas emerged between them amid the mockery.[58]

While everyone in the audience laughed and talked among themselves, Joan finished up her statement and took the vote. Each board member voted yes; Joan's suggestion of a three-foot-high fence—with an allowable foot for the extras—passed unanimously. (See figure 8.) A huge sense of relief swept through the room as everyone realized that the hearing on this issue—which had taken over an hour—was finally done. Danboro's residents with residual liberal sensibilities were able in that moment to feel like insiders—and not "sightseers"—in their own town. Amid this release, Joan thanked everybody for their efforts, and then leaned over the table toward the audience and exclaimed (as if asking for forgiveness), "I thought this was going to be twenty minutes!"

TEMPERING THE PREVALENCE OF NEOLIBERAL SPACE MAKING

The public hearing for this couple's proposed six-foot-high ornamental security gate became a forum for the subtextual display of class anxieties, which were exacerbated during the economic boom years of the late 1990s. The decision not to grant the full six feet demonstrates an effort to temper the prevalence of neoliberal space making through the policing of

Figure 8. The gate, as built.

aesthetic regimes. Jay and David—as representatives for the prospective purchasers—became signs of class transformations in the United States and their associated shifts in moral logics in regard to private property. This infused and doomed their legal strategy and persuasion tactics by evoking ever-present anxieties in town. Once these anxieties became dominant during the meeting, especially after the reference to sightseers, there was an irrevocable shift, pushing the prospective purchasers' security concerns and aesthetic desires out of the realm of the possible for the majority of the debate. A palpable feeling emerged that the purchasers, David, and Jay were—despite the fact that Jay was a long-time resident himself—making an aesthetic request that was overstepping the boundaries of architectural (and thereby fiscal and discursive) inclusion and exclusion in the town. Their deployment of patriarchy (i.e., the fear of a wife being left alone at home while her husband is away) effectively justified the couple's class desires. But, strikingly, an apparent mobilization of racial anxieties through coded language was not able to overpower the subtextual class anxieties at play.

This commonsense reaction to neoliberal space making continued to be present in Danboro long after this debate. Several years later, I called the office of the Danboro Zoning Board of Adjustment to ask for clarification on a few issues. I explained to the woman who answered the phone that I had questions about having a six-foot-high security gate across a driveway. In a panicked tone, she told me that I would need to speak with the clerk. Before I had a chance to explain why I was asking, she transferred me to the clerk, who immediately told me that Danboro does not allow six-foot-high gates in the front of one's property. If I wanted to do so, she added somewhat hostilely, I would need to submit an application for a variance. When I had the chance to explain that I was asking for research purposes—and not as a resident who was looking to build such a structure—she seemed profoundly relieved. She rattled off the name of the couple's street off the top of her head, asking if it was *their* application that I was asking about. It was quite indicative of the significance of this request that after several years and hundreds of cases, that street (in a town with over 750 streets) was still so present in her mind. Still present, too, was the feeling of being flabbergasted by the request, which came through when she informed me that no one had *ever* made *that* kind of request before the couple had, nor had *anyone* done so since.

Granted, all applications for relief of zoning ordinances test the limits of a property owner's entitlement vis-à-vis the public good and a governing municipality. But the rupture during the public hearing for this proposed gate opened a window onto how this tension was articulated in cultural, moral, aesthetic, and visceral terms during the late 1990s. Those on the upwardly mobile side of the growing middle-class chasm who hold a dominant neoliberal sensibility could always afford to buy a home in the town. There is no way for a town to zone out the relatively rich. But through restricting the accoutrements allowed on properties, the zoning board can send the message to those who are considering buying homes in Danboro that Danboro wants to stay a town that is at least trying to hold on to postwar liberal logics of private property. As the reaction of the next-door neighbor revealed, a person's moral approach to property does not necessarily map onto the size of their house.

This debate revealed a spontaneous, commonsense reaction that closed the gate for the moment on neoliberal architectural space making in the town. It was not articulated through an intentional effort against neoliberalizing space, unlike developed antigentrification movements. Yet its political and economic effect, through limiting the height of gates, was comparable to an ideological effort. It was an "agentive moment"[59] that proved contrary to Gramsci's expectation that common sense is, more often than not, a conservative cultural logic that needs to be transformed into coherent political consciousness for there to be political effects. In the late 1990s, a conservative reaction to gating was counterhegemonic, since the production of space was heading in the class-divisive direction of which Lefebvre had warned.[60] Of course, had this debate taken place ten years later amid the economic crisis, perhaps this discussion might not have taken place on the level of the subtextual, since the structural conditions and moral logics that shaped landscapes of middle-class life had by then become explicit topics of public discourse.[61]

This last stand of the liberal sensibility, however, was overshadowed in Danboro by the variety of ways in which people were resolutely driving after class in other contexts in their everyday lives: their homes, their relationships, their cars, their schools. As the next chapters reveal, the anxieties thrown into relief during the debate, which led to the proposed six-foot-high ornamental security gate being denied, were at the same time—quite paradoxically—fueling pervasive non-architectural means of gating. Much like the couple's proposed gate, these vehicles for rugged entitlement offered a "feeling" of security, even if they were not truly secure. And they did so in a way that often was a "detriment" to others (and at times, themselves), further revealing the regulative relationship between class anxieties, objects of display, aesthetics of security, and changing material conditions undergirding middle-class life.

4 Driving after Class

This chapter shifts our focus away from the common sense articulated at Danboro's town hall and brings us into the intimacies of everyday life for one particular family, for whom I worked as an "ethnographic babysitter" a few afternoons per week for sixteen months. Seeking to sustain an upper-middle-class lifestyle, parents like those in the Sillen family often work long hours in high-level professional-managerial jobs. They frequently depend on the private service sector to accomplish the bulk of their domestic chores and responsibilities. I was hired to help undertake everyday parenting jobs—a role that ranged from sandwich maker to homework tutor, from sympathetic ear to disciplinarian. But as is often the case in suburbia, my main job was—literally—to drive after class. On any given afternoon, I was picking up five-year-old Sam from preschool or karate lessons or the YMCA, or taking eleven-year-old Doug to soccer practice or guitar lessons or to a friend's house, or getting fifteen-year-old Julia from school or her volunteer job or her SAT tutor. Through this positioning I became a witness to (and sometimes unwitting participant in) efforts at figuratively "driving after class."

The Sillens lived in a subdivision of moderately sized colonial-style homes—the type of houses that used to be the norm in the town. As the previous chapter revealed, the changing architectural landscape and moral logics of property in Danboro created anxieties for many people in town about the security of class locations. As this chapter shows, so, too, did the volatility of professional-managerial work, which compounded anxieties about raising children in the late 1990s and about who would be granted the power and authority to influence the children and to be in a position of proximity, intimacy, and vulnerability with the family. These anxieties shaped practices that in turn led to other anxieties and practices, all of which created new subjects and spaces—the Bourdieuian "structured structures" that are "structuring structures."[1] In this chapter, I take great care to bring to life the subtleties of subject formation and to depict how subjectivities matter in shaping practices, spaces, and sentiments that in turn shape other people's subjectivities—ultimately asking what futures are being produced through this ever-shifting dialectical process. The aspects of daily life illustrated in this chapter elucidate how the pressures of precarious class position intersected with, were compounded by, and generated further class anxieties, consumer desires, habits of expectation, unfulfilled aspirations, gendered predicaments, racial fears, and class-encoded suspicions.

The ethnographic moments explored may be located inside the Sillens' home, at the mall, and during car rides to and from after-school activities. Yet the desires, sentiments, and practices explored here—like those revealed in the debate about the proposed six-foot-high ornamental security gate—are inextricable from anxieties about the ability to attain and maintain a piece of the shrinking middle-class pie. With the lack of an elaborated macrostructural analysis in the public discourse, anxieties instead played out in everyday struggles and ambivalences. Much in the way that the locus of anxiety and "activism" in Danboro's town hall played out in regard to the gate and those who proposed it, concern and policing in the Sillen family typically engaged "local" things and issues rather than a broader critique of structural shifts undergirding the volatile climate. Whether this involved yearnings for particular consumer products, enjoyment of objects of class distinction, efforts to keep new carpet clean, frustrations about being too busy, excitement about learning the intricacies of the stock market, gendered reactions to working mothers, or racialized anxieties about babysitters and school spaces, they are analyzed for how they are both reflections of the political economic moment and conditions for producing neoliberal subjects.

As Karen Brodkin Sacks reminds us, "Not only is class experienced in historically-specific ways, but it is also experienced in racially specific, gender-specific, and kinship-specific ways."[2] Racialized, gendered, and class-encoded hopes, desires, expectations, habits, sentiments, and thus ultimately new people (in the Gramscian sense) were being shaped within the dynamics of the Sillen family. This "learning," however, was countered by its underbelly: discomfort, ambivalence, exhaustion, and profound questioning of the disciplinary practices and structuring forces in all of their lives. This enormous ambivalence on the part of both parents and children reveals that despite playing the game and divining its hidden rules, they all felt as if something was off or missing or wrong. These feelings of unsettling doubt, however, were more often than not obscured by the overwhelming habit of driving after class. Unable to imagine a way out beyond nostalgia for easier days or imagined other places, and lacking in their midst the conditions of possibility for significant habit-change, the members of this family—each in their own way—continued to fuel up for the ride.

The story that I tell here is "SOOOooo Danboro," despite the fact that Bonnie and Kevin Sillen grew up comfortably middle-class and had moved their family to Danboro from a small city in the Midwest. The cultural politics of a class moment are refracted through the dominant common sense and the particularities of place. Like many of their neighbors who are post-Brooklyn, the Sillens were struggling in part because of the changing class structure, and they were doing so in a way that was "normative" in the town. They, like so many families in Danboro, came to feel trapped by what their lives had become there. It is a testament, I believe, to the power of place and the predominance of rugged entitlement that the ethnographic moments I observed and experienced in the everyday lives of the Sillen family—despite their different trajectory—resonate with so much that was "there" in Danboro during the late 1990s.

"CHOOSING SIMILARITY"

I originally inquired about this job to make extra money to fund my research. It was not until several months into working for the Sillens that

I decided to ask them for retroactive permission to include their family in my project. So the first time I drove over to their house on a Sunday afternoon I was simply a student looking for extra money. Bonnie welcomed me at the door and led me to the den, where fifteen-year-old Julia was working on the computer and eleven-year-old Doug and five-year-old Sam were lying on the floor playing Nintendo 64. Julia's long, dark-brown hair was blown out straight, and she was wearing a form-fitting sweater, M.U.D.D. bell-bottom jeans, and Steve Madden platform shoes—the uniform of choice among Danboro girls at the time. Doug was sporting baggy pants, a soccer T-shirt, and a necklace made of silver-plated beads. His hair was messy, although clearly made to look that way with a little bit of gel. Sam was wearing Gap jeans with an oversize Pokémon T-shirt. Bonnie introduced me to the children, eventually prodding Sam to say hello after his older siblings had paused to glance and wave my way. All three kids quickly returned to what they had been doing, but they could still hear our conversation because we had sat down at the kitchen table, and the den and the kitchen were combined within one huge room.

Bonnie had straight brown, shoulder-length hair, which was neatly styled, and wore nice gold jewelry and a watch with her simple yet well-fitting Banana Republic stretch pants and silk shirt. I had seen a lot of moms in Danboro looking put together like this, even on Sunday afternoons. But during this interview—and in fact throughout the entire time that I was working for her over the course of the sixteen months that followed—there was something anxious in her seemingly confident presentation of self, as if she had something to prove or rather to establish.[3] Her apparent confidence was tinged with a hint of uncertainty, perhaps provoked and exaggerated by my presence: who I was (a white middle-class Ph.D. candidate), what I represented (high cultural capital, low economic capital), and what role I played in her home (a low-wage service worker).

It was during this first meeting that it became clear why she wanted to hire someone like me. Speaking over the beeping sounds of the video game, Bonnie told me that she had been disappointed with the housekeepers she had had in the past. She found that things would often slide when one person was responsible for "doing the floors" *and* taking care of the kids. She said that she also "hated having those depressed women who would go onto the porch and cry that they missed their family in Ghana."

So, she decided to do things a little differently this time. She hired Katarina, a Polish woman, to clean once every two weeks. Now she was looking for an "all-around responsible person" to take care of her children a few afternoons per week, and she wanted someone who also could help the kids with their homework.

Bonnie had been doing all of this work herself for some time because she had been laid off from her previous job doing research at a university medical center. Bonnie made it a point to note that her dismissal was due to the fact that the grant she was working under was not renewed. I nodded in empathy, commiserating with her about working in worlds so dependent upon grants. Bonnie then told me she had spent some time doing other kinds of work, like residential real estate and part-time tutoring. But now she was going back to work as a "professional"—as she defined her job status—at a pharmaceutical company, which is why she needed someone to take over many of the "mom tasks" for her. When Bonnie finished her overture, she assured me that she had "great kids," that she and her husband were "very educated" (he had a Ph.D. and she had a master's degree) and that this would be a good job, "not like working for a blue-collar family."

Bonnie's disparaging, racialized remarks about previous babysitters did not surprise me. Danboro is a town in which many adults freely shared this type of racial commentary. Her desire, as well, to hire someone white, educated, and from a middle-class background corresponded with discussions at that time about families who were "choosing similarity" to shore up their children's habitus in a time of increased competition.[4] What did feel out of the blue was her comment about their not being a blue-collar family. The more I thought about it, however, her need to assert their class positioning (and their cultural capital) made complete sense when juxtaposed with her narrative about moving in and out of "professional" jobs. Her well-dressed manner, too, on a leisurely Sunday afternoon exuded what Bourdieu refers to as the middle classes' "concern for 'seeming.'"[5]

This "concern for 'seeming'" came to matter quite differently in the late 1990s. The power and privilege of being in the middle class—and the very stability of a middle-class positioning—had radically diminished. In a volatile economy with a neoliberal state offering minimal support for middle-class families, and in a town with architectural reminders of the shifting middle-class terrain, there was far more at stake in appearing "as if." The very fact that Bonnie no longer wanted a working-class babysitter of color is revealing in this regard. In the post–World War II period—when the middle class dramatically expanded—acquiring a maid or a nanny of color was a way for those who were newly middle class (and often "not quite white") to achieve a sense of having arrived. The shift to middle-class neighborhoods (and for some, middle-class work) was often not enough; a servant "below" enabled them to construct and reflect their new positions of power and authority.[6] Granted, there were many families in Danboro who had working-class domestic workers of color. The buses from New York City on Sunday nights were full of women (and a few men), often recent immigrants from the Caribbean, who stayed for the week in Danboro before returning on Friday evenings to Brooklyn where they lived.[7] But could it be that during the late 1990s entrenchment of neoliberalism, with heightened anxieties about class stability, a working-class babysitter of color no longer enhanced a sense of class and race security for families like the Sillens?

As Bonnie began to interview me, her yearning to have someone with similar cultural capital and class credentials was even more evident. When she asked me about what I was doing in my life, her face lit up when I mentioned that I was working on my Ph.D. in anthropology at the University of Michigan. At first I assumed that her excitement was because she and Kevin had lived in the Midwest. But when I tried to connect with her through a boy-did-it-snow-a-lot-out-there reminiscence, she seemed eager to move on to inquire about other aspects of my life, particularly where I had grown up. Her eyes once again opened wide with interest when I told her the name of the coastal New Jersey town in which I was raised. Once again, I naively took her interest to be a form of bonding, albeit this time through Jersey geography. But as she inquired more about my childhood and youth in the town, it became clear that her interest had more to do with what it was like growing up in my well-known, upper-middle-class hometown.

I still had naive faith (or rather hope) that Bonnie would want to know about my experience working with children. I tried to inform her about my many summers as a camp counselor and a group leader working with children who were Doug's and Julia's ages. But every time I brought up this expertise, her attention seemed to drift off, as if she were not interested. It was only Doug, who I had assumed was engrossed in his video game, who sat up and took notice when he heard the name of the camp where I had worked. He asked me if I knew a couple of girls from his school who had attended the camp. I knew of one of them, so he and I chatted a bit more, after which I turned back toward Bonnie, still expecting to be asked more about my child-care experience. Instead, she jokingly inquired if I had a good memory because the kids have crazy schedules. I responded with a good-humored yes. She then asked me if I had a safe car. When I said that I drove a Nissan Pathfinder, she was extremely happy to hear that it was an SUV.[8] Without any more questions, she asked me what I thought I should be paid. A bit perplexed at that moment, I asked her if she wanted any references or to hear more about my credentials. Nope, she said as she waved her hand in a sign of disregard for those technicalities. She really wanted it to work out with me. In fact, she was not going to interview anybody else, she adamantly declared.

Bonnie's husband, Kevin, walked in the door at this point. He was not much taller than Bonnie, and looked a bit disheveled after running errands all day in khaki pants, sneakers, and a stretched-out sweater. Bonnie jumped up and ran over toward him, excitedly rattled off my credentials, and highlighted that I was a Ph.D. student. Before Kevin had a chance to respond, she took out her calendar and pointed to the days that I would be able to work. While she was asking Kevin about his vacation days, in the hopes of trying to coordinate our schedules, I could see that he was a bit overwhelmed with the barrage of information and questions. With an annoyed tone and wandering eyes that indicated discomfort, he cut off Bonnie's flow of arrangement making and suggested to her that they discuss this all later. I don't know what they discussed, but Bonnie called the next day to find out when I would be able to begin. We made plans for a Sunday afternoon a couple of weeks later, so that she could give me a rundown on all of my responsibilities and take me to all the places to which I would be driving the kids.

When I arrived at the house this second time, Bonnie gave me a tour first of their home. After chatting for a moment in the open foyer with a chandelier dangling above, we walked up the stairs to the platform on the second floor, off of which were all of the bedrooms. Sam, being the youngest, had the room nearest to his parents, with walls covered in Pokémon posters, sports banners, shelves of books and toys, and family pictures from vacations and family celebrations. Doug's room was just down from Sam's—clearly that of an impending teenager. His walls, too, had sports banners and pictures of famous wrestlers and hockey players; he also had shelves lined with soccer trophies, CDs, and a high-quality sound system. Just across from Doug's room was Julia's room—clearly that of the girl in the family, with pink walls, decorative wallpaper, and a full-length mirror. Bonnie then led me back downstairs, pointing to the formal living room and formal dining room. Bonnie explained that they did not use those rooms much, unless company came over; she preferred, therefore, that the children not spend much time in there so that it stayed neat. We then walked back into the combined kitchen and den area that made up the back part of their house. She opened and shut lots of drawers and cabinets in the kitchen, revealing where I could find everything that I needed to make the kids' lunches or to whip up dinner if she was running late.

Bonnie then drove me around town to show me where I would be taking the kids. I knew most of the places, since I had been living in the area for almost four months, but there were a few nooks that were tricky, like Sam's preschool. It was a tough place to find since it was embedded in the back end of a strip mall on a particularly busy section of Route 2. Bonnie swung her car past the preschool so that I knew which door to enter when I picked up Sam, after which we made our way to Doug's various soccer practice fields, including the well-kept municipal soccer fields nestled in the woods behind Danboro Middle School. After a quick drive-by of the parking lot next to the fields where Doug would be waiting, we decided that Bonnie did not need to take me to the hospital where Julia volunteered. The development in which I lived was just down the street, so I knew exactly where it was.

On our way home, Bonnie told me that she had "a really good feeling" about me; she knew we were going to "make it work." She assured me that she was "fair" and not a "bad" person, and that I wouldn't be working "for" her as much as "with" her. She underscored that she did not see me as an "employee," but more as a "friend," so I should feel free to come and talk with her about anything. There were, in fact, times during our ride that afternoon when we were chatting like new friends. We talked about her hopes and concerns for her children and had a nice conversation about how I was managing to live in the New York area on limited grant money. Bonnie joked with me that despite the fact that she had once lived as a graduate student, she could no longer remember how she was able to live on so little. Her geniality was warm and welcoming. And yet there was a palpable undercurrent of tension in the car that afternoon that was present in our relationship during the sixteen months that I worked "with" her; it kept in view the ambiguous, and at times provocative, dynamic when a domestic "employee" is someone of the same "kind" who could also be a "friend."

When we got back to the house that afternoon, Kevin wrote down the keypad code that opened their garage doors, as well as the code for the security alarm system for the house. Even though they had gotten my name from a woman we knew in common, I was still a bit surprised that they were so trusting of me, so fast. There were many scary child-care stories at that time, including one of a babysitter who had kidnapped the children in her care, making many parents exceedingly anxious about whom they put in charge of their children's welfare. But perhaps in a historical moment when middle-class security was being eroded, a white Ph.D. candidate from an upper-middle-class town was the right "kind" of babysitter to further cultivate their children's habitus. What more was there to ask? As I walked out of the house with these thoughts in mind, I was curiously relieved when Bonnie asked me if I could bring a copy of my driver's license the next time that I came over. At least they were going to make sure I had a safe driving record.

ALL CONSUMING: LEARNING HABITS OF ANTICIPATION AND DESIRE

It was a typical afternoon a few months into my time working for the Sillens. I had parked on the street in front of their house and was walking up their driveway, on which there was a regulation-size basketball hoop for fifteen-year-old Julia and eleven-year-old Doug, and a plastic, miniature version for five-year-old Sam. Sam's little hoop was lying toppled over on the grass, as it always was. All it took was a little gust of wind to knock it on its side. It always struck me as a metaphor for the instability of their middle-class positioning. As I walked past, I lifted up Sam's pint-size hoop, waved to the Mexican-American man trimming the front hedges, and let myself into the house by tapping in the code on the security pad that opened one of the garage doors. I walked through the garage and entered the laundry room, where I took off my shoes. The Sillens had just laid down new bone-colored wall-to-wall carpeting in the den, and no one was allowed to wear shoes on it. In my socks, I walked over the new carpeting, waved hello as I passed Katarina, who was folding clean-smelling laundry on the couch in the den, and made my way to the tiled kitchen. My first task was to prepare lunches for the next school day.

While making Sam's favorite sandwich—cheese, butter, and peanut butter on potato bread—I was thinking about a conversation that I had had a couple of months earlier with Bonnie before the new carpet was laid down. She was talking about how financially strapped she and Kevin felt and was nostalgically recalling their life in the Midwest when Julia and Doug were little, before Sam was born. Even though she and Kevin had made far less money during those years, she said that it had felt like they had more. Together they now earned over $150,000 per year (which placed them around the top 26 percent in household income in the town), in addition to stock options Kevin received through his job at a communications technology company, but it never felt like they had enough. It was not just because the New York metropolitan area is such an expensive place to live, Bonnie emphasized. With the kids getting older, the things that they needed and wanted—clothes, video games, soccer cleats, karate lessons, SAT tutors, CDs—ate up so much of their money. Plus, she added, they also ended up buying what she referred to as "stupid things."

As "stupid" came out of her mouth, Bonnie pointed to carpet samples lying on the couch in the den as an example. Bonnie was in the process of looking at samples because she had noticed that the old carpet was looking a little raggedy. The kids hung out in the den all the time. I glanced at the carpet to see if it looked as run-down as she thought. It did not strike me as that bad, so I told her that I thought the carpet looked just fine. As I spoke, Bonnie closed her eyes, turned her face away from me, and shook her head from side to side, indicating that what I was saying was something she did not want to hear. She was already set on laying down new carpet, she explained, despite knowing that it was "stupid." While she was talking, I noticed that all of the samples were shades of white and cream. When she solicited my opinion on the colors, I asked her if she had thought about choosing a darker color. That way, she wouldn't have to worry about it getting dirty again. "No," she quickly and adamantly replied. She really liked the bone-colored sample; she was set on it. When the new rug came in, she pointed out, no one would be able to wear shoes on it or eat snacks in the den.

It might be easy to dismiss Bonnie's yearning for the new carpet as a trivial consumer desire, but Bonnie's aesthetics of interior design can also be viewed as a means of consuming class security—that is, providing a temporary appeasement of class anxieties through acquiring a consumer item that is common in one's milieu and mirrors back a feeling of equivalence. It is also an instance of the type of nagging longing for consumer items that is indicative of the culture of hyperconsumption that puts increasing strain on families' purse strings, and into which children are being habituated in increasingly cunning and often aggressive ways.[9] Take, for example, one afternoon I spent walking around the mall with Sam after I picked him up from preschool. Bonnie had bought a piece of clothing at the mall that did not fit her correctly, and she needed me to return it. Since I was going to have Sam with me, she gave me a few dollars so that he could pick out something for himself. As she handed me the money, she told me that she always felt like she "*had to* buy something for Sam" when she was at the mall with him. She wasn't sure why; she just felt like she did.

When Sam and I got to the mall, we decided to have a snack. Over Chicken McNugget Happy Meals at McDonald's in the food court, he told me about all of the stores that he liked: Kay Bee Toys, Noodle Kadoodle, the Warner Bros. Store, and the Disney Store. Sam knew exactly where each of those stores was located. In fact, he made it a point to note that there were *two* Kay Bee Toys stores, one on each of the two levels of the mall. *Very handy*, I thought. No matter on which level of the mall you're walking, your child can drag you into a toy store to beg you to buy something. When we finished our food, Sam led the way. Our first stop was at a video-game store. Sam's birthday was still a month away, but he already knew what he was getting: *Yoshi's Story,* a Nintendo 64 game. Sam was very excited to show it to me. As we walked through the front doors of the store and entered the pop-music-filled space, Sam's eyes grew wide with excitement. He glanced around the room at the rows and rows of video games, dragging me toward the Nintendo area. As we walked past the other brands of games, I asked Sam about the differences between them. He rattled off an explanation of the distinctions, particularly the pros and cons of having Nintendo versus Sega. I made sure to listen very attentively, for Sam's comportment suggested that he was a bit put out by having to explain something that was SOOOooo obvious. While Sam was sharing all of this information with me, I found myself quite amazed. I often helped him with his homework, so I knew that he could barely read and often struggled to recognize some letters of the alphabet. Considering that he had not yet entered kindergarten, this was quite normal. What was striking, however, was how incredibly adept he was not only at recognizing a good portion of the video-game collection in the store, but also at articulating a broad taxonomic knowledge of their relationship to one another. It is, of course, quite common for kids his age to become enthralled with the order of things in their midst, so it is easy for us to dismiss these kinds of obsessions as being part and parcel of a developmental stage. But as the next couple of stops on our stroll revealed, Sam also was learning particular habits of consumption and expectation.

After we left the video-game store, Sam tugged my hand and dragged me into the Warner Bros. Store. We were immediately surrounded by the sights and sounds of Bugs Bunny and friends. I followed Sam as he browsed the vast array of offerings in the store's sections, each of which contained items from the most popular Warner Bros. shows and films. When we got to the section devoted to *The Flintstones*, Sam got very animated. He loved watching *The Flintstones* on the Cartoon Network, and since he knew that he was allowed to get something for himself, he decided to pick out a little stuffed Dino. Together we walked over to the register, where I paid for Dino with the money that Bonnie had given me just for this purpose.

With his new purchase in hand and some time left to kill, Sam knew exactly where he wanted to go next: the Disney Store. It, too, was arranged in sections according to the most famous and most recent Disney movies and characters. We wandered from section to section, spending most of the time in the *Toy Story* section. Sam was enthralled with a Buzz Lightyear toy that flashed bright lights when different buttons were pushed. After we played with it for a while, I noticed that it was time for us to head home. While making our way out of the store, Sam and I spotted a section of toys that neither of us recognized. We stopped and stood there for a moment, pondering who and what these characters might be. Soon into our conversation, one of the salespeople walked over to us. She looked directly down at Sam, smiling as she explained to him that these were characters from *Mulan,* the Disney film coming out that summer.

On our way to the car, Sam talked incessantly about how excited he was to see *Mulan.* He skipped as he talked, his words blending together in excited anticipation. I often saw this same embodied enthusiasm when he spoke about the fact that he was getting *Yoshi's Story* for his birthday. Bonnie and Kevin bought the children games only for special occasions. In order to play the games that they did not have, they would rent games from a local game store. Video-game rentals open with scenes from other games, just like film rentals with their promotional trailers. Since *Yoshi's Story* was the hottest new game at the time, the *Yoshi's Story* trailer came on almost every time a Nintendo 64 game was rented. When it popped up on the TV, Sam would start to jump in exhilaration, reminding me that he was getting *Yoshi's Story* for his birthday.[10]

On our drive home, Sam continued to talk about all the things that he was excited to get, to play, and to watch. As historian Lisa Jacobson explains, it was during the early part of the twentieth century that children like Sam were first "enlisted" and "cultivated" as consumers.[11] Through mass marketing in juvenile magazines and on the radio, often by way of clubs like Post Toasties' Junior Detective Corps, corporations set the conditions for children to empower themselves as consumers. Children learned—for the first time—that they could "cross the boundaries of dependency" and make up for what they lacked in the "power of the purse" through their "power to nag and persuade."[12] Mind you, companies charting this new terrain did so with great reservation and hesitation; they feared upsetting parents, particularly mothers, by overstepping their authority to make consumer decisions in the home. Now, as Jacobson discusses, the power dynamic has moved so far in the other direction that parents often feel impotent in the face of excessive marketing and advertising directed at their children.[13] Many parents in Danboro told me that they worried about being a "bad parent" if they did not buy their children the things that all the other kids had, for fear that their child would feel left out or "deprived" or even ostracized.[14] Bonnie was not sure why she felt like she *"had to"* buy something for Sam every time they were at the mall. But as Jacobson's work reveals, companies have long made a concerted effort to cultivate just this sentiment—a dynamic made more extreme in the 1990s with the magnification of advertising toward children, the intensification of hyperconsumption, and the expansion of consumer credit.

This type of consumer learning, which leads to habits of anticipation and desire, is just one of the many ways that children and youth learn about that which they ultimately feel they "want" and "need." When the costs of things that children desire are added to expenses for all the "stupid things" that parents also crave, the financial stress on families is compounded as corporate capital's earnings swell. Children not only become habituated to this type of consumer expectation, but, as the next set of ethnographic moments reveals, they also learn subtle forms of self-regulation for consumer items, with implications beyond the fiscal.

"I JUST HAVE TO GET USED TO IT"

One of my duties was to make sure that the children didn't dirty the new bone-colored wall-to-wall carpeting. Sometimes, they ignored the rules. Every once in a while I'd spot an empty plate with crumbs on it, resting rebelliously on the fireplace ledge next to the television in the den. Other times, I'd catch the children making a quick dash over the rug with their shoes on, following a failed attempt to leap all the way over it. More often than not, however, they actually policed themselves and those around them. I always watched in amazement when Sam would hold up his little hand, all five fingers firmly poised in the "stop" sign, in the face of one of his friends who was about to walk onto the rug. He always reminded them to take their shoes off, pointing to a good spot to leave them. When the new rug was first installed, Sam told his friends about the new rule all by himself. He demonstrated for me during an interview exactly how he told

them. His body went rigid and his tone mimicked that of parental authority as he declared, "Don't step with your shoes on the carpet!" Sam
explained to me that most of his friends have been good about remembering on their own, except for his friend Joey. One time, Sam explained to
me, "[Joey] came. He had his shoes on. He went halfway to the first square
[of the rug]. *Then* he went down and took his shoes off."

One afternoon, when Sam did not feel like taking his shoes off, I
watched in amusement as he crawled on his knees all the way across the
rug, carefully making sure that the tips of his shoes stayed well above the
carpet the entire time. Similarly, when Doug and Julia were in the garage
getting into the car and realized they had forgotten something in the
house, they would often go to another door instead of using the nearby
back door to avoid the rug altogether. This was particularly the case in
winter, when shoes were much less easily slipped on and off. In those
instances, they would run out of the garage and around to the front door,
which opened onto a tiled foyer. This maneuvering to avoid the rug would
get particularly tricky if they had left something upstairs. The new carpet
also covered the stairs and the platform leading to the bedrooms on the
second floor. There was no way to leap over a two-story obstacle. A similar
predicament occurred when the kids wanted to play in the backyard or on
the back deck, and then come inside to hang out in the carpeted den to
play Nintendo 64, watch television, or instant message with their friends
on the computer. The most direct route was through a set of sliding glass
doors that opened directly into the den from the back deck. When the kids
had friends over and the weather was nice, they often left their shoes on a
mat next to the glass doors. This way, there would be easy access to their
shoes for going out, and a convenient spot for tossing them when they
came back in.

On separate occasions, I asked each of the kids if they were bothered by
the fact that they could not wear shoes on the new rug. When I posed the
question to Sam, at first he uttered, "I mind." But then he immediately
switched his answer to "I don't mind," adding, "It doesn't bother me. I just
have to get used to it. Now I just don't care." Sam may have been worried
about saying the right thing—unlike Doug, who instantly declared the
whole thing "a pain." But, he added with a boastful swagger, "I never took
my shoes off." Julia, on the other hand, was comfortable admitting that

she did *try* to follow the rules, despite the fact that "it's annoying." As she pointed out, "Let's say I'm down here with my shoes on, all ready to be picked up, and then I realize that I forgot something like in my room. . . . That's annoying like when you're already dressed and ready to go, and then . . . just to go upstairs you have to take all your shoes off and everything. Sometimes I don't even care, I just like run upstairs." This was particularly tough for Julia when she had friends over. One time when her parents were out of town, a few of her friends came by, and each of them ended up bringing other friends. Julia did not want to ask them all to take their shoes off. "I felt bad saying, 'Take your shoes off,'" she explained. So most of the night she kept thinking to herself, "Oh shit, the carpet."

This concern for keeping the carpet clean was not unusual in homes in Danboro. One afternoon, I was picking up Doug from a friend's house. His friend's little brother—clad in socks—answered the front door when I rang the bell. He yelled to Doug to tell him that it was time to go. Doug yelled back that he'd be ready in a second; he just needed to run downstairs to the basement to get his shoes. His friend's family also left their shoes at the door, and their house was perched on a small hill, so their garage led into the basement rather than onto the main floor of the house. Meanwhile, Doug and his friend had been eating marshmallows in the kitchen when I arrived. Doug still had half of a marshmallow in his hand as he ran down the stairs to get his shoes. His friend immediately followed after him, stopping at the top of the stairs to emphatically and somewhat nervously yell a reminder to Doug that he'd better not get marshmallow on anything or he'd get into big trouble. They, too, had just gotten new carpet.

Julia and Doug both told me that a lot of their friends' houses are "no-shoe zones." Doug added, "Some kids I know, I can't even go into their [bed]room." When I asked him why, he bellowed as if he was one of his friends' moms: "Because I'll mess it up! It's too dirty! You're gonna make it too dirty!" When I asked him where he and his friends hang out, he matter-of-factly stated, "Basement. Go outside. Living room." I asked Doug what he thought about this way of living. He said that it didn't bother him that much. Plus, he added, "it's cool to have a nice house, especially for when people come over." Julia, too, admitted that despite all that is annoying about their new rug, she likes living in a "neat house."

I went back to the Sillens for a short visit a year after I had completed my fieldwork. Kevin and Bonnie were going away for the weekend, and they asked me if I could stay with the kids while they were gone. One of the first things I noticed was that the Nintendo—which the boys had played every afternoon in the den on the new rug—had been moved down to the basement, taking them down with it. Their time on the rug (and thus the literal and symbolic "dirt" that they brought with them) was reduced. As Mary Douglas explains, "pollutions" are not easily eradicated, despite "strenuous efforts that are made to bring the inward heart and mind into line with the public act." The "contradiction between external behavior and secret emotions," she points out, "is a frequent source of anxiety," which—ironically—is produced through "the act of purification itself."[15] Sam spoke to this point when he said that remembering to take their shoes off before walking on the rug was something that they "just have to get used to"; their self-policing was (ideally) supposed to give way to embodied habits—the active mode of objectification known as "subjectification"[16] that fascinated Foucault. But in light of the children's irreverence and their everyday oppositional "tactics"[17]—of which their parents were well aware—it clearly was not working.

The children were participating in caring and sacrificing for this object of class presentation and control, often at the expense of feeling like they were included in all aspects of their own home. As Bourdieu illuminates, "[T]he 'book' from which the children learn their vision of the world is read with the body, in and through movements and displacements which make the space within which they are enacted as much as they are made by it."[18] What are the implications when children come to understand at a very young age that it is "normal" to have a lot of spaces in which they are not allowed or are provisionally welcomed? What kinds of habits, desires, and sentiments are produced through this kind of self-policing and (eventual) displacement for the appearance of "nice" and "neat"? The children were learning that a part of being in a relatively privileged class position (and thus being able to have these objects of display) is accepting and becoming habituated to their own marginalized space and place so that objects of privilege (and presumably their privilege as a whole) can be maintained. Is this dynamic, while not new even if it might matter differently in these new conditions, a small part of a larger process that prepares them (and their parents) to accept as normal and unquestioned things about the capitalist order of things that they might otherwise interrogate? Bonnie may have deemed the new carpeting a "stupid thing." However, it (and particularly the policing and sacrifice required to keep it clean) were powerful ways that the children were becoming habituated to a way of being that was required for the display of tenuous class attainments and the satisfaction of anxious class yearnings.

HABITS OF DISTINCTION

As with the status conferred by a "nice" and "neat" house, the children were also being habituated to an upper-middle-class way of "being-in-the-world"[19] through experiences of hierarchy and distinction in settings such as sports teams. Doug was on a special soccer team in Danboro for advanced players of his age whose skills were a step up from those playing in the town's recreational leagues. Unlike those teams, which played against each other, Doug's team traveled around the state to compete against teams from other towns. Each member of Doug's soccer team was given a nice, fine-quality windbreaker that proudly displayed the Danboro team logo, along with matching jerseys and sweats. They also were given huge professional-style duffle bags with the number of their jerseys monogrammed onto them. All of their gear—cleats, shin guards, water bottles, extra clothing, and even soccer balls—fit easily into these bags, which were almost as big as the boys themselves. Whenever I picked up Doug at his practices, I couldn't help but watch in wonder as he lugged his bag from the field and hoisted it up into the car.

One afternoon after practice, with his bag successfully thrown on the back seat, Doug excitedly told me about a special soccer clinic that was being run for his team. A couple of British players from a professional team in England had been flown in for the week to teach them new skills. Doug was enamored by all the cool moves that they were learning, highlighting the neat tricks and unique drills that they got to try. While Doug was talking about the British players—their funny jokes, their patience, and their charisma—I got the sense that he and his teammates loved having this special clinic in part because it gave them a break from their regular coach, who was notorious for being tough. Whenever Doug described his practices to me, it was often about all the yelling and the extra running that they were made to do when they made mistakes.

On our ride home that afternoon, I asked Doug about all of the gear that they had and the expense that it must have taken to fly in professional players from England. I figured that the cost of being on the team was a sizable part of the financial pressure Bonnie frequently spoke about. Doug explained, however, that there were not that many costs. The team was given most of its gear for free through his coach's business: a sports-clothing line. A lot of the extra paraphernalia that they got, like water bottles, were free things that his coach got as promotions. I glanced at the water bottle out of which Doug was drinking; sure enough, it bore the insignia of a company. As Doug continued pondering the way that his team was able to afford all of these perks—particularly the players from England—he wondered if perhaps his coach's company had a connection with them and sponsored the players' team in England, though he wasn't sure. I asked Doug about the other teams that they played against in their league: did the teams from other towns have such nice gear and participate in special clinics? Doug said that his team did look the most put together at their games with their matching bags and all. He then perceptively, yet unapologetically, uttered that they had all this stuff because of the money in Danboro. Their parents could afford to have these English guys come.

Doug was already well aware, at age eleven, of the ways that power and privilege—obtained through being in a place with money and business connections—grant access to certain things. And some *free* things, no less. He was quite articulate about the privileges associated with growing up in a town like Danboro. Most people in Danboro with whom I spent time during my fieldwork were quite comfortable discussing the fact that Danboro was a (relatively) well-off place, at least within the realm of the middle classes. The question is, What becomes of that consciousness for children like Doug? Will he always like being on "that" team, the one whose objects of distinction enable him to stand out? Or, as the next set of ethnographic moments broaches, will the growing pressures and sacrifices entailed in those benefits one day make him question not just the positioning he has always known or the corporate-sponsored freebies, but the system itself?

"IT SUCKS BEING SO BUSY"

Doug's contradictory consciousness in regard to his privileged position was thrown into relief amid his frustration with his busy schedule. One afternoon, he was scrambling to finish up his homework while eating an early dinner. With a few bites still in his mouth, he raced around the house putting together everything he needed for soccer practice. We had to get him to practice on time or else his coach would make him run extra laps. Mind you, his grueling soccer practice was just the beginning of his evening. When it was over, I was to pick him up and take him directly to his guitar lessons. Just before we ran out the door, while I was mixing a Gatorade drink in the water bottle that he took to practices, Doug complained to me about his schedule. He kept going on and on about how he had no time; how he never had any time; how "it sucks being so busy."

Doug's situation was somewhat extreme because of his traveling soccer team, but many children and youth in town faced similar pressures, prompting many parents in Danboro to wonder, "When do they get to be kids?" One day, I asked Sam if he was excited about turning six. His birthday was a month away, in July. I expected him to enthusiastically talk about getting *Yoshi's Story*. Instead, with a powerful sense of anticipated relief in his voice, he explained to me what he was really excited about: "That I won't have any school. I can rest sometimes." Julia, too, envisioned their daily life as jam-packed, with weekends as no exception. I once asked her what it was like on a "normal" weekend, since I was with them only during the week. She complained to me, "Uch, it's chaos. There's just like so much to do. . . . Everybody's running." This type of scheduling pressure began to receive public attention during the late 1990s, raising questions about the effects on kids of this approach to providing them with a competitive edge.[20]

The predicament of busyness in Doug's life took on a whole new perspective in a conversation I had with him a couple of months later. On our way to the track where his soccer team was doing stamina training, I asked him the usual "How was school today?" question. In an overwhelmed and frustrated voice, he told me that he didn't understand why we have elementary schools. He explained to me that he gets that everyone has to learn to read and write, but he still didn't see the point of it all. I threw out a reminder of all the important things that are learned, during which he blurted out, "It's so annoying that we have to go to school and be so busy when we're young. Then, we have to spend the rest of our life working all the time." This sentiment was echoed several months later when I asked him during a formal interview what he thought it meant to become a "teenager" or an "adolescent." He responded, "I think I'm just entering more and more work. . . . I have to do the stupid exercises my coach gave me. Now I'm going to go to middle school. It's twice the work. . . . More and more work as you get older."

I wasn't surprised to hear these words from Doug. He had a pretty frantic schedule, as did many of the parents in his midst. What did amaze me was what came out of his mouth next that day in the car. He informed me that he wished we had "a society like communism because they don't have to work so much." He then hesitantly added, "They do have to wait in long lines like in Russia, but it seems so much better there." I wasn't sure where he got his understanding of communism and Russia, but I was struck by this potential seed of radicalism. That is, until a few months later when Doug walked in from school, dropped his backpack, and asked me if I had any stock tips for him. Somewhat bewildered at hearing this question from someone his age, I said that I didn't know that much about the stock market, but why was he asking? He said that his dad had opened an E*Trade account for him with some money so that he could start learning how to invest. Seeing this as a moment for a subtle intervention, I told him about socially responsible funds. He said that he hadn't realized that you could choose stocks that way, but his main goal, he explained, was to make enough money to buy a car for himself when he turned seventeen. His dad was going to give him two hundred dollars each year, plus a little something extra on special occasions.

It was about a year after this conversation that I was back at the Sillens for the weekend when Bonnie and Kevin were away. During my first night there, Kevin called to check in, and Doug picked up the phone. After telling his dad that we were all fine, Doug proceeded to tell him about a stock he had purchased that afternoon. The next day, I asked Doug how his stock market "adventures" had been going.[21] He said that he had been really into it ever since he and his dad opened up his E*Trade account. He told me about the online research that he does on different companies;

how he gets stock tips from people; and how the first thing that he does when he gets home from school is check his stocks. With the serious comportment of a young, enthusiastic day trader, he told me, "You don't want to see me on a day when my stocks aren't doing well."

Doug's critique of his frenzied life and initial desire for that which could be provided by a supportive state (even if not articulated as such), combined with his embrace of the stock market's ability to generate capital and enable self-sufficiency, exposes contradictions inherent in the shift to neoliberalism (and underscores that nothing hegemonic, like neoliberal ideology, is ever truly hegemonic). Yet the odds seemed to be working against the possibility that the buds of his critical gaze would bloom. When I asked Doug about his Russia comment nine months after he first made it, he said he did not remember saying it. In fact, he seemed shocked that he would have said anything about wanting a communist-style society, remarking, "I would never say that." He then added, "I would rather be busy than always be at home all [afternoon]. . . . It's boring. In a sense, I do like to be busy sometimes. . . . At least I have something to motivate me." Where Doug was growing up, the hectic, advanced capitalist lifestyle was seen as normal, accepted as unfortunately just the way it is. It was, after all, part of the plan for the building of the suburbs during the Cold War. As famed homebuilder William Levitt infamously remarked at the time, "No man who owns his own house and lot can be a communist. He has too much to do."[22] There was an old church that I often passed on my way to the Sillens' house. It was built when Dutch settlers occupied the area and was located next to fields where a crucial battle was fought during the American Revolution. One week, their announcement sign on the side of the road proclaimed: "Jesus is coming. Look busy." Levitt would have loved it. A lot.

Just as much as parents worried about their children's lack of time to be "kids," they, too, craved time for themselves to feel more "human" and to be "better parents." Over dinners together during one summer when Kevin was working late, Bonnie constantly voiced her concerns about working so much. She often jokingly asked, "Do you think I'm a bad parent?" Although it was couched in a humorous framing, there was something poignant in her apprehensive question. This same concern came across when I was talking with Stu (whom we met in chapter 2), who commutes to New York

City each workday. I had asked him about his sense of Danboro as a place to raise children, to which he responded, "That's probably a bad question to ask me. I get to spend so little time at home. . . . I leave the house at six [or so] . . . in the morning, and I get home at seven-thirty at night." Some parents, like the prospective purchaser requesting the six-foot-high gate, had to travel out of town for work for extensive periods of time. The same was the case for Shari's husband, Jay. To express to me how often he was away for work, Shari (who had confused my project with *the* projects) used the island in her kitchen as an object lesson. Despite the fact that there were four members in her family, she had, without realizing it, had the island built with only three chairs. Jay rarely ate dinner with them.

THE GENDERING OF BUSYNESS

Despite the fact that Danboro was full of many people—both young and old, male and female—who were overworked in their daily lives, my questions to Doug and Julia about the problem of busyness ended up leading down a gendered path. One time I asked Doug what he thought about the hours that his parents worked each day. Considering his ominous sense of adult life, I assumed that this question might provide a springboard for getting to what Doug may have had in mind when he uttered the Russia comment. Doug's response to my question—despite the fact that I asked him about his *parents*—was in regard to his *mother.* "I'm actually proud to have a mom that works," Doug explained to me. "Because compared to other kids, their moms sometimes work part-time. Most of their moms just sit at home and do nothing."

Julia, too, when I asked her specifically if it bothered her that her *parents* worked a lot, replied with thoughts on having a working *mother:* "I'd rather have my mom work than not work because that's when she's happier. . . . Like when she's working, she says, 'Oh, I don't want to go to work.' But I know that she can't just like sit home. And um . . . my mom has always worked ever since I was little. And that's what I'm used to. I like having that kind of role model instead of someone who just sits home." Julia did note, however, that it bothered her sometimes, particularly when she came home from school. "I want her to be home sometimes. . . . I hate having to like sit down at ten at night and talk. . . . I wish we had like more time to talk and, um, things like that." But at the same time, Julia explained that she understood why it was so hard for her mother: "She comes home and then she has to . . . arrange all the car pools and everything. . . . Late at night she's up making phone calls." Because of the continued gendered discipline of upper-middle-class childhood, women still do the majority of the domestic work, and problems with *parents* having to work often end up getting understood as a question about working *women,* and not the current nature of work for *everyone,* men included. In fact, their father was equally busy; yet his busy work life was so normative that it was not remarked upon or questioned.

Bonnie, too, was caught in this dearth of available narratives for criticizing the intensity of professional middle-class work lives. This was most evident when she made sense of the sacrifice that one of her colleagues felt that she had to make for her career. Over dinner one night, Bonnie told me about a conversation she had had earlier in the day with Diane, a thirty-six-year-old coworker who was about to get married. They had been discussing Diane's wedding plans when Diane mentioned that she was not planning on having children. Bonnie told me that Diane was more committed to her career and did not want to have kids if she would not be able to raise them properly. As Bonnie was telling me the story, she commented on several occasions that Diane's perspective was "off" and that she would surely regret her decision one day. Bonnie did not include in her understanding of Diane's predicament that perhaps what was "off" was the nature of work for everyone, and that the conflicts between career and motherhood that she and Diane experienced might each in their own way be a reflection of the rearticulation of long-standing gender roles amid exacerbated anxieties about class stability. With limited space in the public discourse for such an analysis, as seen in its noted absence in Doug and Julia's commentary as well, it was not surprising that Bonnie did not see that when she worried about how her work life was affecting her own children, she was reacting in a different way to the same structural limitations that prompted Diane not to have children. In a moment during which economic shifts were making it increasingly difficult to maintain a "professional" status, anxieties about balancing work and family were compounded, and projected into child rearing.

ANXIOUS FUTURES

As Cindi Katz has noted, the quickening "backbeat of anxiety" among the middle classes has led to "parental involution," or "the embellishment and elaboration of parenting tasks and concerns that tend not only to absorb parents completely—if sometimes resentfully—but also to . . . deflect attention from the political-economic and other structural reasons for their insecurities."[23] This was most evident in Bonnie's contradictory hopes, desires, and concerns about Julia's career aspirations. Much of what Bonnie and I discussed was Julia's future. During my initial drive around town with her, she told me how impressed she was that Julia already knew what she wanted to be when she was older: a pediatric oncologist. Bonnie was unmistakably moved as she considered that she might be the inspiration for her daughter, sharing with me several times how incredibly proud she was of Julia's determination to enter a field that was both important and challenging, albeit depressing. Bonnie's eyes welled up as she mused that Julia's early conviction must have come from watching her work as a researcher. But there was a palpable apprehension in Bonnie's voice, which she later explained was her concern that Julia was so directed at such a young age. She found it weird that Julia did not seem to waver at all, seeming quite unlike a teenager who was supposed to be filled with adolescent indecision.

Just as I was about to ask Bonnie more about what it was that worried her about Julia's early commitment and diligence, she asked me in a seemingly guileless and curious tone where I had gone to college. When I said that I went to the University of Pennsylvania, she appeared ecstatic. With rapturous enthusiasm, she told me that I *had* to talk with Julia about colleges because she really wanted Julia to go to an Ivy League school. Considering that we had just talked about Bonnie's concern with Julia's excessive directedness, it seemed a bit odd that she wanted me to have this conversation with Julia so early in her high school career. But as further conversations with both Bonnie and Julia revealed, Bonnie's hunger for a certain kind of class future for her children (and herself) overshadowed her ambivalence about what it might take to get there and what might get lost along the way.

One evening, Bonnie told me how upset she was that Julia had not received a scholarship to attend a premed summer program in Europe.

Julia had been accepted to the program, but it cost six thousand dollars. If she and Kevin spent six thousand dollars for the program, Julia would not be able to receive a car when she got her license, which she had been expecting. Bonnie was particularly upset about the whole thing because she believed that the girl who got the scholarship must have lied on her application. Bonnie found it hard to fathom that this girl was really a musician and also had time to run a program for underprivileged kids. Ironically, I later learned, Bonnie had filled out Julia's application for her—itself an ethically questionable act.

That night, as our conversation continued, Bonnie nervously divulged that she was really panicked about Julia's future and did not know what she was supposed to do. "She just *has to* go to an Ivy League school," she declared. "I don't know what I'll do if Julia doesn't get into medical school." Bonnie was worried that if Julia did not go to the summer program, she would end up "wasting" her summer working at a local day camp, which would in turn hurt her future chances. Julia had already spent the summer after her first year of high school participating in a special program for teenagers at a prestigious medical school on the East Coast, but Bonnie felt that it was not enough. I tried to interject my thoughts on the benefits of taking time off from stress, or what Julia might learn about life through a summer job. But, just as when I tried to offer my thoughts on the samples for the new bone-colored carpeting, Bonnie let me know that she was set in her ideas. She did not want to hear my thoughts on the matter, although when we began to talk about how important it was for Julia to apply for these things on her own and thus to be an active participant in shaping her future, Bonnie granted me one concession: she would leave the decision about the summer up to Julia. Europe, or a car? It would be Julia's choice.

Julia often complained to me that her mom was too invested in what she was doing. "I honestly do want to be a doctor," she told me one afternoon, "but I . . . don't want it to come from her. I think it should come from me. . . . Even if she didn't pressure me, I still think I would have wanted to become a doctor. But like, I don't know." Julia said that she felt like her mom was a lot more upset than she was when she didn't get the scholarship for the summer program. But at the same time, Julia admitted, she did understand that her mother was "crazy" about these things because she had never finished her Ph.D. Bonnie and Kevin started having children when they were very young, while Bonnie was working on her master's degree. Julia understood her mother's predicament, but she felt that her mother had made a choice since you can't have everything. While it has always been nearly impossible to "have everything," the economic shifts over the last twenty-five years have made it increasingly difficult for all but a few people. Would Bonnie have felt and projected her own unfulfilled professional ambitions as powerfully if it wasn't getting harder every year to find and maintain a "professional" job, not only for her, but also for her children's generation?

"IT JUST SEEMED SO, LIKE, DIRTY"

Despite the fact that Julia was in high school and had friends who were able to drive, I spent a good amount of time driving her from place to place. Sometimes I'd get an apologetic phone call from her during an afternoon when I was off, requesting a ride home from school after having missed the bus. But our usual time together was every Tuesday, when I drove her to her volunteer job at the local hospital. Julia was trying to put in enough hours to qualify for a college recommendation from the supervisor of the program. During our many afternoons sitting in traffic on Route 2, Julia spoke about her plans to become a doctor, particularly all that she was doing (and not doing) to put herself in a good position to get accepted into a good college program. It was during this time together that the racial implications of class perseverance were revealed, particularly the ways that racial fears increase busyness and self-sacrifice.

In light of the pressure on Julia fueled by personal ambition and parental anxiety and desire, I was surprised to learn that Julia was not attending a special, prestigious medical program at one of the local high schools to which she had the option to apply. The medical program, which provided intensive training in medical and natural sciences research and academics, seemed to me perfect for Julia's pursuits. But Julia was attending instead a global studies program in another school. I was curious about whether it had to do with the fact that the medical program was housed in Milldale High School, the school in the district with the highest percentage of students of color and students whose parents hold working-class jobs.

During one of our car rides on the way to the hospital, I asked Julia why she was not enrolled in the medical sciences program. She said that it was because she didn't want to go to "the Mill," as the school was often called. She had gone to visit the school when she was in the eighth grade and was "turned off," she explained, because it was such a small, old, and rundown school. Plus, she added, the kids there didn't seem "nice," and there were a lot of kids who were from a "bad crowd." When I asked her more about this in a formal interview—to see if she might mention the race and class makeup of the student body at the school—her answer was similarly elusive:

> I don't know, like, it's a smaller school. And like I didn't feel like there were people that I could relate to. . . . I guess like I wanted to be around a few people that like, I don't know. . . . Just . . . I didn't want to go there. It didn't seem like a good school, like . . . I went there for a day to see it. . . . I mean I heard that it wasn't in a good area, but I saw it. I don't know. It wasn't that people were mean, but it just seemed so, like, dirty and like. I don't know.

Julia's hesitant pauses and excessive use of *like* and *I don't know* suggested that she was uncomfortable speaking about her reasons for not wanting to go to the school. Her use of *dirty* and claims about not seeing people that she could "relate to" implied racialized and class-based anxieties in regard to the school space.[24] She was not the first student to try to avoid Milldale High School for this reason. One girl I knew, who lived in a middle-class development in Milldale Township that was zoned for Milldale High School, applied for a special program at Danboro High School so that she did not have to attend "the Mill."

Thrown into relief during this conversation with Julia were the further racial implications of my position as her babysitter. Not only was I hired because I was "like" them and not one of those "depressed women who would go onto the porch and cry that they missed their family in Ghana"; my services were needed, in part, because Julia was going to a school much farther from her house to avoid being among kids from a "bad crowd." I was driving her to volunteer work each week, presumably because she and/or her mother figured that it would help compensate for the fact that she was not in the medical program. Julia was made busier because of this added extracurricular activity that, incidentally, was a sacrifice in other ways: she hated every minute that she worked at the hospital. According to Julia, her supervisor was "a real bitch." When racial fears intersect with class aspirations and efforts to shore up educational credentials, busyness and sacrifice take on a whole new appearance, and a key effect of neoliberalization on space—increased segregation of youth and adults along race and class lines—gets exacerbated.

But even as Julia did not want to be with those ranked lower in the racial and class order of things, neither did she want the daily pressures of being among those at the upper tiers of the middle class. This was part of why Julia was happier at Milldale Township High School, which housed the global studies program, than at the closer Danboro High School. Bonnie used to complain to me about the fact that Milldale Township was almost a fifteen-minute drive from their house. The school district provides buses for the day-to-day commute, but on weekends she and Kevin were constantly driving Julia to and from the houses of her friends who lived near the school. Julia kept reminding her parents that it was only two more years until she would have her license and would be able to help out with the driving. On several occasions, Bonnie confessed to me that she was not going to let Doug go there because of the hassle. In fact, she thought about asking Julia to switch back to Danboro High School. But Julia *really* loved Milldale Township, which Bonnie felt largely had to do with the fact that Julia had always hated the dress and appearance pressure within Danboro schools. The kids in Milldale Township were from families who were a rung "lower" in income,[25] Bonnie expounded, which is why the people in their town were less "snobby" and "more welcoming." Julia was constantly telling her how the kids there were so much nicer and friendlier than the kids in Danboro. On several occasions, Julia and I discussed what it was that she relished about the "mellowness" at Milldale Township High School. She explained to me that there was a strikingly different feel among her new group of friends than when she was with her old friends from Danboro Middle School. The Milldale Township crowd was a bit more "down-to-earth," as she described them. They were less concerned with having designer bags, fancy cars, and the latest clothes.

Julia enjoyed the feeling of release from the class-encoded pressures she experienced among her Danboro friends. Her discomfort and ambivalence in regard to that which is "SOOOooo . . . Danboro" set the conditions for her to find relief among those who paid less attention to various forms of display. It is ironic that the racialization of class aspirations, which led her to attend Milldale Township High School (and not "the Mill"), enabled her to question some of the class-encoded desires in her town. And yet, this inadvertent intervention into a certain kind of classed way of being was still racial: Julia was more comfortable being among those who were a step "down" in class than with the possibility of racial mixing. She may have questioned certain forms of class display, but she continued to pursue class, to leave the racialization of class unquestioned, and to enjoy the privilege of safe ascendancy.

EMBODIED CLASS DISPLAY

Another irony was that Julia's presence among her new group of friends at Milldale Township slowly transformed that site of class relief into a place with somewhat familiar concerns with embodied class display. Julia had told me that what she most appreciated about her Milldale Township friends was their "healthy" relationship to food. Unlike her Danboro friends, who she said were "so skinny" and "don't eat anything" and who constantly said, "Oh, I'm fat. I'm fat," her Milldale Township friends "don't care." She described for me what it was like when she went out to dinner with her different groups of friends: "Like when we go out in Danboro . . . we won't even like have dessert or anything. And in Milldale, they get like three desserts for two people. It's just, it's a difference." The difference, however, diminished through Julia's presence at the lunch table each day. She was on Weight Watchers, so she always brought a diet lunch with her to school: tuna fish in a container with a few baby cut carrots, a piece of fruit, a water bottle, and six miniature flavored rice crackers. Over time, Julia explained, her lunch table "slowly but surely lost the chips. . . . By the end of the year, every single girl at my lunch table was eating [her Weight Watchers diet lunch]."

Granted, Julia was perhaps exaggerating when she said that they don't eat anything in Danboro. However, most of the girls whom I knew in

Danboro were concerned with their weight. For Julia, it began when she was fourteen. When she woke up every morning, the first thing she thought about was whether she would have time to run during the day. And when she looked at other people, she could not help but wonder if they dieted as well. In fact, the whole topic of body image came up in my interview only because Julia brought it up. I had asked her a stock question that I asked all of the kids: "Is there something random that is always in your head, which you think might be weird, but is something that is present for you all the time?" Julia, like Danielle and Lauren, whom we met in chapter 2, answered this question by telling me that they think about their weight and their body and what they eat, *all the time.* But as Julia explained, "It's just the way I am now. It doesn't bother me. But . . . sometimes I wish like I didn't think about it. But I do."

Just as Julia and her brothers habituated themselves to the demands of the new bone-colored carpeting, Julia was "used to" policing her body, despite her ambivalence. Her body was another object of class display, for the benefit of which she learned to sacrifice pleasure. While body-image issues are typically explored in regard to a relationship between control issues and internalized gendered restrictions, the body is also a site for the crafting and display of class appearances, with particular impact on girls.[26] According to Julia, her mom was really supportive of her in this regard, unlike some of the other mothers in Danboro, who were constantly telling their daughters to diet or who would not accept the fact that their daughters were anorexic or bulimic. But much in the way that Stu and Linda and Nancy and Eric struggled to work against that which is "SOOOooo . . . Danboro" in raising Danielle and Lauren, the pressures were "out there" and quite powerful. They even, as in Julia's case, came to transform spaces that used to be a site of relief from those very same pressures.

AMBIGUOUS OTHERS: GOSSIP, RUMOR, AND SUSPICIOUS HUMOR

When Bonnie first interviewed me, I assumed that the fifteen months I was going to spend with her family would bring to life nuances of middle-class anxieties, pressures, and sensibilities. But I never anticipated the intensity of suspicion of others that would be revealed. Bonnie's suspicion about the girl who had won the Europe scholarship is one example, but others were far more extreme. One evening Bonnie and I were waiting for a woman named Sandy to come over. Sandy was the mother of Gordon, one of Sam's friends. I had picked up the two boys earlier in the day at the local YMCA, where they were dropped off each afternoon by a yellow school bus after having attended a summer day camp outside of town. All sweaty, slightly sunburned, and a bit exhausted, Sam and Gordon came back to the house and played video games most of the afternoon. When Sandy arrived, she and Bonnie chatted while I helped Gordon put on his shoes. I could hear Sandy telling Bonnie about a group of executives who had been at her house that afternoon.

When Sandy and Gordon left, Bonnie and I sat down for dinner as Sam went upstairs "to rest." The minute Sam walked out of the room, Bonnie remarked to me that there was something fishy about Sandy, who had just gone through a divorce and had taken over the mortgage on her upscale home in Milldale Township. That, in itself, was not so bizarre, Bonnie pointed out. What was peculiar was that Sandy claimed to be comfortably supporting herself and her son through consulting work with executives. According to Bonnie, no one (i.e., in the group of mothers of the boys who played together) seemed to know exactly what kind of "consulting" Sandy was doing with these executives, aside from the fact that she coached them about career changes. A great deal of suspicion had arisen among the women about what exactly this "coaching" was all about. Bonnie winked and coyly smiled at me as she joked about what it was they all thought Sandy was *really* teaching these men.

I asked Bonnie what made them all think *this*. Bonnie told me that there was a lot of weirdness surrounding Sandy's comings and goings. When she went away for work—which was quite frequently—she never left the babysitter a contact number; rather, she told the babysitter to contact her ex-husband if they needed anything. And before Bonnie had applied for her new job at the pharmaceutical company, Sandy had mentioned that she had coached several executives who worked at that company. When Bonnie got the job, she thought it would be fun to grab lunch the next time Sandy came to the corporate campus. When she invited

Sandy, Sandy said that she was no longer going to the headquarters for meetings; the executives were now coming to her home. Bonnie couldn't understand why "big executives" would drive over an hour to her home. The clincher for Bonnie and her friends, however, was the time when, during the divorce, Gordon mentioned something about how his daddy used to get upset because of all the men that came over to their house.

It all seemed a bit far-fetched to me that Sandy was a prostitute, although it would not have been the first time an executive prostitution ring was run out of a quiet suburban home. During that summer, the notorious "Morristown Madam" was arrested for running a bordello for suburban businessmen out of her Victorian mansion in northern New Jersey.[27] Yet there were hordes of people doing all kinds of coaching during those years, the type of consulting work that has since come to typify efforts to create neoliberal self-managers. It would not have been surprising if Sandy was a self-made guru. Nevertheless, I took up Bonnie's request to be more attentive in my conversations with Sandy to see if I found out anything suspicious. To be honest, I looked forward to this bit of intrigue. I needed something to spice up the painfully boring spans of time that I spent waiting for Sam's bus in the hot, smelly gym at the YMCA, though I never did discover anything particularly out of the ordinary about Sandy. She seemed to me to be like a lot of the other moms: friendly, attractive, in shape, often showing up in her gym clothes, chatting on about her son. But regardless, Sam began spending less and less time with Gordon, eventually seeing him rarely if at all. Near the end of my fieldwork, I asked Sam why he didn't hang out with Gordon anymore. I was curious to see if he had picked up on any of the suspicions. He simply replied, "I don't know. I just don't see him a lot."

As Luise White points out, gossip, like other forms of social control, "traces the boundaries" of a community; "[i]n that talking, a world of value and behavior is constituted."[28] Yet these values and behaviors are not necessarily those immediately apparent, for they are often "an individual's own ideas about his or her self."[29] From what I knew of Bonnie through our relationship, I suspected that Sandy's success may have been a threat to her tenuous sense of being a "professional." If Sandy were a prostitute, she would no longer be provocative for Bonnie in that regard, particularly once she and her son were pushed out of the Sillens' lives—

much like the zoning board's rejection of the six-foot-high ornamental security gate and all that it symbolized. Moreover, as White reminds us, a rumor brings to life "the passionate contradictions and anxieties of specific places with specific histories."[30] The collective production of this rumor among the mothers in Sam's crowd reveals that Bonnie's concerns were indicative of something far more widespread among those in her class positioning during those years. Alongside anxieties about racialized and class-encoded others, there also was anxiety about imposters within.

I, too, was the subject of curious qualms. One cold, wintry evening I was browsing in the coat section in Nordstrom at the mall during an end-of-season sale. While trying on one of the coats, I spotted Bonnie walking past me in the reflection in the mirror. Our eyes met, and she smiled and started to walk my way. As she approached, the first thing that came out of her mouth was, "What are you doing shopping when you're so poor?!" I was taken aback by her comment, even though it was said in a humorous tone. I responded by laughing in kind, after which I asked her opinion about the coat, making sure to point out that it was on sale. I got the feeling that she *needed* me to be "poor."

This moment, however, came to look more like a suspicious inquiry a few weeks later when I asked Bonnie's permission to include her family in my study. While we were talking about the process of writing up my research, she asked me whether I would have to go back to Michigan at all. She said that she was asking because her friends found it weird that I was in Danboro, and yet my degree was going to be from Michigan. Kevin also wondered about this, she added. I explained to her the nature of ethnographic research: practically all anthropology students go away from their home institution to work on their dissertations. While I was spelling this out, she took a quick step back, pointed to herself, and then clarified that *she* understood my situation. It's just that it came up among her friends when they were discussing the story about a babysitter who had kidnapped a child. Bonnie then laughed, and with a joking smile on her face asked me, "Do you have any intention of stealing my kids?!" I laughed (albeit a bit awkwardly), and assured her that I had no desire for any full-time kids in my life at that time.

Bonnie was presumably joking. But there was something profoundly unsettling in that moment. Could she have really thought that I was a legitimate threat to her children? It had been almost a year since I began working for her, and she never hesitated when she ask me to drive the children anywhere in my car; when she asked me for advice about the children; or when she used me as a sounding board to process her feelings about being a "bad parent." Plus, she always seemed quite comfortable gossiping with me about Sandy and other people in her life. As Max Gluckman points out, "The right to gossip about certain people is a privilege which is only extended to a person when he or she is accepted as a member of a group or set."[31] But this "acceptance," Georg Simmel would suggest, brings with it "dangerous possibilities" when "close relationships" are formed with a "stranger."[32] I was "like" Bonnie, and yet I was hired from the outside to work "for her," despite her claims that I was working "with her." Our relationship may have been idiosyncratic in terms of what we forged together during my time working for her, but there is always a constellation of "nearness" and "remoteness" in such a stranger.[33] Perhaps my ambiguous positioning as a soon-to-be Ph.D. service worker in her home aroused anxiety about the tenuousness of her class positioning. Or perhaps the intense cultivation of appearances bred suspicion that things weren't as they seemed.

Fortunately for me, the gossip among Bonnie and her friends about my anomalous role did not inspire her to push me out of their lives, as occurred with Sandy. Perhaps Bonnie resolved the contradictions that I embodied through the beautiful birthday present she gave me that summer: an antique-looking necklace made of black stone and brushed copper that she purchased at Nordstrom. Three or four times over the course of the following week, she told me that she spent a lot of money on the necklace, as if it was something that I needed to know and of which I had to be continually reminded. But was it really a gift for *me*, or was the necklace placed around my neck to mirror back to Bonnie a *feeling* of class security every time I walked through her door, with the repetitive uttering of its value a comforting reminder to herself of what *she*—and not *I*— could afford?

Discussions of white middle-class families who are "choosing similarity"[34] focus on how families resolve their discomfort with the intimate power differential of employing a working-class person of color in their home, while at the same time firming up their children's class habitus. An au pair from Europe or a local college student allows them to have a serv-ant without feeling like they have a servant. But perhaps choosing similar-ity also enables employers like Bonnie to create—through their relation-ship with their middle-class servant—a sense of power and authority *within* the middle classes, not unlike how Bonnie felt vis-à-vis Sandy, or how Julia felt in the school that she chose to attend, or how Doug likely felt while wearing sports gear that no other teams could afford.

Near the start of this chapter, I mentioned the relief that I felt at the end of my interview for the job when Bonnie asked me to give her a copy of my driver's license. I preferred to be a victim of doubt rather than be devoid of all misgivings simply because I was a white, educated young woman from the right class background. But as I drove up to the Sillens' house each afternoon after these moments, my feeling was slightly altered. I still parked, got out of my car, and lifted up Sam's pint-size basketball hoop. But I began to wonder: in this climate, is anyone able to truly prop up this metaphorical object, so easily susceptible to unpredictable gusts of wind?

THE LIMITS OF DOUBT

The daily experiences of the Sillen family—particularly the ways in which things, people, and ways of being were policed, pondered, questioned, and often accepted with hesitant resolve (both consciously and through embodied forms)—provide a window onto the contradictions of neoliberal capitalism during the late 1990s, as complicated by gendered ambiva-lence, racial fears, and class-encoded suspicions. Granted, many of the struggles and strategies faced and embraced by Bonnie, Julia, Doug, and Sam are not "new." However, they were exacerbated by the growing chasm in the shrinking middle class, and thus came to matter quite differently during the late 1990s, making it more likely that anxieties about class positioning played out in a nervous and somewhat aggressive struggle for the appearance and maintenance of privilege—a "feeling of security"—rather than in coalitional efforts to diminish the class divide.

In the lore of the American-dream narrative, families like the Sillens have it all. And yet they have it tenuously, as the economic crises that ensued ten years later revealed. Many families I knew in Danboro felt these same pressures, leading them to wonder if the stresses in their daily lives were worth it for them and their children. Most were well aware—at least, on some level—that they were heading in a direction that was unsettling, if not problematic. And yet, there was so much that they had hoped for through their move to Danboro, which kept them driving on despite their doubts. On occasion, they searched for the brakes. But more often than not they were unable to reach them or realized that they did not even know where they were. So off they continued, sensing that the road down which they were rapidly driving was not the idealized route that they had envisioned when they moved to Danboro. With little time to stop and imagine another direction in which they would like to head, they fueled up instead on nostalgia, whether it was for the Midwest or Brooklyn. And they continued buying "stupid things."

Among the members of the Sillen family and the other families I knew in town, there were many moments of doubt and questioning that could have turned out to be truly "agentive moments" in regard to the current order of things, generative of "radically new habits that lead in radically new directions."[35] But as the next two chapters reveal, the class anxieties and pressures revealed in the daily lives of the Sillens and other families in Danboro were fueling what I call "vehicles for rugged entitlement." Whether it was through driving around town in SUVs (chapter 5) or politically maneuvering to ensure that Danboro's teenagers did not end up being redistricted into the high school that Julia chose not to attend (chapter 6), these forms of "gating" worked against the possibility that ambivalence and doubt would lead to habit change that would counter the dominant common sense.

5 Vehicles for Rugged Entitlement

On the afternoon of her first automobile accident, seventeen-year old Wendi was driving her white Chevy Blazer down a road that winds its way through a few of the older subdivisions built in Danboro during the late 1970s and early 1980s. As she cruised along, the view outside her window was mostly of houses that were quite similar to each other, all resembling the Sillens' moderate-size colonial-style home. At one point, however, a brand-new home awkwardly protruded. There had been a colonial on that lot as well, just like the ones nestled up against it on either side, but it was torn down to make room for a larger, more contemporary home. As Wendi continued farther, she passed the entrance to a new upscale subdivision that was under construction, with houses on the same scale as those in Tarragon Hills—the subdivision in which the couple had hoped to build their six-foot-high ornamental security gate. Shortly after she passed the new development, Wendi approached one of the structures in Danboro that had yet to be improved upon or plowed to make room for more (bigger) houses: the 120-year-old Danboro Bible Church.

At the church, Wendi turned right onto a particularly well-traveled street. Like many old farming byways in highly developed suburban areas, it was invariably busy. Impatient drivers used it as a shortcut to avoid the frustrating bottleneck and numerous traffic lights on Route 2, the multi-lane highway that runs through town and that Linda did her best to avoid on Saturdays. During the late 1990s, this narrow thoroughfare was particularly overburdened. There had been little development of the transit infrastructure to match the car-purchasing fervor and housing boom. Efforts to deal with overcrowded schools also came too little, too late. Just across from a barn-red flower stand that Wendi passed on her right was the entrance road to two of the five elementary schools in town, one of which was notoriously overcrowded.

As reminders of the shifting terrain of class positionings, these changes were unsettling to many people in town. Perhaps some people felt a momentary reprieve as they spotted the old Danboro Bible Church, presuming that *it* was protected and secure. (It, too, was knocked down a few years later.) For Wendi, however, the modifications in her midst were not something often remarked upon. What was foregrounded for her was the thrill of being able to move through her hometown all by herself, in the driver's seat. The economic prosperity of the late 1990s meant that, like many teenagers in Danboro, she was given a new car to drive when she got her license. Her Blazer was her ticket to mobility. She relished the new-found feeling of freedom. What Wendi mostly noticed when she drove around town, music blaring out of her car stereo, were the cute Abercrombie & Fitch–clad boys on the front lawns of their homes.

As Wendi passed the entrance to the schools, she noticed that a Blazer driving ahead of her was slowing down, or so she thought. Then she realized that it had actually come to a complete stop, so she frantically slammed on the brakes and jerked the wheel to the right to veer off to the side. Despite her efforts, her brakes gave out and she smashed into the Blazer in front of her with the left front end of her car. That Blazer, in turn, smashed into a Mercedes that was stopped in front of it. When the sound of smashing steel gave way to silence, Wendi began crying and hyperventilating. She was okay, but she realized that she had just caused a huge accident. She continued to shake as she emerged from her vehicle, even though she could see that everyone was okay. She walked toward the family that was riding in the other Blazer. As she drew near, she instantly recognized them. The mother and daughter, who were from the neighboring town of Westbrook, had come in to shop the week before at a store in the mall where Wendi worked. Wendi told me how nice they were to her after the accident (unlike the couple in the Mercedes, who spoke only to the police), assuring her that everything was okay. They explained that they had stopped because the Mercedes ahead of them had stopped and was waiting to make a left turn. Wendi could not see the Mercedes, so she assumed that they were just slowing down. Their Blazer had blocked her view.

A few days after the accident, I was helping Wendi's mom carry groceries into the house from their garage. Wendi was upstairs in her bedroom getting ready to go out with some friends, with the radio blaring and her blow dryer running on high. Wendi could not possibly hear the conversation that her mom and I were having two stories down. Regardless, her mother whispered to me as we walked through the basement and made our way up the stairs to the kitchen; she did not want Wendi to know how much she worried. With a catch in her voice, she told me that she had just come from the mechanic where Wendi's Blazer was being fixed. Her eyes welled up with tears as she described the horror of seeing the damage. She told me how thankful she was that Wendi was in a Blazer because she shuddered to imagine what could have happened if Wendi had been in a smaller car.

I, too, was concerned about what could have happened to Wendi. We had spent a lot of time together that school year. But I also was struck by other visions during the first few days after hearing about her accident. I kept picturing Wendi within this protective border of steel. She was still new to driving, but because of this expensive and expansive armor, she was somewhat sheltered from injury. So was the family in the Blazer in front of her, who could also afford the luxury of a sport-utility vehicle (SUV). Yet if Wendi (or the family in the other Blazer) had gotten into an accident with a smaller car (and not a fortified Mercedes), who knows what might have happened to the other driver and passengers. SUVs at that time were three times as likely as midsize cars to fatally injure the other driver in a collision.[1] (See figure 9.)

Furthermore, quite paradoxically, Wendi's accident may have been caused—in part—*because* she was in an SUV. SUVs at the time were at least half a ton heavier than cars with the same amount of seating. The extra weight was positioned higher off the road in order to enable sufficient ground clearance for off-road driving. When drivers like Wendi slammed

Figure 9. Editorial cartoon by Gary Markstein, 2000.

on the brakes, the bulky, excessive weight shifted forward, putting extreme pressure on the front brakes. This is perhaps why Wendi's brakes gave out when she tried to avoid hitting the Blazer in front of her. Moreover, the tires that were typically put on SUVs compounded this dynamic. Designed with grooves for off-road driving, they provided diminished traction when SUVs were driven on paved surfaces. It was much harder to stop an SUV in time.[2]

In the late 1990s, the sport-utility vehicle was effectively taking over the roads. What are we to make of the growing popularity at the time of this cumbersome apparatus that (supposedly) protects its passengers in a way that puts others in exaggerated harm's way while often causing accidents in the first place? What does it say about the state of citizenship when public-awareness campaigns about these effects affected the consciousness of SUV drivers but not necessarily their conscience? What were teenagers like Wendi learning, aside from how to drive, when they developed their driving sensibilities in an SUV? And how might we view SUVs through the lens of class anxieties during those years, even if not articulated as such by their drivers?

Even your nest egg will be protected.

Figure 10. Land Rover advertisement, 1999.

Most advertisements in the late 1990s were selling SUVs through high-lighting their rugged, go-anywhere-at-any-time nature, showing them climbing mountains—even if most consumers were buying them to drive to work or the mall and to drop the kids off at school. They subtextually offered the promise of a masculine replacement of the family car—adventurous and risk taking, unlike a tame, boring minivan or station wagon. Yet a few ads here and there, while rare, spoke to the volatility of the economy. Take, for example, a Land Rover advertisement from the *New York Times* of October 22, 1999. (See figure 10.) The center of the half-page spread is composed of two pictures of Land Rover SUVs facing away from each other: one, the more pricey Ranger Rover County; and the other, the more affordable Discovery Series II. Underneath these pictures are the small-print details about each vehicle, including their features and their lease deals. But the first thing that catches your eye as you turn to this page is the declaration in large, bold-print letters emblazoned across the top of the advertisement: "Even your nest egg will be protected."

The image of the SUV-as-financial-protector also was used in a full-page ad for CIBC World Markets that appeared in the *New York Times*

"Business" section of February 23, 1999. The top half of the page is composed of a photograph of the top portion of Wall Street (the actual street), with its looming buildings, minimal light, and crowded feel. Most of the image is in black and white, aside from a bright red Hummer that is driving down the street with a driver and two passengers, all of whom are wearing suits. The declaration at the top of the page states, "You want a bank that's out there for you. In good times and bad." A glance down to the bottom of the page reveals the tag line: "The Drive You Need Now."

A commercial for Wendi's Blazer that aired during those years is vague enough to tap into a range of anxieties, financial and otherwise. The commercial begins with a shot of dense fog, the kind that can turn the light of day into the darkness of night. It is unclear at first exactly what we are watching, although a blurred, circling light starts to come into view. As the image draws closer to the light, we are able to see that the light is coming from atop a lighthouse that is perched on a small, rocky island. As our perspective draws even closer, we are made to realize that it is actually a Blazer that is spinning around on the top of the lighthouse. The light that we have been seeing all along is emanating from its headlights. As the commercial comes to a close, the advertisers for Chevrolet tell us what it is that the Blazer provides: "A Little Security in an Insecure World."

This chapter explores the ways that SUVs helped draft the travel map of our political-economic road trip and how they can be viewed as a metaphor for feelings of insecurity in the late 1990s. Much like the proposed six-foot-high ornamental security gate, SUVs are objects of display and security implicated in questions of community, and complicated by a nexus of fear, anxiety, and desire. They, too, provide what Joan, the chairperson of the zoning board, referred to as a *feeling* of security," even though they are not truly secure. And they are a potential "detriment" to others, and, at times, even to their own drivers. I draw on the time that I spent with Wendi and the thoughts that she shared with me during an interview at the end of her first year of driving. We discussed her (four!) accidents, her embodied experiences behind the wheel, her fears and anxieties while driving in vehicles other than SUVs, and her opinions about other drivers on the road. My analysis reveals how her vivid and poignant words and incidents metaphorically resonate with the discourse on class and citizenship in the United States, as it was articulated within the anxious middle classes. I also suggest that the popularity of SUVs, particularly for use among new drivers, means that they are much more than a trope for the boom time and a consumer item that was good for the U.S. economy in the late 1990s; they were also vehicles for the development of neoliberal sentiments and subjectivities among youth like Wendi. As Gramsci's writings remind us, developing proclivities are not always as trivial as they may initially appear. Particularly in moments of economic and political transition, ripening tendencies have the potential to play a significant role in the regulation of the political-economic system.[3]

There has been much critical discussion about SUVs in the years since Wendi's accident, addressing their rollover tendencies and incidents involving defective tires; their death-defying size, weight, and drivers; their poor emissions standards and shamefully low fuel economy; their environmental impact and role in increased traffic on the roads; not to mention their part in amplified oil dependency and wars in the Middle East.[4] I add to these discussions a view of SUVs through the lens of rugged entitlement, as it was developing among those teetering on the edge of the chasm separating the middle and the upper middle classes. The tag line for the *Wall Street Journal* during those years suggested that one needed to be prepared for "Adventures in Capitalism," yet it was not just any capitalism, but a form of capitalism that created growing inequality, a stock-market bubble, and the looming possibility of a crash—all underexamined by an increasingly corporate-biased media. I would argue that this is part of the story of why SUVs started to take over the roads at the end of the twentieth century. I regard SUVs much in the way that scholars and cultural commentators view the uptick in gated communities and nanny cams during those years: as a private solution to the limited offerings of a "shrunken state,"[5] a way of purchasing a private safety net and some semblance of control. Yet, like gates and nanny cams, SUVs can leave people feeling (and often being) more insecure.

The sport-utility vehicle is thus a metaphor and a "sign" of the times in the Peircean sense. It has an iconic, indexical, and symbolic relationship to the cultural politics of class in the late 1990s. As I was listening to Wendi's words and thinking about SUVs while they were becoming normalized during the volatile economy, I could not help but hear and see metaphoric resonances with neoliberal capitalism and its newly dominant structure of feeing. It is generally not standard ethnographic practice to employ the narrative device of poetic metaphor to illuminate cultural, political, and economic conditions. Anthropologists tend to study metaphors and other tropes as a window onto how powerful beliefs, concepts, and ideologies shape people's social worlds (material conditions included) through everyday communicative practices.[6] Yet I would argue that as it is part of my job as an ethnographer to see the ways that unspoken, emergent, not-yet-discursive affects like insecurity and desire become manifested in things like SUVs, metaphors are particularly useful explanatory devices for this type of interpretive move. They enable us "to index, to point, to throw into clear relief."[7] As E. Valentine Daniel explains, "Metaphors [may] wrench words from their context. But if they destroy, they also reveal."[8] Poetic metaphors specifically enable us to make sense of the social world through what Peirce describes as a "play of musement," or "spontaneous conjectures of instinctive reason."[9] Included here are the "spontaneous conjectures" from my fieldwork in the late 1990s. Within a few years of my time in Danboro, SUVs had become recognized as a sign of the excesses (if not also the insecurities) of that moment; they are now the kind of "root metaphor"[10] that anthropologists have long studied. This discussion is in part a window onto the metaphor of the SUV as it was in formation, showing how a poetics of the SUV can help us make sense of the conditions and sensibilities in which SUVs—and rugged entitlement—were forged.

REGULATING THE U.S. ECONOMY THROUGH NOT REGULATING SUVS

When these thoughts about SUVs began to develop in my mind during the summer of 1998 after Wendi first told me about her accident, I began looking for critical discussions in the media on SUVs. Whereas in subsequent years nightly newscasts would feature stories about their dangers and the growing backlash against them, there was minimal attention being paid to this growing presence on the roads at the time, aside from concerns about rollover tendencies. I became (admittedly) somewhat obsessed with clipping articles from newspapers, assuming that the larger implications of SUVs would (or rather, I hoped would) enter into public consciousness. As my pile of clippings began to grow, I noticed that most of the incisive analysis was written by Keith Bradsher, then Detroit bureau chief for the *New York Times*. Bradsher had been reporting on the business side of SUVs, particularly how the dramatic sales of SUVs, especially among the affluent, were reviving Detroit automakers after a twenty-year slump. In February 1997, one of Bradsher's colleagues at the *Times* asked him about an issue that had not yet been seriously addressed in the media: "What happens when SUVs hit cars?"[11] This provocative question ended up fueling a five-year investigation by Bradsher, leading him to become one of the most trenchant of SUV muckrakers.[12] In revisiting some of Bradsher's insights into how this unsafe and fuel-inefficient vehicle came to dominate the economy in the late 1990s, we can appreciate not only how SUVs are a product of neoliberal logics, including regulatory loopholes, shortsighted optimization, and luxury-market focus, but also how they became an iconic vehicle for rugged entitlement.

It is, of course, no stretch to bring automobiles into a larger discussion of cultural, political, and economic conditions within the United States. As many people have claimed (and lashed out against), the twentieth century was—in part—a story of the conquest of the automobile and the growth of car culture.[13] Throughout the twentieth century, the automobile industry profoundly shaped the American landscape. Henry Ford not only enabled the masses to afford a Ford; he (and particularly all that falls under the rubric of Ford*ism*) created the conditions for corporate power to infiltrate and conflate what it means to be a worker, consumer, and citizen in the United States.[14] On a mundane level, the confluence of these two dynamics led to the situation in which we find ourselves today: the majority of people in the United States *need* cars for their everyday mobility, and car culture has crept into the subtlest aspects of our lives. In fact, when I was talking with Shari (Stephanie's mom) about the idea of "adolescence," she said that the biggest change she noticed in Stephanie was the sense of independence that developed once she was able to drive, much like what Wendi was feeling on the afternoon of her first accident.[15]

Equally powerful has been the extraordinary influence of the automobile industry's "private-pressure groups" to access the "public purse" and sway public officials.[16] In the 1920s, when roads were still better fit for horses, "tire manufacturers and dealers, parts suppliers, oil companies, service-station owners, road builders, and land developers" successfully lobbied for *public* funds to be put into rebuilding roads and constructing parkways and highways to support this form of *private* transportation.[17] From the early 1940s to the mid-1950s, this lobbying group expanded dramatically to include "the Automobile Manufacturers Association, state-highway administrators, motor-bus operators, the American Trucking Association . . . the American Parking Association . . . . oil, rubber, asphalt, and construction industries; the car dealers and renters . . . banks and advertising agencies that depended upon the companies involved; and the labor unions."[18] With heavy contributions from the automakers, most notably General Motors (GM), it was a force to be reckoned with. Tapping into Cold War anxieties about nuclear threats and the atomic scientists' calls for "Defense through Decentralization,"[19] they successfully lobbied for the Interstate Highway Act of 1956. Once it passed, 75 percent of federal transportation funds were spent building highways, with a mere 1 percent for mass transit. Add in those who were waiting to pounce—particularly professional real-estate groups and home builders' associations—and there were all the ingredients for entrenching American dependence on automobility through a new vision for achieving the American dream: low-density suburbs like Danboro.

Throughout the postwar period, the automobile industry continued to wield profound political influence through the intimate relationship between its executives and federal officials; the immensely powerful union of its workers, the United Automobile Workers (UAW); the local-ness of its dealerships embedded in the everyday life of their communities; and the industry's location in key swing states during federal elections. It was, in Bradsher's terms, a "freewheeling collection of industrial giants that could pretty much build what they wanted."[20] The industry also continued to be the bedrock of the U.S. economy through its employment of millions of American workers and its booming success in sales, which was largely built on an American penchant for large, gas-guzzling cars.

It was not until the late 1960s and early 1970s that the auto industry ceased to be such a powerhouse. In 1965, Ralph Nader's *Unsafe at Any Speed* raised profound questions about safety standards and pollution, fueling a movement that led to more regulation of the industry as a whole.

When the oil crisis began in 1973, fuel-economy standards were added to the list of concerns, about which Congress had no choice but to intervene as gasoline prices soared and shortages crippled the country. Yet these regulatory efforts were focused on vehicles classified as "cars," with "light trucks" like pickup trucks and cargo vans escaping regulation, in part because of the political clout of small businesses. Jeeps and others SUVs were a very small portion of the market at the time, so safety and environmental activists largely ignored them.

As successive recessions pounded the economy and oil prices remained dramatically high, many Americans were no longer driving big cars made by Ford or General Motors or Chrysler. All across the land, roads were being taken over by small cars manufactured largely by Japanese and German automakers. The supremacy of U.S. automakers came to a dramatic halt, as did many of their production lines. It was not just wounded national pride that led Washington to become deeply concerned with the decline of the Big Three and the smaller U.S. automakers. The U.S. economy as a whole was at stake, and the first company gravely at risk was American Motors Corporation (AMC), which had bought Kaiser Jeep in the late 1960s.

The Jeep is the lynchpin of this whole story. With the broader environmental movement in full force at the time, the Environmental Protection Agency (EPA) set out to enforce the Clean Air Act of 1970. However, regulators and politicians realized that AMC would end up going out of business if Jeeps were held to the same emissions standards that were being drafted for vehicles classified as "cars." AMC did not have the engineering capabilities to make cleaner engines for Jeeps, and its rivals in Detroit (particularly GM) were mired in competition to stay afloat amid the American turn to small cars. Needless to say, GM was not particularly interested in selling their new emissions technology to AMC. The EPA, not wanting the Clean Air Act to be responsible for putting AMC out of business, drew on what is known as the "truck chassis definition" (i.e., defining a "truck chassis" vehicle as a vehicle built on the same underpart as a pickup truck, which is essentially what the first SUVs were) to exempt Jeeps from the new regulations.[21]

The light-truck exemptions were a relief for the Big Three Detroit automakers as well. They, too, were holding on by a thread, and their one saving grace was their dominance in sales of light trucks, particularly pickups. So when Congress, following the EPA's decision, began work on legislation to double the fuel economy of cars to 27.5 miles per gallon by the model year 1985, the auto industry's "private-pressure groups" went to Washington in full force to lobby hard to ensure that a gas-mileage standard for light trucks was not included in the congressional bill. If light trucks were not included, their fuel-economy standards would be determined not by the EPA, but instead by regulators from the Department of Transportation, which had a much less stringent set of conditions. The lobby was victorious. "Light trucks" were kept out of the congressional bill and held to far lower standards. Since the Transportation Department kept the definition of *light truck* that the EPA used in their decision, Jeeps and other SUVs escaped the tougher regulations.

The "light truck" classification was not the only loophole that set the conditions for the types of SUVs that Wendi and others would be driving in the late 1990s. Size also came to matter. When the Transportation Department and the EPA were drafting the fuel-economy rules and emissions regulations, they were given federal permission to set standards for vehicles with a gross vehicle weight (GVW) of up to ten thousand pounds. GVW is the maximum cargo load recommended by the manufacturer. Vehicles on the high end of GVW are mostly huge pickups for serious work, so the EPA and the Transportation Department decided that it didn't make sense to focus their efforts on those vehicles. They decided instead to develop regulations for light trucks up to six thousand pounds. Automakers jumped at this loophole, building light trucks (which at that time were still largely pickups) that were six thousand pounds or more to avoid these new regulations. "In other words," as Bradsher remarks, "automakers shifted to beefier, less energy-efficient pickups even in a time of rising gasoline prices rather than try to meet regulations that they deemed too stringent."[22] When the Ford Explorer was introduced, it would have a GVW of around six thousand pounds.

To further the new fuel-economy rules, Congress decided in 1978 to add an incentive in the tax code for people to drive smaller cars. If a car's gas mileage was five miles or more below the standard in the congressional bill, it would be deemed a "gas guzzler" and require an additional tax. (In 2003, on some sports cars, this amounted to over seven thousand dollars added to the price of the car.) When this new tax was being drafted, light trucks were initially considered for the tax as well. However, after much lobbying on the part of the automobile industry and rural lawmakers, light trucks were made exempt from the code. They also were exempt from other safety regulations that were being developed at the time, enabling them to have longer stopping distances, less durable tires, higher bumpers, and decreased vehicle stability (i.e., being prone to rollovers). Suffice it to say, as Bradsher notes, "[t]he result has been a public policy disaster, with automakers given an enormous and unintended incentive to shift production away from cars and toward inefficient, unsafe, heavily polluting SUVs."[23]

Eyeing the victories for light trucks, automakers began to think hard about what was going to happen when Americans wanted bigger cars again; they were not going to be able to find them among "cars." The way to satisfy the American desire for gas guzzlers (albeit a desire that had been created by the automakers themselves) would have to come from "light trucks," despite their legal definition as "automobiles which are not passenger automobiles."[24] Sure enough, in 1983, relief came in the form of the Jeep Cherokee, which AMC had been developing behind closed doors. It was an instant success. All the time that AMC was lobbying to save their company under the banner of producing vehicles for plumbers, builders, and farmers, they were trying to design a Jeep that could become the new family vehicle for people craving the space that they lost when they gave up their gas-guzzling station wagon. Using the same underbody as pickup trucks (i.e., lowering a new body down onto a previously designed pickup-truck frame) meant saving costs on developing new parts and new production lines, not to mention not having to develop technologies to meet new regulations from which "light trucks" were exempt. As Gerald Meyers, a top executive at AMC during those years, explained, "It escaped regulation. . . . It was a dream for us—we didn't have the money to do anything, and we didn't do anything. . . . I wasn't doing the sociological thing, I was keeping a dying company alive, I had the blinders on."[25]

The other automakers watched in envy at the amazing success of the Jeep Cherokee and the Cherokee Limited that soon followed. They all looked to cash in on the success of these vehicles, which brought enormous profit from each vehicle because of the minimal manufacturing expenses.

As each automaker entered the SUV market and capitalized on this cheap and easy road to profit during the 1990s, the auto industry as a whole rebounded in a dramatic way. Contrary to the more familiar story that it was the Internet boom that fueled the economy in the late 1990s, Bradsher argues that the auto industry was a major force, thanks to the sales of SUVs. As he points out, "GM and Ford each had greater sales than IBM, AT&T and Microsoft combined. . . . If the Microsoft Corporation were selling $22 billion a year worth of auto parts instead of $22 billion a year worth of computer software, Bill Gates would probably be an obscure GM vice president that nobody ever heard of."[26] SUVs restored the financial health of not just U.S. automakers. Through not being regulated over the years, they ended up regulating the U.S. economy as a whole. Automakers began to realize at this time that their future did not lie in the sales of cars for the everyman, contrary to what Ford came to realize during the early part of the twentieth century. The luxury market would be their mainstay. Through good economic times and bad, through oil prices high and low, the affluent could ride the fiscal waves comfortably in the driver's seat of their SUVs, for they do not feel the effects of economic downturns in the same way.

As the automobile industry strategically harnessed the regulatory loopholes created for light trucks, they set the conditions for SUVs to "displace the family car."[27] Pushed to the side was the ideal of the station wagon and the minivan. The most infamous marketing guru during those years was a Frenchman named Clotaire Rapaille, who incidentally had training as an anthropologist. He preached about the human need for reproduction and survival. Through a Jungian framework, he provided a psychological story to the auto industry about how SUVs tapped into people's most basic instincts. The United States, in his opinion, was a place particularly ripe for such a vehicle. Americans were irrationally fearful of crime and other violence, he suggested, as evidenced by the gated communities that were being built and the private security forces blooming up everywhere. "SUVs are . . . armored cars for the battlefield," he once remarked.[28] Like many other things that were becoming mobile, sport-utility vehicles are evidence of the mobility of this sensibility about protection.[29] Through this vision, marketers focused their efforts on the fantasy of being a rugged person who takes up a lot of space, can't be run off the road, and has the freedom to go anywhere at any time, without being marked as a parent embedded in domestic realities. With an advertising budget that accounted for one in every seven dollars spent in the United States, the automobile industry spent a great deal of that money "subtly or blatantly undermin[ing] people's confidence in cars."[30] But what marketers did not plan for, and what helped sales of SUVs, was that people were buying them for their teenagers.[31] According to Bradsher, advertisers knew that they were promoting a car that was not particularly safe, but they were not promoting them for use by teenagers, nor were they advertising them as a safe family car. Yet SUVs began to be bought in droves for these purposes in places like Danboro.[32]

"A LITTLE SECURITY IN AN INSECURE WORLD"

On the afternoon when Wendi and I spoke about her accidents, we sat around her kitchen table. It was a warm, sunny afternoon, and she had just been outside lying in the sun by her pool. Her thick, curly hair was pulled back in a ponytail, and she was wearing an Abercrombie & Fitch tank top that matched the color of the stripe that ran down the side of her Abercrombie & Fitch shorts. I had spent a good amount of time at this kitchen table, hanging out with Wendi and her friends or having an afternoon snack with her mom, who was able to arrange her work schedule as an assistant at a law firm so that she could be home when Wendi was done with school. Wendi was not involved in after-school activities like Sam, Doug, and Julia. The only time she was busy was when she had to pick up part-time jobs to help pay for the damage to her car after her accidents.

From where Wendi and I sat, we could see the pool and the small wooded area at the back of their yard. The woods concealed a creek, which was the dividing line between Danboro and neighboring Milldale Township. In the winter when the trees were bare, you could see the houses on the other side of the creek, which were exactly the same models as those in Wendi's housing development. The developments were built during the housing boom of the 1980s, on the same scale as all the larger homes built in the area at the time. The main difference between the two developments was the value of their homes. The houses on the Milldale Township side in the late 1990s were valued at around fifty thousand dollars less. According to Wendi's mom, this was because they were zoned for Milldale High School, the high school in the regional high school district that Julia chose not to attend. On several occasions, Wendi's mom shared with me her concern about what might happen if their development was rezoned for Milldale High School—a possibility that had emerged during high school redistricting debates occurring at the time. (See chapter 6.) She was worried that their property value would drop, which would greatly affect the financial security they assumed they would have when they sold their house after Wendi left for college.

The redistricting question had yet to be resolved, so Wendi's mom was not yet sure about the security of their finances. But there was one thing secure in Wendi's future. Her parents were going to buy her a new car in her junior year of college, when her insurance would go down. They had done the same thing for her older sister, who was a senior in college at the time. Wendi already knew exactly what she wanted: a Toyota 4Runner—another SUV. When I asked her why she wanted the 4Runner, she explained, "[Because] it's a truck and it's just so slick."[33] This was not an uncommon response among teenagers in the United States at the time. A study conducted by General Motors in 1999 found that 90 percent of teenagers said that they preferred SUVs to all other classes of vehicles.[34]

When I asked Wendi to elaborate on why she liked trucks, there was a sense of urgency in her voice as she responded, "Because I'll die if I don't have a truck." I asked her why in a perplexed tone, after which she emphatically clarified: "No, no, no—like, literally, I will die. . . . Because if I get into an accident, and I'm driving this little car and I get into an accident with a [Mack-like] truck, I'll die. . . . The fact is that it's really dangerous for me to drive like with a little car. I could go underneath something. I could . . . like, you know, I could die." Wendi then told me that she also loves driving an SUV because "you're so much higher off the ground. . . . When I'm on a highway . . . I feel like I can see more." Wendi's voice then took on a more serious tone as she continued, admitting that she feels "a little more scared" when she drives a smaller car like her mother's midsize Toyota coupe: "If I'm behind a truck, I can't see if like there's an accident there, or if there's something I have to veer around."

I do not want to take away from Wendi's very real fears—dreads that are not unfounded when you grow up in a state that is one of the most densely populated and "roaded."[35] Mack-like trucks are undoubtedly enormous vehicles, and driving among a cluster of them on a highway can be quite disconcerting. Yet Wendi's concern about a truck blocking her view is ironic when you consider that her first accident occurred because she could not see past another Blazer. It, too, blocked her view (just like a Mack truck would have), thus making that advantage dubious. When her words are reread metaphorically in terms of class anxieties, the Mack-like trucks to which Wendi refers look less like monstrosities barreling down the New Jersey Turnpike. They seem like codified obstacles to a continuance of the lifestyle in which she has grown up. Wendi's fear of dying in a smaller car, particularly from going "underneath" something, could be read as an impending "fear of falling" out of the class in which her parents raised her. As Barbara Ehrenreich notes, "The 'capital' belonging to the middle class is far more evanescent than wealth, and must be renewed in each individual through fresh effort and commitment. In this class, no one escapes the requirements of self-discipline and self-directed labor; they are visited, in each generation, upon the young as they were upon the parents."[36]

I do not think Wendi, at that point in her life, feared losing her class positioning. But her parents, like most parents in her hometown, grew up in working-class and lower-middle-class urban settings. As they shifted upward in their class positioning through their professional jobs, they moved to the suburbs—the last hurdle toward achieving their dream. They were so thrilled to have been able to provide their daughters with the accoutrements, connections, and sensibilities of the upper middle class. But just as parents are scared about what could happen to their teenagers while they are out on the road, they are also aware of the roadblocks and potholes that can derail the classed route on which they have placed their children. This was very much on the minds of parents whose children were attending the overcrowded school across from where Wendi's accident occurred. Half of the sixth-grade classrooms had been pushed out into trailers. I was in one of those temporary structures the day before school opened that fall. A few parents were there to complain about the detrimental effects that this situation was going to have on their children's lives. One mother questioned her assumption that her child would benefit from their recent move out of their old "poor" neighborhood in Brooklyn to this supposed "rich town."

It is as if the day Wendi's parents gave her the Blazer to drive was one of the last moments when they would be able to pass their privilege on. It would soon be up to Wendi to do with it what she would. On several occasions, Wendi recounted her mother's joking reminders to her about how she'd better get a "fancy job" when she was older because she was an "expensive girl." It is no wonder that Wendi's mom felt better knowing that Wendi was driving in a Blazer. As the commercial suggested, the Blazer provides "A Little Security in an Insecure World." But as more people bought SUVs, particularly the luxury behemoths that dwarf older SUV models, Wendi's Blazer (like her positioning among the middle classes during a time of diminishing U.S. global economic power and diminishing state entitlements and safety nets) could no longer provide the same feeling of security. Being "higher off the ground" is an advantage only when one is behind a smaller vehicle. No longer was it just Mack trucks (icons of the working classes) that could squash her Blazer or block her view. There were probably just as many SUVs (or people in the middle classes) hindering her view or towering over her on the highways.

INTRINSIC HAZARDS, ESSENTIALIST FAITH

It is important to note that Wendi's Blazer, like her class positioning, was leased, not purchased. But the uncertainty of her class security, whether or not she consciously experienced it, goes beyond the fact that this (somewhat) elevated position on the roads might one day need to be returned. There were some fundamental flaws in its purported safeguarding defense. It is likely that the size and weight of her Blazer were part of the reason she could not stop in time. The statistics on these likelihoods were—admittedly—not well publicized at the time. However, Wendi had two small run-ins in her Blazer after her first big accident. Each incident further revealed how her Blazer's enormity—the very reason that she felt protected from injury—likely played a role in causing her accidents in the first place. Regardless, Wendi continued to have an essentialist faith in her SUV-as-protector, which enabled her to maintain the integrity of that belief despite first-hand evidence to the contrary. As Gordon Allport remarked in regard to this type of essentialist thinking, "It is a striking fact that in most instances categories are stubborn and resist change. . . . If we are accustomed to one make of automobile and are satisfied, why admit the merits of another make? To do so would only disturb our satisfactory set of habits."[37]

Wendi's first little run-in after her big accident happened one afternoon while she was parking at the mall. Spotting an open parking space, she started to turn her Blazer into the spot. As she pulled in farther, she "just went too far forward," as she described it. She ended up scratching the car parked in the spot facing her car, leaving a touch of the white enamel from her Blazer on the front corner of the other car's hood. Wendi never told her mother about this little collision, and she didn't leave a note for the owner of the other car, who was not there at the time. "It was like a two-second thing. Then I left. I bolted," Wendi explained. "A compound would have taken it off. You couldn't even tell it was off my car, so I left."

Not long after Wendi misjudged the parking spot at the mall (and fled the scene!), she backed into her friend Eddie's sedan. It happened one night when she and her friends were over at their friend Jason's house. When she arrived, there were two cars parked in Jason's driveway, which was very long. The cars were pulled in all the way up against the two-car garage, so Wendi pulled up behind one of the cars to park. When it was time to leave at the end of the night, Wendi and her friends hopped into her Blazer, not noticing that her friend Eddie had parked his car right behind hers. As she hit the gas to back out of the driveway, she immediately hit Eddie's car. Eddie "flipped out," according to Wendi. His parents had just bought him the car, an Infiniti sedan, and it was the first time he was driving it. Wendi explained that Eddie had "pulled [his car] up *very, very* close, and since I'm high up, I couldn't see that there was a car. Plus, my windows are tinted. Plus, his car is black and it was nighttime, so I didn't see his car. . . . It's not my fault. No one else in the car saw it. You know?" Needless to say, Eddie was not appeased by this explanation when the accident first happened or by Wendi's various pleadings of "I'm sorry." But eventually, everything was okay between them. Wendi bought Eddie a nice apology card, and it turned out that her Blazer had left only a couple of scratches on his car, which were barely visible. "It [was] like nothing. You [couldn't] even see it," Wendi pointed out.

In a section below, I explore the question of citizenship and the paradox of responsibility and "fault," which are quite glaring in these two incidents.

But here I focus on what it means that Wendi's faith in her Blazer-as-protector was unwavering, despite experiences and understandings that continued to expose its intrinsic hazards. The length and width of her Blazer made it hard for her to judge the parking space. And the height of her vehicle, which made her feel as if she could better see what was coming ahead, created a blind spot in regard to that which was positioned behind her, particularly when, like Eddie's car, it was lower down. Moreover, when we continued to speak about her uneasiness in smaller cars, she said that it was about more than size alone, but also about air-bag release. She explained, "I'll suffocate. They told me that because I'm so short, if the air bag ever goes out, it'll burn my face, probably break my nose, and I'll suffocate." Since air-bag release has little to do with the size of a vehicle, I asked, "So trucks hit . . . differently?" She replied, "No, in general . . . in a truck, it's less likely for me to get into such an accident where the air bag is needed. You know, like, it'll protect me more." I then asked her, "But don't air bags just go out anyway?" She told me that hers never came out in any of her accidents. I decided to stop pushing the point. Psychological essentialism "refers not to how the world is but rather to how people approach the world." It may be bad metaphysics, Doug Medin contends, but it often proves to be good epistemology.[38] Wendi *has* been protected in *each* instance, and *her* Blazer's air bag *never* released.

It was, however, when I asked Wendi about the damage in her first accident that her deep-seated essentialist faith in her Blazer was most powerfully revealed. I had asked her about the damage to the other Blazer. She—at first—said, "Their car wasn't that bad." But then she qualified, "It was bad, though . . . it wasn't like terrible where they couldn't drive it." According to Wendi, this was "because it was a Blazer." Yet when we spoke about the damage to *her* Blazer, she described it as "literally, like, compressed." There was no pause between her comments. Wendi went straight from claiming that there was minimal damage to the other Blazer *because* it was a Blazer right into how her Blazer was "compressed." While Wendi was speaking, I kept picturing her mother's face on the afternoon when she had just seen the damage to Wendi's Blazer, her eyes brimming with tears. I also could not help but think back to a conversation I had with Wendi a few days after that conversation, when I called to see how she and her mother were doing. Wendi told me that she had just gotten off the phone with the mechanic, who was deciding whether or not the Blazer would have to be totaled. Clearly, Wendi's car had been in bad shape, despite the fact that it was a Blazer. To press Wendi on this point, I asked, "But your car was a Blazer, too?" Wendi responded, "Right, but . . ." She then paused—and didn't finish her sentence.

Wendi did not have a reason why *her* Blazer had been so crushed, despite the fact that she believed that Blazers (by their nature) were safe from this kind of damage. It was as if the details of her accident revealed an insignificant aberration. This is typical essentialist reasoning, in which contrary evidence is "perfunctorily acknowledged but excluded." This process of "re-fencing," as Allport refers to it,[39] is central to psychological essentialism, whereby "people act as if things (e.g. objects) have essences or underlying natures that make them the thing that they are. Furthermore, the essence constrains or generates properties that may vary in their centrality."[40] For Wendi, SUVs are *essentially* vehicles that protect her, without which she feels that she could literally die. The various properties that do the protecting, such as height and ability not to be squashed in an accident, "vary in their centrality" in Wendi's thinking, maintaining the essence of what her Blazer means to her (i.e., a protective border of steel).

Wendi's feeling of security in her Blazer was likely due in part to the fact that the public discourse in her midst at that time celebrated the safety of SUVs. But when read through the lens of the class metaphor, Wendi's words again are striking in their correspondence, this time in regard to rugged entitlement. She conceives of her SUV as a safety net, yet the structure that makes her feel protected contains an air bag— something that she believes could at any moment cause her grave damage. She convinced herself, or at least always needed to believe, that her Blazer would ensure her safety, despite the fact that it also likely caused her accidents in the first place and was almost totaled in her first accident. People were becoming increasingly anxious about the shifting configuration of the middle class. When everyone else is getting their hands on what is supposed to be protecting *your* view from above, perhaps the ever-present intrinsic threat of the metaphorical air bag must not seem so bad. But will Wendi always defend her SUV, as many people continued to do in regard to other privatized responses to the limits of neoliberalization, like overmortgaging and expanded credit, if she starts to realize that *it* might have been a part of the reason she crashed?[41]

TRANSFORMING WANTS INTO NEEDS (AND THEN BIGGER NEEDS)

This question gets more complicated when we further consider habit production among people who are driving SUVs. Wendi learned to drive in her mother's old Blazer, the exact same model that she was driving during her first year on the road. Her driving sensibilities were produced in a sport-utility vehicle—feeling high above the road, safe behind the wheel, and protected while among the other cars and trucks driving around her. For Wendi, as for all of us when we first learn to drive (or learn to do anything), these early moments are significant starting points for habit production.[42] These ways of being—especially once they become second nature—play a pivotal role in regulating the capitalist system and further transforming the class structure itself. It is therefore significant when Wendi talks about the fact that she feels unsafe in smaller cars; when she explains why she wants her next automobile to be another SUV; and when she reveals her essentialist faith in this "class" of vehicle. Many people bought their first SUV for a host of personal reasons. Wendi said that her mom got the Blazer because "she wanted to get a truck because, you know, those were like what's 'in.' You know, 'Time to get a truck!'" However, once an object of desire, the sport-utility vehicle has become an object of necessity in many people's eyes. What was a "want" has become a "need."

Gramsci was fascinated with Henry Ford's ability to create such desires in people.[43] Ford was a master at taking a luxury item—a car—and creating the conditions for it to become a consumer object that every family had to have (and eventually *needed*).[44] We may technically be in a post-Fordist moment when it comes to the means of production and the accumulation of capital. However, this aspect of Fordism—that is, the infiltration of the needs of corporate capital into people's everyday lives, with a good amount of help from the state—continues today in all of its rearticulated glory. If Gramsci were still around, I imagine he would be intrigued by this situation, which represents an extreme version of this aspect of

Fordism. These kinds of vehicles have become a matter of life and death in Wendi's eyes, and she likely might feel she needs a particular bracket of income when she is older in order to fulfill this "need."

Wendi, though, had doubt, discomfort, and ambivalence in regard to her SUV, much like the contradictory consciousness among the Sillen family members in regard to their vehicles for rugged entitlement. I asked Wendi at one point, "How do you *feel* when you're driving your car?" I expected her to say that she felt powerful and in control, which is what most other teenagers in town told me when I asked them about their experiences with driving their SUVs, including Lauren (Stu and Linda's daughter) and Danielle (Nancy and Eric's daughter). But Wendi said, "I feel like this powerless little thing in like this huge car. . . . I feel like this little cute little girl. All my friends laugh at me." I asked her why she felt "powerless." She continued, "Because I'm so small, you know. I'm like five-two. I can barely see over the wheel. . . . All my friends will come in the car and be like, 'You look so cute driving the big car.'"

You could say that it is quite ironic that the same vehicle that made Wendi feel safer (because she liked to see what was coming down the road) also made her feel powerless (and created difficulties in regard to her range of vision). But much like other means of driving after class, the anxiousness created by the structure itself could very well have been adding fuel to her "need" for this "class" of vehicle (despite the gendered discomfort it entails). This is much like living in a gated community, or having an overmortgaged home, or having new carpet to keep clean. Wendi's expectation of feeling secure in her Blazer had become regularized. As E. Valentine Daniel points out, "Expectations are of the nature of habit. The more our expectations—conscious and unconscious—are satisfied, the more regularized and ramified our habits become."[45] The way that Wendi feels she *needs* an SUV is not unlike Sam's *anticipation* of the next Nintendo game to be released or Bonnie's *craving* for "stupid things." These are all "habits of expectation" that were continually being elaborated within the neoliberal capitalist culture in which Wendi, Sam, Bonnie, and other people in Danboro (and beyond) were continually becoming.

Wendi's essentialist faith in her Blazer was able to counter the force of her doubt, although her need and doubt likely will require a bigger SUV in order to be fully satisfied. Wendi's Blazer is now quite small in the hierarchy of SUVs on the roads, much like her parents' positioning among the middle classes. So while her expectation of feeling secure in her Blazer had become regularized, this habituated need will likely require an increasingly larger SUV to provide the same sense of security. This is, of course, part of how the capitalist system thrives. New desires are produced and satisfied for just a brief period of time, so that consumers eternally seek and long. But in a moment with decreasing safety nets, the desire to seek that which will make people feel secure is even more pronounced.

CREATING CITIZENS

Adhering to Gramsci's understanding of consumption requires that we go beyond viewing new "needs" on the part of Wendi and other SUV drivers as mere reflections of a new consumer niche, which was created through the production of new types of subjectivities. As Gramsci (and Ford) knew quite well, these new subjectivities also are linked to the ways that people are being and becoming *citizens*.[46] What type of citizenry is produced or exaggerated through the pervasiveness of sport-utility vehicles? An episode of *The Simpsons* that first aired during the winter of 1999 offers an incisive and irreverent critique of SUV drivers-as-citizens. Marge, the mother of the family, is given an SUV by her husband, Homer. Over the course of the episode, Marge transforms into a dangerously aggressive driver whose road rage lands her in driving school and ultimately leads to her license being revoked. In one scene, Marge's two children climb into the back seat of her SUV. Lisa, the conscience of the family, advises, "But, Mom, I read that sport-utility vehicles are more likely to be in fatal accidents." To which her brother, Bart, responds, "Fatal to the people in the *other* car. Let's roll."[47]

I asked Wendi at one point what she thought about concerns that had been raised in regard to SUVs. She said she had not heard that there were any problems, so I shared with her some of the findings that I had learned about through the writings of journalists like Bradsher, explaining that if a Blazer were to get into an accident with a little Toyota, for example, the person in the little car would have a much higher chance of major injury or death than if that person were to get into the same accident with another little car. Wendi listened and nodded while saying, "Yeah," as I elaborated. I then asked her what she thought about the idea that people should not buy these big vehicles because it is unfair to those who cannot afford to have this extra layer of protection when they are on the road. Wendi's immediate response was to say that if someone is driving a little Toyota and *they* cause the accident, it is their fault, especially if they are drunk driving or something. I then brought up the possible scenario that *she* caused the accident and the other person got hurt. She responded, "Well, sorry, but I'm—" But before she had the chance to finish, I added that the journalists are "just saying, like, well, rich people . . . can afford to buy them and . . . the poor people can't and so—" Before I had a chance to finish, she said, "Yeah, but there are, like, those old used ones you can afford to buy, because, you know, they're not so new anymore."

Wendi's comments could easily be disregarded as evidence of nothing more than "typical" teenage self-centeredness. The "egocentric adolescent" is one of the more readily available narratives for making sense of explanations provided by teenagers. But Wendi's ability to so easily reason herself out of this predicament is more revealing, I would argue, of the instantiation of liberal ideology in the form of neoliberalism, whereby blame and responsibility are understood solely within the logics of the market and individual choice, rather than the limiting conditions of possibility in which people are continually becoming. According to this logic, if someone dies while driving drunk, compassion is not likely to fall on their side, even if they would *not* have become a fatality if the other car had *not* been a sport-utility vehicle. The idea that it is tragic that everyone does not pull out of their parking spots with the same advantages is rarely accommodated within that perspective. People are more likely to say that "they" could have bought a used one. It is thus somewhat to be expected within this ideological climate that Wendi believes that they can, but that they must be *choosing* not to.

It is also telling that Wendi caused several accidents, while *sober*, and yet her image of a threatening driver on the road is a drunk. The irony, of course, is that SUV drivers like Wendi (i.e., those who have not been hurt by either intrinsic or external hazards) learn that you do not have to be responsible when you have a protective border of steel (or at least an imagined one). You do not even have to feel accountable. While Wendi did receive a ticket after her first big accident, she left the scene after her mall incident without getting caught, and felt that it was not her "fault" when she backed into her friend Eddie's car.

This contradictory relationship to the predicament of individual responsibility is not only at the core of liberal ideology, as Uday Mehta contends.[48] It is also the crux of what it means to be among the middle classes in a liberal democracy that tends to provide more safety nets for capital than for people. There is a "feeling" of being protected. And yet, as Ehrenreich points out, one's cultural capital gets you only so far; those "in the middle" come to learn that they are actually *not* protected in many ways.[49] The anxiety that emerged from this dynamic in the late 1990s set the conditions of possibility for the intensification of rugged entitlement. Concern for the collective good got shifted to the backseat.

Wendi's fourth accident threw into relief this vulnerable sense of security. The accident occurred one afternoon when she was merging onto Route 2, the gridlocked state highway that runs through town. She could not remember whether she pulled too far out or whether the other vehicle, which was already driving on the highway, pulled too far into the shoulder as she was merging. Regardless, Wendi's Blazer sideswiped the other vehicle, which was another (much bigger) sport-utility vehicle, a Chevy Suburban. The Suburban suffered little damage, aside from a flat tire. Wendi's vehicle, on the other hand, initially lost one of its side mirrors. Then, a few minutes after the accident, the whole front-end fender popped off. According to Wendi, the two women in the Suburban were really nice to her. In fact, during our discussion about her first year of driving, she acknowledged her good fortune, remarking, "Thank God I've always gotten into accidents with nice people!"

Is it just "nice people," or is there something to the fact that they have always been people driving the same "class" of vehicle? When an accident happens among people from within the same "class" of drivers, it is easy to forget the danger that these automobiles could have to others who are not as fortunate. Sure, some of the wind was taken out of the tires of the Suburban, which momentarily brought it closer to the surface of the road. But I kept imagining Wendi's side mirror, lying crushed in the road, limiting her range of vision of what is behind her. We cannot predict how

Wendi's (or anyone's) developing habits, desires, and sentiments will play out in the future, but it behooves us not to lose sight of their production and their relationship to political subjectivities, with implications for citizenship. We need to keep these moments in view.

As Wendi's first year of driving reveals, SUVs in the late 1990s not only were vital to the workings of the U.S. economy; they also were embedded in the habits, desires, and sentiments of their owners. Wendi, like many other drivers on the road, had an essentialist faith in the power of SUVs to protect her, despite the fact that they—like middle-class privileges—do not guarantee security for their occupants. Despite this illusion, however, the effects of vehicles for rugged entitlement like SUVs were (and are) still quite real. They provide a *feeling* of security; embody a potential "detriment" to others (including by way of oil wars and global warming); and set the conditions for creating neoliberal subjects who are often unwilling to give up this (supposedly) privileged position on the roads, regardless of what it means for other drivers or themselves or the terrain as a whole.

From the perspective of an upper-middle-class teenager growing up in suburban New Jersey, it was hard for Wendi to grasp that she might be an unwitting participant in the entrenchment of rugged entitlement through her seemingly harmless everyday habits and desires, as it can be for many of us in our daily lives. Wendi knew only the comfort and familiarity of sameness. The possibility of consciously experiencing a "fear of falling" was not realized. Yet Wendi was surprised when the front end of her Blazer unexpectedly popped off. And in the mid to late 2000s, it came as a surprise to many to learn about or to experience the dramatic rise in bankruptcies and foreclosures among the middle classes. The sudden loss of a fender is a powerful image of the loss of protection, yet political possibility lies in these moments of vulnerability.

WHAT ELSE MAY HAVE CAUSED THE CRASH?

As we drive further into this century, we bring with us the quickening trend of further divisions along class lines in the United States and the transnational community of which it is an inextricable part. Like so much that has become mobile, the sport-utility vehicle purports to enable its drivers to become unhindered and free. Yet driving in an SUV will never be able to satisfy the need for feeling free yet secure, with an unobstructed view of the road ahead. There will always be Mack trucks barreling down the highways, not to mention ever-larger SUVs. As we continue with this "highway arms race," as Bradsher has described it,[50] we further entrench our society in a dialectic that eternally seeks to appease class anxieties that are unable to be satisfied through vehicles for rugged entitlement. There is always the likelihood, as we saw in Wendi's first accident (and in the economic crash) that the brakes will give out. Only *real* (and ideally, secure) entitlements—such as education, health care, Social Security, and child care—can truly provide "a little security in an insecure world." But can this security be realized with most attention being paid to Mack trucks and other SUVs?

Recall that in Wendi's first accident, she was unable to see the car that had stopped in front of the other Blazer, a Mercedes—a vehicle that signifies the bourgeoisie. The damage to the Mercedes was minimal. It got only few scratches. According to Wendi, the couple that was driving the car also was okay, though on the accident report they claimed to have received neck injuries. Wendi found this to be a bit shady, so she assumed that they were going to sue her, particularly because they never spoke with her after the accident. They spoke only with the police—representatives of the state. But Wendi never did hear anything from the people in the Mercedes. She heard only from the police, who gave her a ticket for careless driving.

It was no surprise that Wendi got a ticket. The rules of the road are very clear when it comes to determining fault in this type of accident. As every teenager learns when preparing for the written part of his or her driving test, it is a driver's responsibility to stay at least two car lengths behind the vehicle ahead. Because of this rule, blame is automatically placed on the vehicle at the back of the line; the details of the incident are inconsequential. But let's face it: in reality, very few people actually stay two lengths back. As most drivers are well aware, the cause of rear-end accidents (and thus blame) is far more complicated. Speaking metaphorically, with the economic crash in mind, the Mercedes (the bourgeoisie) could have eased into its location, or it very well might have stopped short. Either way, we can be pretty sure that it was focused on where *it* was going, not the vehicles behind it.

Like class relations and the economy, the dynamics between drivers on the road are far more complicated in practice than described on paper. The "rules" do not often capture the complexity of reality, even in instances with no malicious intent. During the economic crisis that hit in 2008, people whose mortgages were foreclosed or who were forced to default on loans were deemed "at fault" for living beyond their means. Like the Blazer at the back, they were considered to be to blame for their predicament, despite predatory lending and credit practices that ensnared people in too much debt, or a national ideology that continue to promote an upscaled suburban American dream that was no longer sustainable or as attainable. Just as the Mercedes escaped blame, so, too, at first did the banks and the policy makers. But in a moment when the landscape of the roads was being dramatically altered by SUVs, much like the class structure itself, it should have been time to rethink the rules of the road. The bigger the SUV, the higher and heavier it tends to be, making it far easier for it to crash. Two lengths back was no longer enough.

In the years that followed the 2008 economic crash, some started to become optimistic about the future landscape of the roads. Energy prices and political concerns forced a decline in the sales of SUVs, and it became cool to be "green" and drive Minis, Smart Cars, and hybrid vehicles, even among those not feeling the economic crunch. At the same time, it has become very normalized to share the roads with SUVs, even huge ones—a concern unto itself. Just as car companies anticipated, elites whose pocketbooks are not fazed by the rise in oil prices, and whose consciousness is not fazed by environmental or other concerns, will continue to drive their Suburbans and Hummers, offering an even more stark representation on the roads of the growing class divide, not to mention an even larger safety imbalance when different classes of cars collide.

The nation's headlights also started to shine on the bourgeoisie, bringing the elite into critical view. People started thinking more about all the Mercedes (and big SUVs) that were just sitting there, waiting to make a left turn, hidden from view because we (as a society) were so focused on the Blazer that was driving ahead. All kinds of "unlikely coalitions"[51] began to emerge among members of society who were driving smaller vehicles, so to speak. But during the time of my fieldwork, before the economic crash, this was rarely the case in Danboro, as the next chapter

reveals through a discussion of a redistricting debate about student placement in the regional high school district of which Danboro High School is
a part. Like the situation in the elementary school across from where
Wendi's first accident occurred, Danboro High School (among other
schools in the district) was extremely overcrowded. Rather than forming
a coalition with those of all classes who were being affected by this situation, parents in Danboro joined forces with those from the neighboring
town of Westbrook (where the family in the other Blazer was from) to try
to ensure that their children would not end up in the school in the district
with drivers of smaller cars, as it were (that is, "the Mill"—the school that
Julia chose not to attend). Vehicles for rugged entitlement, as the next
chapter demonstrates, are found not only in the things that people buy,
whether they are SUVs or "stupid things" or six-foot-high ornamental
security gates. Power and authority are vehicles for rugged entitlement as
well.

6   From White Flight to Community Might

It was nine months before the opening of a new high school in the Milldale Regional High School District, a sizable district encompassing eight towns and almost eight thousand students. The district's board of education had just hired an educational consulting firm to aid them in the arduous task of reconfiguring school zones to fill the new school and to alleviate overcrowding in three of the district schools, one of which was Danboro High School. Many Danboro residents were up in arms at the prospect that their children might be rezoned to another school in the district. The consultants held five public meetings—one at each of the existing five high schools—to create an opportunity for concerned citizens to learn about plans being developed for student placement and to share their thoughts on various redistricting options. The meetings did provide well-attended, open forums. But the process became another site for the instantiation of rugged entitlement, fueling divisiveness in the district and throwing into relief class anxieties, racial politics, and community battles in the late 1990s. As with concerns about SUVs, these debates raised questions about the nature of citizenship at a time when people were feeling crowded and crowded out. On display was another instance of "gating"—a "forting up" of town boundaries, social borders, and the social spaces in which youth come of age.

The five public forums, which are the focus of my discussion in this chapter, proved to be quite raucous affairs, with proclamations that included: "Lots of parents from Danboro have come out and made it clear that *their* kids will go nowhere but Danboro [High School]." "This should not be done to satisfy other towns whose mouths are opened the widest!" "This is not an integrated system. It's segregated. And there are racist dynamics and innuendos." "Why are we being called racist when we just don't want to have our kids move schools?" "It's not about racism, but community spirit!" "We're in the United States of America, and we have *choice!*" "All we want is *choice, choice, choice!*" "Who should I blame when my kid has psychological problems from being moved?" "There are gonna be five thousand new houses over the next year!" "It'll end up like an urban setting with thirty-plus kids in each classroom." "Now I'm going to have to go to a private school." "Danboro would secede." "Danboro and Westbrook are not buying into the concept of a regional district." "You're just telling people what they want to hear, not what needs to be done." "This has been so late to start. . . . Maybe this is a sham . . . and we're just wasting our time!"

These redistricting debates, I suggest, can be read as a microcosm of larger tensions over the relationship between individual desires and collective needs. Being part of a regional school district means that individual residents can be asked to accommodate for the good of the whole—as when redistricting is needed, which had already happened in the district for some towns. Many parents from Danboro and the neighboring town of Westbrook, however, tried to ensure that their children would not be redistricted. Other residents in the district in turn used the public nature of these forums to challenge and denounce their sense of rugged entitlement. (Danboro, in particular, is known in the area as being a place where people have an extreme sense of privilege and entitlement. Indeed, the town is one of the more affluent of middle-class towns in the district.)[1] Much in the way that the zoning board debate in chapter 3 brought to life tensions between residual and dominant sensibilities in regard to private property, this chapter provides a window onto clashes between residual and dominant approaches to public schooling, wherein commitments to regionalism come face-to-face with inclinations toward "competitive regionalism"[2] and limited notions of "community."[3] Here, the differing sensibilities are most pronounced *across* towns in the district rather than within Danboro itself, scaling up our view of rugged entitlement from individual versus community to municipal community versus regional collective, though varying perspectives within individual towns come through as well. While we often think about competitive regionalism in regard to metropolitan regions, the concept is fruitful for the smaller scale, on view here, of towns within a region grappling with limited resources.

As we move from meeting to meeting, it becomes increasingly clear how class relations were negotiated and maneuvered through racial politics, community coalitions, and liberal claims. By paying close attention to *what* was "sayable" (and what wasn't), *where* it could (and could not) be said, *how* it was uttered, and *to whom*, we see how shifts in power and alignment took place through subtle linguistic and discursive forms, much as we saw in the zoning board debate.[4] On view were communicative practices that ranged from heckling, joking, cross-talk, and coded language to emphasized accents, slips of the tongue, and subtle shifts in framing. Used to critique and at times to collude, these strategies policed the boundaries of inclusion and exclusion and created coalitional effects.

Amid expressed concerns from Danboro and Westbrook residents about "community spirit," "choice," and "psychological problems," there was an undercurrent suggesting that racial anxieties were an elusive subtext of vocalized concerns. As Jane Hill notes, racialized coded language "communicate[s] by absence and silence,"[5] through "inferences that the literal content of a text or an utterance invites."[6] But to claim that race is the sole issue here would oversimplify the nature of cultural politics. As Gramsci reminds us, broad cultural forms particular to people's lives shape their common sense. Concerns about children's academic, economic, and emotional success are real and legitimate. This is tricky (i.e., for an interpreter), because educational excellence is a socially sanctioned moral value, and "education"—particularly *public* education—can be an acceptable assertion of class privilege; it is not necessarily linked to racial anxieties or undemocratic sensibilities.[7] And yet, even if the objections of Danboro and Westbrook parents to the plans were not explicitly "about race," the collective *effects* were in part racial. One does not have to *be* "racist" for there to be racial implications; intentionality (individual motives, sentiments, and concerns) is not the question here.[8]

I want to underscore again that rugged entitlement cannot be understood without keeping in mind the changing class structure, newly dominant discursive formations, and a state aligned with neoliberal logics. Parents in Danboro (and Westbrook), I suggest, were asserting their power vis-à-vis other towns in a context in which they may have felt powerless in regard to political-economic shifts shaping their lives and their towns (even if they do not directly attribute anxieties about their children's schools to these conditions). People's class anxieties were increasingly being encapsulated in sport-utility vehicles, driving toward class- and racially segregated spaces in frantic efforts to secure the economic future of *one's own* children. As we saw in the daily life of the Sillen family, these conditions exacerbated a sense of rugged entitlement rather than creating conditions of possibility for towns in the district to come together to collectively tackle their problems, infrastructural or otherwise.

THE MILLDALE REGIONAL HIGH SCHOOL DISTRICT: NAMING, RANKING, RACE, AND RUMOR

When discussions began about options to fill the new school, there was already divisiveness in the district. Before I describe a series of events that triggered discord, it is important to briefly look at the story of how the district was created, which provides some originary clues to its social borders. The eight towns encompassed by the Milldale Regional High School District—Bowen, Danboro, Ellenville, Great Farms, Lenape Crossing, Milldale Borough, Milldale Township, and Westbrook (all pseudonyms)— had been rural farming communities, aside from a small industrial base in downtown Milldale. (See map 1.) All students attended school in Milldale. As the number of students grew amid suburbanization, individual towns created their own elementary and middle school districts. But for high schools, the municipalities decided to pool resources and create a regional high school district. In 1966, the first new school was built and named North Milldale High School. It was located in Danboro (which is north of Milldale) because the majority of its students were from Danboro.[9] As new schools were needed, they were built in the town that would be sending the most students. Eventually, school names were changed to match the name

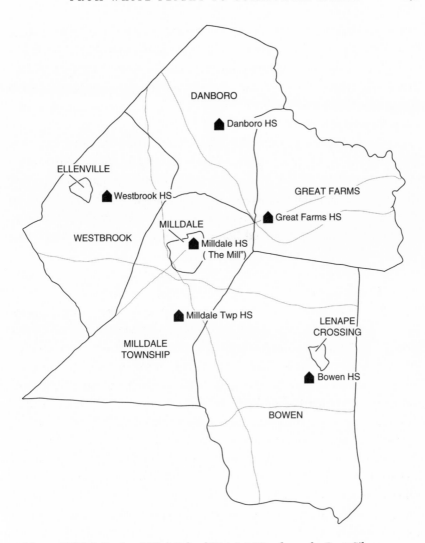

Map 1. Milldale Regional High School District. Map drawn by Brett Silvers.

of the town in which the school was located. By the late 1990s, there were five high schools in the district: Milldale High School, Danboro High School, Bowen High School (which had been South Milldale High School), Westbrook High School, and Milldale Township High School. The school under construction in 1997 was named Great Farms High School because it was located in the town of Great Farms.[10] The switching of school names from district names to town names proved to set the conditions for some residents, particularly in Danboro and Westbrook, to feel that the school in their town was *theirs* rather than being part of a larger *regional district* that had the right to redraw attendance boundaries if need be. As Gramsci points out, "[A] popular conviction often has the same energy as a material force or something of the kind."[11]

Continued efforts to maintain those boundaries (or rather, to create them as "real") took place in the months leading up to the redistricting meetings amid a heated debate in the district over a referendum to remove class ranking. Referendum 5120 (or simply "5120," as it was referred to) was quietly put on the table over the summer with little publicity and passed at a modestly attended board of education meeting. One father proclaimed that residents in the district were "stonewalled" by what appeared to be a secretive process. Some of the loudest (and most organized) voices who sought to overturn the referendum and keep class ranking were Danboro residents. They were galvanized shortly after it passed via passionate emails forwarded around town by the mother of a Danboro High School student. Danboro's public information officer, sitting in her office in Danboro's barn-shaped town hall, joked that this woman was "like a modern-day Paul Revere via the Internet," sending emails that basically said, "The board is coming! The board is coming!" During this time, a parent from Westbrook who also opposed 5120 realized that the members of the board who wanted to overturn 5120 represented 57 percent of the district's residents despite being a voting minority. Each town in the district had one elected member (and therefore one vote). If representation were reconfigured using population percentages, 5120 could be overturned, for Westbrook and Danboro would gain more voting power; they were among the largest towns in the district.[12] He filed a suit claiming that the configuration of representation on the board was unconstitutional. A federal court judge agreed, though state legislators had yet to finish designing a formula for board representation when this redistricting process began.

The "5120" issue, however, proved to be about far more than class ranking and district control. It also tapped into racial tensions in the district. Deliberations over 5120 at first raised typical concerns when class ranking is on the table. Those who wanted to keep class ranking were worried that their children (typically those with high ranking) would lose a distinguishing feature on their transcripts. Those who supported the referendum felt that the majority of students would benefit from not being told where they were ranked. Yet amid these pubic discussions, some suggested that those who wanted to remove class ranking had no concern for (or even understanding of) education because their children were not college bound or did not aspire to top universities. At that point, the local chapters of the NAACP and the Human Relations Council got involved. They felt that there were racial undercurrents in those latter claims, particularly when it was implied that "those" who had no concern for education were parents whose children attended Milldale High School. Milldale High School, referred to as "the Mill," is the school that the majority of the district's African-American and Mexican-American students attend, many of whom come from working-class families. It is the school that Julia chose not to attend because it felt "dirty" to her.

Amid this eruption of race and class (ranking) tensions, rumors circulated that sections of Danboro (and possibly Westbrook), including Wendi's development, might get redistricted to the Mill. The Mill had the lowest student enrollments at the time, so many assumed that students from overcrowded schools might be moved there. As discussed in previous chapters, the "white flight" trajectory of many Danboro residents led people to "see" the racial makeup of downtown Milldale, where the school is located, as "darker" than it actually was, and to infuse their children's habitus with a fearful relationship to it. A teacher from the Mill told me that people from Danboro often asked her if there were metal detectors at the school—of which there were none. I had heard this from Wendi, who once told me that the school had "lots of Mexicans and blacks [and] tough guys . . . [so] they have metal detectors." During a discussion with Stu, I asked him if he thought the fear among many Danboro parents of their children ending up at the Mill was linked to their relationship to Brooklyn. Did they feel that the "darkening" they left behind was back in their lives, as if they were being "forced" to put their kids in the kinds of social spaces that they fled? "Of course!" he replied. With a sense of being aghast at the idea of it, another resident explained, "They want to move Danboro kids into the Mill. Can you believe it? There's gonna be quite a battle!" And there was.

To complicate the situation more, there was a feeling of a kind of "collapse of the state" in the district. Not only was the board unable to make any major policy decisions until it was properly reinstated (including these redistricting decisions, which had to be approved by the judge), but the superintendent had resigned. One mother in Danboro figured that he wanted "to jump ship before it sank." Buzz quickly emerged around the district that Danboro and Westbrook parents were filling the power vacuum and perhaps working furtively with the consultants. This was viewed with great trepidation by many who worried that the desires of Danboro and Westbrook parents would supersede their own, including their commitment to the ideal of a regional district.

This situation fueled not only distrust of the process, but also resentment of the board for the late start and the dearth of information provided. The consultants were hired in December, yet school boards typically hire them in September—a year before changes are to go into effect. This was of particular concern for parents of eighth-grade students; their children were supposed to be making course selections for the following year, and they did not yet know which school they would be attending. For those who might be going to the new school, there had been no official information—only rumors—about the curriculum, the extracurriculars, and the teachers. And most people in the district did not learn until these meetings that the money to build the new school was not enough to build it to its full capacity. The money had been allocated during the housing boom of the 1980s, when the district first worried that five schools were not sufficient to house the growing student population. Yet right after the bond referendum was passed in 1986, the housing market collapsed, and the district decided to sit on the money and wait out the downturn. However, the money budgeted in 1986 was not enough to build the school at its planned capacity of 1,300 students; construction costs had risen considerably by the late 1990s. So while core facilities (auditorium, cafeteria, gymnasium, hallways, restrooms) could be constructed for 1,300 students, there was enough money to build classroom space only for 750. There would need to be another tax bond to build the additional classrooms. And even with the new Great Farms school at full capacity, the district was only a few years away from having more students than all of its facilities were meant to hold. The district needed to build another entire new school or construct additions onto existing schools—and they needed to make a plan right away. And as is the case in New Jersey's school districts, which are funded in large part through property taxes, residents in the district were going to have to foot a good portion of the bill.[13]

Making matters worse, the consulting firm was hired simply to fill Great Farms for its opening year while bringing some relief to the over-crowded schools. Their charge did not include dealing with the need for—and costs of—further construction. And because they were based on Long Island and had little prior understanding of conditions in the district, their learning curve and "expertise" proved to be additional lightning rods for anxiety and frustration through the process. Their initial analysis of projected enrollments in the district, for example (see table 1), was calcu-lated using standardized state formulas, which utilize existing elementary school enrollments. These figures did not take into account the hundreds of new children in the district likely to enter the schools once the housing developments under construction were complete.

THE OPTIONS: MINIMAL, PARTIAL, COMPREHENSIVE, OR VOLUNTARY

Soon after being hired by the board and working with their "stats people" to calculate the (underestimated) projected enrollments for the existing schools, the consultants developed three redistricting options for the dis-trict to consider. I, like everyone residing in the district, received a flyer in late December that included their projected enrollments, details about the options, and dates for the public meetings. The three options on the flyer can be summarized as follows:

- Option 1 ("Minimal Redistricting"): Great Farms residents would, over time, be phased into the new school (i.e., Great Farms High School). In addition, special programs (like the one that Julia attended) located in the overcrowded schools would be moved to Great Farms.

- Option 2 ("Partial Redistricting"): In addition to moving Great Farms students, some Danboro and Westbrook students would be assigned to Great Farms High School, and more Bowen students would be moved into Milldale Township to keep the special programs at Bowen High School.

Table 1. Projected enrollment and percentage of capacity by school and school year.

High School	1997 – 1998	1998 – 1999	1999 – 2000	2000 – 2001	2001 – 2002	2002 – 2003	Capacity
Milldale	815 62%	869 67%	884 68%	1,013 78%	1,123 86%	1,294 99%	1,306
Milldale Twp.	1,388 91%	1,384 91%	1,380 91%	1,353 89%	1,263 83%	1,197 79%	1,518
Bowen	1,876 118%	2,075 130%	2,320 145%	2,496 156%	2,740 172%	2,826 177%	1,596
Westbrook	1,853 111%	1,891 113%	2,024 121%	2,209 132%	2,374 142%	2,545 152%	1,670
Danboro	2,035 119%	2,109 124%	2,248 132%	2,371 139%	2,608 153%	2,802 164%	1,704
Great Farms							750
TOTAL	7,967 93%	8,328 97%	8,856 104%	9,442 111%	10,108 118%	10,664 125%	8,544

- Option 3 ("Comprehensive Redistricting"): In addition to the movement of students in Option 2, all of the special programs from all of the schools would be moved to Milldale High School (i.e., "the Mill").

Significant to note here is that none of these options recommend redistricting parts of Danboro or Westbrook to the Mill. Options 2 and 3, though, do include the possibility that parts of both towns could be redistricted to the new school.

Before the five big forums at each of the high schools at the end of January 1998, there were small meetings at each of the schools on January 7th run by the principals of each school, in conjunction with a newly formed task force of district citizens.[14] When the consultants reviewed the feedback from these meetings, which apparently included vitriol from some Danboro parents about the possibility of their children being redistricted, they decided to create an option 4, along with some general recommendations (e.g., keeping siblings together, not moving eleventh and twelfth graders, and not moving any of the special programs, which are considered crown jewels of each of the schools). Notably, the recommendation not to move special programs makes options 1 and 3 no longer viable, making the new option, option 4, a serious contender:

- Option 4 ("Voluntary Redistricting"): Move Great Farms students to the new school; ask for volunteers from other towns to move to the new school; create a new technology special program at the school to attract students; and build additions onto the overcrowded schools.

Significant to note here is that in option 4, no one would be forced to move schools, except for Great Farms students. But with option 2 still in the running, the possibility remained that parts of Danboro and Westbrook could be redistricted.

Two consultants from the firm—Mr. Broder and Mr. Kelly (pseudonyms)—held the public meetings in each of the existing high schools over the course of eight days.[15] These two somewhat large men—at least large enough in build to make one feel as if they were a significant presence— stood in the front of school auditoriums filled with hundreds of parents and a smattering of students, press, and police officers. Broder was the president of the consulting firm, and Kelly was the community-relations part of the team. They both often referred to their previous, long-term careers in New York public school systems. Broder and Kelly were white and graying, and Kelly, in particular, spoke with a distinctive Brooklyn accent. The meetings were each around three hours long, beginning with opening remarks from the consultants, followed by public discussion that included twenty to thirty speakers each night. Most speakers were from the town or towns whose students attended the host school, though there were speakers from other towns at each of the meetings. Unless otherwise noted, speakers were from the town in which the meeting was held. Aside from several people at the meeting at the Mill and one person at the Danboro meeting, the majority of speakers and audience members were white. (I have chosen not to note the race or ethnicity of the speakers, unless analytically significant.) Microphones were set up in each of the aisles for people to approach when they wanted to share their thoughts. But often, people just spoke from their seats in raised voices. At the start of each meeting, Kelly announced that each speaker had a two-minute limit in order to leave time for everyone to speak. This, too, was protocol not often followed. When I got to the meetings each night, I always found a seat somewhere near the back of the room. I wanted to have full view of the audience.[16]

What follows are highlights from the first two meetings followed by more in-depth accounts and analysis of the last three meetings—all of which are narratively constructed to feel comprehensive, despite being pared down. Each meeting extended over three hours, so there is no way to bring to life the full range of discussions. As such, there are other avenues through which these meetings could have been extensively explored, including the relationship between infrastructure planning, statistical calculations of enrollment figures and school costs, discursive use of those numbers, and various forms of expertise—areas in which there is growing literature within science and technology studies. These issues are still present and set the conditions for the dynamics explored, but my focus here is on the agentive power of rugged entitlement and commonsense reactions to it. The circumstances mapped out above—school names, dramatic overcrowding, class anxieties, racial tensions, conservative calculations, unknown financial burdens, third-party involvement, a short-term "charge" in a district with the need for long-term planning, and the power vacuum—set the conditions for the meetings to become a forum for issues much larger than redistricting options and the question of student placement. These debates became a site on which a broad range of sentiments and anxieties were provoked, played out, and voiced, much in the way that the proposed six-foot-high ornamental security gate became about much more than whether or not it was warranted.

BOWEN HIGH SCHOOL: "PEOPLE NEED TO MAKE CONCESSIONS WHEN THEY MOVE TO A REGIONAL DISTRICT"

The route to Bowen High School takes you past many more working farms than one sees when driving around Danboro. At one point, I thought I was going to be late for the meeting because traffic had slowed down to enable a tractor to pass. But here, as in Danboro, subdivisions were interspersed along winding country roads, with many new housing developments under construction. Bowen's suburban development began later than Danboro's since it is farther south from New York City. But Bowen came to have the largest population among the municipalities in the district (48,903, according to the 2000 U.S. Census), and its vast amount of farmland was quickly developing into homes comparable to those that could be acquired in Danboro, albeit more affordable. With over 30 percent of town residents under eighteen, Bowen had schools that were particularly overburdened. Its elementary schools were bursting at the seams, and Bowen High School was projected to be at 177 percent capacity in six years if student enrollments were left untouched. (See table 1.) Like Danboro High School, Bowen was one of the most overcrowded schools in the district. In light of these conditions, I was not surprised to see a few hundred people in attendance at the meeting at Bowen High School, with an audience that reflected the racial makeup of the town, which is predominantly white (around 91 percent, according to the 2000 U.S. Census).

Bowen's residents were no strangers to the idea that residing in a regional district means that your children might not attend the high school that bears your municipality's name. Bowen had long had too many high school students to fit into Bowen High School, and so some sections of Bowen were already zoned for Milldale Township High School. Most comments that night coalesced around the theme of being a regional district, where ideally *all* citizens (including kids) would make accommodations for the good of the whole, and all decisions would be based on *collective* interests (and not those of particular groups).

Broder and Kelly began the meeting with opening remarks that included a summary of the various options and recommendations. It took only a few minutes for concerns about the power of Danboro and Westbrook parents to arise. One of the first speakers said that she was upset that the proposals all seemed "to cater to Westbrook and Danboro kids." There were a few claps and cheers from the audience, after which she asked why there was an option to move kids out of Westbrook and Danboro, thereby relieving *their* overcrowding; yet, *no* students were moved to the new school from Bowen, which has the most overcrowding of all three schools and is actually *adjacent* to Great Farms, unlike Westbrook. More claps and cheers erupted from the audience. Broder took the microphone and commented that the options were not created to appease any group. In fact, he added with a friendly smile, even if that had been their intention, "we surely did not achieve it." He joked with the audience that after reading the Danboro responses from the January 7th meetings, he thought his consulting group might "need an armored car to drive through Danboro!" Most people in the audience began to laugh, and in this friendly moment, Broder noted that the creation of contiguous districts (i.e., a radical redrawing of the lines) was not part of the plan.

After a few questions about the proposed technology program and about other buildings that might be used as schools to help keep capital costs down, the audience got a taste of what was to come at the Danboro meeting. A woman from Danboro got up to speak. At first she commented that she liked option 4, which received a round of applause from the audience. Then, sounding as if she was on the verge of tears, she fervently declared that *her* kid should be able to be in school with the *same* kids she'd been in school with since the *first* grade: "Who should I blame when my kid has psychological problems from being moved?" The audience erupted into pockets of laughter, sidebar conversation, and yelled-out commentary, washing out her voice. Despite the palpable dissent, she continued, arguing that she pays extremely high property taxes and so *her* kid should be in *her* school. Someone from the audience bellowed out, "It's not *your* school!" After which another audience member shouted, "Go back to Danboro!" Broder chimed in, remarking, "Thanks for the previews of our visit to Danboro!" and then joked, "We [consultants] have already discussed how we're going to bed early the night before the Danboro meeting!"

The discussion then turned toward the need for better long-term planning in the district, including concerns about why tax dollars from new houses were not enough to fund new schools. But soon enough, Danboro concerns returned. The next man to speak asked why the Mill, which was underutilized, was not being filled with people in Danboro who live in the developments that border it. The man's tone and facial expression were serious as he spoke, though the minute the suggestion came out of his mouth, members of the audience began to laugh. He, too, then cracked a smile, with a look of knowing acknowledgment on his face. It was assumed in most corners of the district that most Danboro parents were not okay with the idea of their children attending the school in the district with the largest minority presence. The same man continued speaking, arguing that if this was not how redistricting was being done, this was "not really a *regionalized* district. . . . People need to make concessions when they move to a regional district." He then mimicked the Danboro woman, saying that people cannot assume that *their* kid will go to the school with *their* town name on it. A "Hear! Hear!" burst forth from the audience, after which he wrapped up his comments by noting that when there's "regionalization," the only issue should be "proximity. . . . People should do their homework when they move somewhere."

Broder said that he agreed with the man, though he took a moment to point out that the issue of proximity is not that simple in this kind of district: "This isn't a stable school district. It's growing beyond anyone's dreams—or nightmares. . . . Total redistricting only works in a stable place [with no population growth]. We can't do that here." He then offered the example of New Rochelle, New York, a city for which they had previously consulted. New Rochelle had overcrowding in a school located in its downtown area. The school in its suburban area was underused, so they simply redrew the lines to ease the overcrowding. The housing growth rate in New Rochelle was stable, so the problem was solved once enrollment numbers were reorganized. This is not the case for this growing district, he emphasized. Broder's use of New Rochelle as an example of a stable community was an interesting choice. The redistricting in New Rochelle in large part moved African-American students into a predominantly white school. Perhaps it was a strategic move to imply that they do not "side" with white parents who might not want their children in school with students of color.

The next person to speak returned to the mocking of the Danboro woman, joking with the audience, "I graduated from this district. I went to the Mill for the first one and a half years and then moved to Danboro High School when it was under construction—and I'm not psychologically impaired!" The audience erupted into laughter, and several people began to clap loudly. She continued, "Kids are flexible . . . [and they] will adapt with support at home." There were more claps around the room as many eyes turned in the direction of the Danboro woman. "The *real* issue," the speaker concluded, "is that we need another school or else we'll be throwing our money away. I don't want to pay more, but we don't have another choice." Piggybacking on the sacrifices that will need to be made, another woman added, "I don't want Bowen to suffer because the other towns are too shortsighted to see that we need to redistrict as well." There had been no official discussion about the inevitability of redistricting parts of Danboro and Westbrook at some point, but with overcrowding rates almost as high as Bowen's, it was an expected likelihood in the eyes of many district residents.

The issue of Bowen bearing the brunt of the district problems became particularly pronounced in a tension between the next two speakers. The first conceded that while she liked option 4 (i.e., the option based on volunteers), she understood the long-term concerns, and so she was in favor of adding to Great Farms High School and moving Bowen students there, since Bowen was willing to go. In a furious tone, the next speaker took issue with the idea that *everyone* from Bowen was willing to go to any school. With a tone of anger in her voice, she proclaimed, "I don't want more change. Some Bowen kids are already going to [Milldale] Township. Why bounce Bowen kids around? Danboro kids aren't moved at all!"

Returning to questions posed earlier in the evening about utilizing the space at the Mill and whether the options catered to Danboro and Westbrook, the next speaker asked, "How come no options are to move people to the Mill when the numbers are there? Were you told people would get upset?" Sympathetic to the psychological concerns raised by the Danboro woman, he offered: "If we keep kids from the same elementary schools together, then it's less of an issue." As this man went to sit down, Broder adamantly proclaimed, "No one told us to do anything. . . . No one is going to be moved to the Mill because it will be at capacity in a few years, so it's not worth it." The defensiveness in Broder's tone was striking compared with his affable manner all night, though it would come out in full force the next night at Milldale Township as distrust of the process took center stage.

MILLDALE TOWNSHIP HIGH SCHOOL ("TOWNSHIP"): "WHO DREW UP THESE PLANS?"

Milldale Township High School is the school that Julia attended and whose "mellowness" she enjoyed, which Bonnie attributed to the fact that it was a rung "lower" in income. As in Danboro, there were many parents who grew up in the outer boroughs of New York City, though it was a slightly "whiter" town (88 percent, according to the 2000 U.S. Census). There was a lot of housing development in Milldale Township as well, though nothing like what was taking place in Danboro, Bowen, and Westbrook. It was a more "stable" community, though like Bowen it was quite familiar with the idea of being part of a regional district. Bowen's overflow students attended the Township school; to make room for those students, developments in Milldale Township near the Mill were zoned for the Mill. When I noticed only a couple hundred people in attendance at the meeting (about half the number that attended the meeting the night before, though equally as white), I figured that this was because neither the Township school nor the Mill were overcrowded. There was little possibility that Milldale Township students would change schools.

This meeting began much in the same way as the one at Bowen, with Broder and Kelly reviewing the options. What was different on this night was how they closed their opening remarks. Broder noted that they had received a lot of good feedback at Bowen in regard to ways of modifying option 4. He did not offer details—generally a good strategy to avoid biasing recommendations that might emerge. Yet in foregrounding option 4—the one most favored by Danboro and Westbrook parents—Broder stoked concerns not only about who was being "catered to," as raised at Bowen the night before, but also about who was orchestrating the process and who would be making the final decisions.

Right off the bat, the first person to speak suspiciously inquired, "Who drew up these plans?" Broder responded defensively, "There has been no involvement by the school board. It has all been done by our organization—if you want to shoot the messenger." With so much focus the night before on Danboro and Westbrook parents, foregrounding the school board proved to be—at least for a bit—an effective deflective move, whether intentional or not, for the next few questions focused on the board. "Did the board screw up when they decided to build a school for 750 and not [full capacity]?" the next man asked accusingly. Kelly, the community-relations half of the team, fielded this question. He did not so much answer the question as divert the issue away from the effectiveness of the board: "Our job is to see what you people want. We're not doing a building study. But what you're saying is that we need to recommend a building/construction task force *now*. The worst thing is to mistrust. We need to focus on the kids."

But lack of trust in the process kept resurfacing. After a discussion about why the new school was built out for 750 students and whether other towns objected to redistricting because of the new school or because they were "afraid that they had to go to the Mill," a woman underscored the uncertainties in the district: "We have a minor crisis of confidence in our board. There is fear that a referendum would not be passed because people will feel that if we can't fill [the new school], why build more." A woman from Bowen, whose development was zoned for Township, added, "With all the lack of faith and . . . an election coming [for board representatives], a referendum is risky. . . . Towns are being pitted against one another. People are only gonna vote if it affects *them*." Building on this, one of the next speakers succinctly noted: "The district is in a public-relations crisis [because of] 5120." Broder passionately argued, "You can't give up because it might *not* get passed. . . . If you do not try it, the kids are going to get hurt. This should not be about board politics. . . . Do what's in the best interest of the kids. . . . If you don't start fast and do something, you will have higher class sizes and double sessions." He paused for a second, and then warned the audience, "Don't wait till then." (A "double session"—often referred to as a "split session"—is the term used when a school facility is utilized from very early in the morning until late at night in order to have two full school sessions in the course of one day.)

While the audience let board politics rest, skepticism continued and shifted to the consultants. The next man who got up to speak disclosed that he had been at the previous meeting and had attended all of the board of education meetings over the previous several months. He sounded frustrated and angry as he declared, "Options 1, 2, and 3 were dead on arrival, and Broder confirmed it tonight. Lots of parents from Danboro have come out and made it clear that *their* kids will go nowhere but Danboro. . . . Option 4 is 'the Danboro Plan.'" There were lots of claps from the audience as he continued, "Even though you have said it's yours, it was actually created by a Danboro attorney, and . . . when asked if it was a 'Danboro Plan,' you wavered on that." Broder and Kelly stood quiet and still as he continued, "This is not a solution. We gotta see redistricting. It's fear and ignorance, but I'm not gonna tell Danboro parents that 4 will be passed by the board because of this." He said that he knew from "high sources" that a referendum was already in the works to build onto the overcrowded schools—a recommendation in option 4: "Township and Bowen have already been moved to other schools. Township has the highest taxes, and so we need to have a referendum to reapportion the tax burden. We're discriminated against again, and we're gonna be asked for money for these other three schools." He said he liked the idea of expanding the new school, but he asked, "Will it cost less than additions onto those schools? Taxpayers need to know about this burden." The room erupted into loud and forceful applause.

Broder replied vehemently, "For the record, and based upon my *integrity*, option 4 was developed by [our firm]. Someone from Danboro may have come up with it, too, but there was no involvement. We know Danboro doesn't want to move." He acknowledged, "A reporter asked me if I had seen the 'Danboro Plan.' I told him to fax it to me." It did look similar, he noted, but it did not have a lottery to determine who among the volunteers would go to the new school. Broder then started to talk about the logistics of expanding the new school versus building additions onto the overcrowded schools, rambling on for quite some time, not answering the man's question about costs. People in the audience started to shift in their seats, and at one point a woman and her daughter got up and left. Perhaps sensing people's frustration, Kelly took the microphone and explained that they could not comment on exact costs. As he underscored the dramatic need for added construction, explaining that "adding to Great Farms doesn't do the whole job," I overheard a woman comment to the man sitting next to her, "Why are we being asked to give feedback on these options when a solution would require tons more building and redistricting with that extra construction in mind? So what exactly are we deciding on *now?*"

It was time for another person to have a chance to speak. But before this man asked his question, he declared with a sheepish smile, "I'm not always proud to be from Danboro!" There were many giggles from the audience, and he laughed along for a moment before turning more serious as he asked, "What is the state formula for these [enrollment projection] numbers?" Broder launched into an explanation of the state's requirement of five-year facility studies every five years; how capacity numbers are calculated using available square footage of instructional space and the number of kids enrolled in the elementary schools; and how their firm had completed forty-five of these studies in New Jersey alone. As he continued to explain the nature of these studies and to assuage "integrity" concerns by underscoring their experience, the man who asked the question interjected, "So, the administration hasn't dealt with the future?" to which there was applause. *Abstract* state calculations do not incorporate issues facing *their* community, including growth. One of the next speakers drove this point home when he shared with the consultants something well known in the district and likely to add to the numbers: that many Great Farms kids attended private schools and might want to attend the new school in their town.

This same speaker brought the conversation back to the regional issue: "Why not have an option 5 in which there would be widespread redistricting and all of the schools would be at 125 percent?" This would have everybody share the burden until construction was complete. "Option 4 is protecting Danboro and Westbrook. I'm sympathetic to the parents, but it's got a financial tag attached to it." He added in a sarcastic tone, "The

'Danboro Solution' might be different, but how about another one where *all* towns would be able to choose *their* school as their primary school?" The audience erupted into laughter and bits of cheering, after which he remarked, "We *need* to break the idea that schools belong to municipalities. If we don't move in that direction, there are going to be more problems down the line." Kelly nodded as he spoke.

The next man to speak declared himself to be from Danboro, albeit unapologetically. He said that he liked option 4, and added in a somewhat angry and frustrated tone, "It's *not* a Danboro plan—but a *district* plan." He then looked the consultants in the eye and commented in a chummy way, "It's a shame you weren't here when we were dealing with the ranking issue!" Murmurs erupted from the audience at this seeming collusion. He self-assuredly continued to speak, as if the construction recommendation in option 4 was a guarantee. He suggested having split sessions while construction was under way to avoid redistricting: "If you ask parents who went to high school in Brooklyn or Queens, we had split sessions. We didn't feel that our education was hurt." To which Broder responded, "*Respectfully,* you were fortunate that it was not a mess where you were with split sessions because they're usually a mess. You *will* see changes that impact education [like curriculum that can be offered]." Kelly then chimed in, warning that split sessions "should only be used in emergency measures"; they are not as easy to do in small schools, unlike in "huge" city schools. He then admonished, "You need more space. You have three years. You've got a choice now: make a schedule, stick with it . . . or your kids will be affected." In a divisive tone, the man from Danboro uttered as he sat down, "If 5120 [the referendum to remove class ranking] is not rescinded, we won't have a district [i.e., Danboro would secede]!"

There was a brief moment of calm in the meeting as the next few comments skirted controversial issues, with composed questions about busing routes for volunteers and the possibility of incorporating recent births into projected enrollments. But soon enough, the divisiveness returned when a woman spoke in an angry tone comparable to that of the man from Danboro. She began by referring to him, and then looked toward the consultants: "Tell Westbrook and Danboro to *deal*. We need to change the names of the high schools. . . . We shouldn't have changed them. *It ain't their school.* Danboro is *our* school!" Continuing to fume, she explained that "by not giving black and Hispanic kids a chance to opt [for the new school], we're gonna have another lily-white high school and it's not gonna pass constitutionally." The next speaker heightened the focus on the racial implications of the plans, asserting, "Your firm is tap-dancing around [the Mill]. Why leave one so low? Take out a map and let the chips fall." It was exactly these issues of segregation and respectful engagement with the Mill that took center stage in the meeting at the Mill four days later.

MILLDALE HIGH SCHOOL ("THE MILL"): "THIS IS NOT AN INTEGRATED SYSTEM. IT'S SEGREGATED."

When you walk into Milldale High School, there is a noticeably different feel from other schools in the district. It was the first school built in the district, and there are moldings and other decorative details not found in the newer schools built in the modern style of the 1960s and 1970s. It also is appreciably smaller, providing a more intimate feel, particularly as you walk through the hallways. The audience at the meeting also was different. At this meeting, there were many more people of color, particularly African-Americans and a few Mexican-Americans and South Asians. The diversity in the room reflected the diversity of the two communities whose children attended the school. According to the 2000 U.S. Census, Milldale Borough was 74 percent white, 28 percent Hispanic/Latino, 16 percent African-American, and 3 percent Asian, and Milldale Township was 88 percent white and 5 percent each African-American, Hispanic/Latino, and Asian.

Four days had passed (including a weekend) since the Township meeting, during which an article emerged in a local paper that highlighted some of the questions raised at previous meetings, including racial anxieties of those in other towns and who was in control of the process. It was thus no surprise that shortly into Broder's introductory remarks, he underscored: "No one is making us do anything." In an adamant tone, he added that regardless of what people may believe in regard to their doing things for certain political reasons, "We're objective." He said that while that article and other articles published since the process began have focused largely on "politics . . . *our* concern is the youngsters . . . and, *respectfully,* that should be everyone's concern." But as the discussion in this meeting underscored, concern for "youngsters" does not override political concerns; processes through which student-placement decisions are made—whether by groups of citizens, consultants, boards of education, judges, or state laws—directly affect the spaces in which those youngsters come of age.

In a defensive tone, Broder resumed his opening remarks, albeit in a way that felt quite rushed in comparison with previous meetings. He quickly explained why their firm did not recommend moving students from overcrowded schools into their school, offering a somewhat confusing discussion about state numbers and how their school would be at capacity within five years. He acknowledged the limits of using state formulas to calculate capacity, which do not take into account sprawl or different usages of classroom space, such as special-education classrooms where the number of students needs to be lower for instructional purposes. He then moved quickly through an explanation of why the options did not include major redistricting, offering once again the example of New Rochelle, New York, as a "stable" community" versus this "dynamic" one. In light of all of these issues, he explained, there were problems with the first three options, which he did not bother to explain—unlike at previous meetings. With option 4, he continued, there would be minimal redistricting, and the schools that were way over capacity would be given the option to choose Great Farms High School. As he closed his remarks, he steadfastly declared, "Option 4 is *not* a Danboro plan."

Broder looked relieved when the first person to speak asked a benign question about the new school and how its lack of a track record might affect kids when they apply to college, though the respite was short-lived. The following speaker got up and passionately proclaimed, "I love this school because of the racial balance!" Many people in the audience clapped appreciatively, after which she asked, "I have heard that you have to make a racial balance in the five (and now six) schools. Are you going to address it? Do you have to?" Broder explained, "Anytime you redistrict, you need to be concerned with the racial balance. . . . If there are changes, you need to seek approval from the state." In this district, he pointed out, "[the Mill] has the highest minority population in the district," but since no students would be moved from this school, "there will be no racial-balance changes with the options."

Despite state concern only with changes to schools with existing minority populations, residents' concerns with creating another "lily white" school continued. The next speaker asked why kids that could walk from the Mill to Great Farms were not being given the option to choose the new school yet those far away in Westbrook were. Broder started to explain how they were moving only kids from schools with higher growth rates, but she interrupted him and remarked in a frustrated voice, "You're not answering my question!" In an angry tone she declared, "*So*, some towns can opt and others can't. You *need* to open moving to *all* students or else there's going to be another can of worms and legal issues opened up." She then made reference to "the Danboro plan" and said that although she understood that the numbers were higher in Danboro and Westbrook, "this should not be done to satisfy other towns whose mouths are opened the widest!" There were loud claps around the auditorium.

The fact that some towns in the district had never had to send their kids to another district school was raised as part of the problem in the next comments. One speaker, the man who had made the comment at the previous meeting that option 4 was a "Danboro plan," pointed out that he lives in Milldale Township, and that residents of Bowen and Township have been doing redistricting already, and it has worked. "And we feel more a part of the district versus our neighbors to the north [i.e., those who live in Danboro]." He added that option 4 "mirrors the . . . Danboro Plan—a do-nothing plan. . . . [And] you don't know what volunteers you'll get." Piggybacking on his comments, the next woman to speak at first fired off a series of questions: "What if no one volunteers? What about busing [routes]?" If only ninth and tenth graders attend the new school to start, "how does that affect after-school activities with no varsity teams?" But before the consultants could respond, she abruptly switched her tone and remarked with futility in her voice, "Danboro and Westbrook won't send their kids, which is what this is about anyway!" As this comment came out of her mouth, a woman sitting in front of me, presumably from one of those towns, blurted out, "That's not true!"

The racial-balance problem returned in full force in the next man's comments. Speaking calmly and gently, he pointed out that he was president of the Milldale chapter of the NAACP and was on the county's Human Relations Commission and Fair Housing Board. He looked the consultants directly in the eye as he explained that he loves this country; he was in the military; and he was putting back into the system now that he was retired. He said he assumed that they were familiar with the class-ranking issue, to which Broder and Kelly nodded. He noted that the NAACP was "ready to move forth" in regard to issues raised in an article published the previous year in the *Star-Ledger* (a highly reputable northern New Jersey newspaper).[17] The article discussed a 1993 Harvard University study that revealed that New Jersey schools were the most segregated in the nation: 54.6 percent of African-American students and 44.4 percent of Latino students were together in the same schools that were over 90 percent minority students; the rest of the schools were predominantly white. He continued speaking in a calm, explanatory tone as he underscored, "Milldale Regional is one of these school districts."

He explained that when the NAACP discusses 5120 and these redistricting debates, the problem with segregation is key: "This is not an integrated system. It's segregated. And there are racist dynamics and innuendos. . . . The NAACP's position is that three schools are overcrowded, one is under, and that they need to take into account desegregation laws." While he was speaking, two white people got up and walked out of the auditorium. He continued, "The NAACP will work with the district to overcome this." One of the key problems, he pointed out, is that "Danboro and Westbrook get more influence through weighted votes on the board and can vote down what's not in their best interest, thus furthering segregation." The woman sitting in front of me, who had just blurted out, "That's not true!" leaned toward her husband and murmured something about the Fourteenth Amendment. The man from the NAACP then asked the consultants, "Do you know of any desegregation plan?" They simultaneously responded no in self-protective tones. The law to which Broder referred earlier only ensures no *further* segregation; it does not require districts to address *de facto* segregation already in place.

The consultants were further backed up against the wall as the next set of questions cast doubt on the practices of their firm, ethical and otherwise. One of the speakers, an African-American woman who was a member of the redistricting task force, chastised them. All eyes were on her as she spoke in an extremely angry and adamant tone, at first noting that she was originally excited to work with the expertise of a consulting firm.

However, the whole experience of working with them "reduced [her] zest and zeal. . . . What expertise is being brought?" she inquired as she looked firmly in Broder's direction. She then added that she was asking her question, "in your words [i.e., Broder's words], *'respectfully.'*" She continued to vent, adding that there had been "no thought or imagination" in their approach. A big round of applause erupted from the audience, after which she commented, "Experts should have anticipated these issues. . . . You're underestimating our community, and [think] that we'll sleep through this." She then addressed their use of language more directly, remarking, "Don't keep saying *you people*. It's not very P.C." Kelly often used *you people* when speaking to the audience at the meetings, particularly during his opening remarks. It had always struck me as a patronizing choice of phrase, yet public administrators in New York City who grew up in the outer boroughs commonly use it. But within the context of this meeting, it had racial implications.[18] Much in the way that the lawyer at the zoning board meeting could not control the referent of *sightseers,* Kelly's choice of phrase—regardless of intentionality—was open to a variety of interpretations.

The task force woman then explained that she was curious about something: "Since we got to see all three options, why not see an option 5 with just redrawing the lines? This is what my community suggested." The audience burst into deafening applause. It was the loudest show of support for a comment that night. As the noise died down, the consultants stumbled over their words to apologize if they "offended people with their phrases." Then they said that even with redrawing the lines, it would still be "impossible" to fit everyone since drawing the lines won't fix "the problem." Upon hearing their response, she sat down with a huff, and several people in the audience eyed their neighbors with looks of frustration on their faces. The "problem" was not just overcrowding. As the next woman to speak remarked, "A totally segregated school will be created through Great Farms High School. It's all going to further polarize the communities."

A particularly poignant moment occurred when the next speaker, an elderly African-American man, slowly got up from his seat to speak, wobbling as he sured up his footing. He shared that his six children all graduated from this school, and that when he first moved to Milldale in 1962, it was the only school in the area. He began to map out the history of the district and how the towns around Milldale didn't want to build their own high schools, so the district was created, "and we built the schools for them." As more and more houses were being built, he reminisced, "I knew we were gonna need a new school. . . . I'm a construction man." He continued to speak slowly; it was clear that it was physically difficult for him to get the words out, but he kept on. As he continued, one of the consultants interrupted him and asked, "Sir, is there something particular about the options that you'd like to share?" The man shook his head no, and said that he wanted to offer a historical perspective. I noticed a few people with disturbed looks on their faces when he was cut off. With all the questions being raised about racial implications, this elderly African-American man, who had been living in the area since before the first housing development in Danboro was built, had been silenced. He slowly sat down without finishing his remarks.

The next woman to speak picked up where he had left off, though at first she remarked, "Why can't Danboro and Westbrook kids come here? . . . It's a great school!" She then pointed out that when the idea for Great Farms High School first came up, it included redistricting. "Why is it being run by Danboro?" she asked. Adding more historical perspective, she noted that "they" (i.e., Danboro) wanted to leave the district once before, but they realized that it would cost them too much. "So let them build their own school . . . or send Mill kids to Great Farms High School and the Township and give [the Mill building] to Danboro!" The audience erupted into deafening laughter and applause. Echoing this sentiment, another speaker looked toward the audience and stated, "The consultants are telling us what we already know: Danboro and Westbrook are not buying into the concept of a regional district."

After a few other comments and questions were raised, including those about busing routes, the adaptability of kids, and redrawing the lines, concerns about the process returned as a woman voiced concern about the limited information provided. "You never gave us the monetary figures," she stressed, noting that elderly citizens in the district vote simply based on the price tag. "We can't make intelligent decisions." To which Broder quickly replied, "The board never told us to deal with costs." Complicating concerns about what had and had not been shared, the next speaker, who pointed out that his wife was the woman on the task force who had spoken earlier, asked the consultants if they were really just "presenting" information each night. His feeling from having attending the meetings at the other schools was that the information was not being presented in the same way at each of the schools. Many people in the audience nodded their heads in agreement with his framing concerns.[19] As to why this was the case, one of the next speakers offered his thoughts. In an extremely frustrated tone he argued, "This has been so late to start. . . . Maybe this is a sham. And the board knows what they want—and we're just wasting our time!" Broder replied defensively, although in a calmer tone than he had been using the rest of the night, "There is no indication to us that there is some prearranged plan." Whether or not there was a "prearranged plan," concern about a mounting influence of Westbrook and Danboro was stressed as a woman pointed out that there were sure to be four hundred to six hundred parents at the next meetings at Westbrook and Danboro. "What effect does that have?" she asked. Lots of people clapped, and continued to do so as the next man to speak emphasized her point by stating, "I live in Danboro—and I hear the whining!" Though coming to the defense of the consultants, the next speaker emphasized, "Board members are not here. Take note! Let's not put these guys on the spot. They were hired very late [because of the] ineptness of our board of education."

Among the last speakers was a cluster of parents from Danboro and Westbrook, who, like the man from Danboro who had just spoken, challenged the stereotype of parents from those towns. One of the speakers, who began by saying that he was from Danboro but that "not all people from Danboro think the same," asked for more information on the new school. The speaker that followed him said that he lived in Westbrook, but that his kid was in the medical program at the Mill. "Westbrook is so close to the Mill. Why send them to Great Farms High School? I'd rather have my kids here—although," he joked with a smirk on his face, "most won't say that in Westbrook." That was surely the case at the meeting at Westbrook the next night!

It was time for the final speaker, who pointedly asked the consultants, "What will you take forward with the feedback from tonight?" Broder replied that "the obvious [things] that . . . emerged" were to redistrict along the lines of proximity to the new school and do a total redistricting, "although we don't see redistricting as a viable option"; he also noted that some people there felt that "you can do a temporary fix; but you can't do that. . . . Option 4 moves you toward the resolution." He made no mention of the segregation issue, or the NAACP's offer to help with the process. As people got up from their seats, I saw a lot of looks of frustration. I imagined that most people left feeling that it was a waste of their time, as had been suggested earlier.

WESTBROOK HIGH SCHOOL: "IT'S NOT ABOUT RACISM, BUT COMMUNITY SPIRIT!"

The next night, as I walked through the halls of Westbrook High School on my way to the auditorium, I ran into Liz, who had just come from cheerleading practice. Liz was friends with Lauren and Erika. Many kids in Danboro had friends in Westbrook, even though the two high schools were great rivals and Danboro was considered a bit higher in the hierarchy of the middle classes. Westbrook, too, was full of families who had moved from Brooklyn and, more recently, Staten Island. Family friendships and connections from old neighborhoods moved fluidly across municipal lines. If you recall, the people in the other Blazer in Wendi's first accident, who were really nice to her, were from Westbrook. After chatting with Liz for about fifteen minutes, I realized that I was missing the beginning of the meeting, so I quickly and quietly made my way into the auditorium. There were several hundred people in attendance—the most at any of the meetings so far. This turnout was what those the night before had anticipated. But unlike the diversity of the crowd at the Mill, this was a very white crowd, aside from one African-American family. Westbrook was the "whitest" of the large towns in the district (92 percent, according to the 2000 U.S. Census). Race proved to be a central topic at the meeting, interwoven with (and among) different notions of "community" and who was considered a part of it. This was the most spirited meeting so far: the outbursts and cross-talk here made the passionate moments at the Mill seem tame in comparison.

As I found my way to a seat, Broder and Kelly were still amid their introductory comments, with Kelly explaining how the projection figures were done with present elementary kids in mind. To which a woman from the audience yelled out, "There are gonna be five thousand new houses over the next year!" Many in the audience nodded their heads in agreement. Kelly explained that it wasn't their "charge" to deal with that, after which a collective huff emerged from all corners of the room. Westbrook was one of the three overcrowded high schools, and with a great deal of farmland ripe for construction, a whole new section of town was rapidly emerging. Broder then began to speak, stressing, "We're not here promoting any options. . . . We're just presenting information . . . and will present the options with the community reaction to the board." He then turned to a discussion of option 4, during which there were claps from the audience, particularly when he said there would be minimal movement of kids. Some disagreement started to emerge, however, when he emphasized the need to deal with this right away—or else the district would find itself in the situation of having overlapping sessions (i.e., "split sessions"). "You don't want that," he told the audience. Amid murmurs in the room, one person yelled out, "It's not that bad!" Broder did not address the remark, but rather kept underscoring the need to make a decision on these issues and take action *right away*.

It was time for audience participation, and among the first people to speak was a man wondering how option 4 could work when it depended so heavily on volunteers. (Unlike most speakers at the meeting, he was committed to the idea of a regional district.) He was curious if there was any basis for the projected number of students who would opt to move. Broder acknowledged that there was no basis for the numbers, after which the man remarked that there was "no common sense to sending Westbrook over Danboro to Great Farms High School. Why isn't this geographically based?" he inquired. "You're just telling people what they *want to hear*, not *what needs to be done*," he accused. Broder did not address this man's allegation, but rather simply pointed out that the issue of proximity "has come up a lot," and explained that they were in the process of coming up with an option 5: "We're having a meeting tomorrow morning [to come up with a plan] to move kids in overpopulated schools to the one closest to them, if space is available." This sparked extensive conversation in the room, likely because the Mill was the closest school to some parts of Westbrook. Over the conversational hum, the man who was speaking revisited the volunteer issue. He turned toward the audience and asked, "How many parents will volunteer?" Around ten to fifteen hands went up. (The projected number from Westbrook was sixty.) He had a look of victory on his face, to which Broder responded, "Well, first we'll need to educate people about the new school."

After some discussion about the problematic figures and other possible ways of shifting kids around, the next woman asked why in some of the options ninth and tenth graders were considered okay to move when eleventh and twelfth graders were not. There were lots of claps from the audience, after which Broder replied, "Kids are adaptable." As these words came out of his mouth, there was an outburst of dissent from the audience. The woman who asked the question interjected, "When they are younger, yes . . . but when they're older, less so." People continued to speak out, and one woman yelled that it's not so easy for high school kids to make that kind of change. Broder tried to calm the audience down, and then explained, "I've dealt with lots of schools and kids over the years. Kids with the proper orientation will adjust well. It's the parents that don't." Some people looked offended by his comment, although there were a few loud individual claps. The same woman continued to speak. In an angry and frustrated tone, she made it known that she had worked in education for twenty years and saw how kids react: it's the youngest kids who do well. Broder responded, "It's sometimes the case, but *not* a generality [that older children do not adjust well]." She momentarily shifted topics to comment about the risk that this would place on scholarship opportunities for ninth-grade varsity players, after which she added, "Basically, I don't think *anyone* should move." Broder smirked as he responded, "We can't fill Great Farms High School that way," to which she obstinately replied, "I don't care!" The next woman to speak suggested that it might be easier to fill Great Farms if all Great Farms kids were moved right away, including the eleventh and twelfth graders. Broder responded, sounding frustrated, "Before you said no ninth and tenth, and now you're saying move all Great Farms kids since they are 'those kids' and not 'ours.'" Perhaps realizing the implications of her suggestion (or not), she changed the topic and asked about the curriculum at the new school. Broder briefly commented on the offerings, then returned to the topic of moving the "other" kids: "You have a right to an opinion. . . . But you can't have it both ways. It doesn't fit."

The next speaker said that she wanted to address the article published the day before, which had mentioned Westbrook as one of the "elite" towns in the district with racial concerns about the redistricting process. She explained that she and her husband "researched this town forever" and moved to Westbrook for what it offers. "Why are we being called racist when we just don't want to have our kids move schools? And when did Westbrook become 'the elite'?" Her voice turned bold and angry, mixed with a sense of hurt, as she rhetorically asked, "How can they call my town racist when they don't know us?" There was great applause from the audience, which continued as she explained that it's not about the other places. Her kids have watched everyone else in town grow up, and they just want to become a Bulldog (the Westbrook High School mascot). "It's not about racism, but community spirit!" As the applause became louder, she added, "I'd rather be in an overcrowded school and have loyalty. . . . You can tell I'm furious," she remarked, after which she asked a series of questions about the sibling rule, varsity sports, and the making of boundaries. She then vented: "The board hides from us! This should have been decided by January 1st. It's shameful! Now I'm going to have to go to a private school." *Community spirit* can be a code for racial politics, and since her comments suggested that she was more comfortable with the idea of creating a new community in a private school rather than in one of the other schools in the district, there are class implications as well. Not everyone in her community can afford a private school. As she started to ask another question, Kelly jumped in and said, "In fairness, you're over the two-minute limit." Perhaps after the awkward silencing the night before, the consultants had decided to enforce this rule evenhandedly.

Shortly after, a ninth grader from Westbrook took the floor. She was the first teenager to speak at any of the meetings,[20] though her question ended up becoming the first of several that highlighted that short-term consultants hold abstracted understandings of place. "I don't like what you're doing," she began, and then explained that she was concerned about what opportunities would be lost without older kids to learn from. "Why can't the special programs go to one school so that all Westbrook kids can go to school in their town?" Broder explained that the feedback they had received from the district had been "overwhelmingly against moving all the special programs to Great Neck." People in the audience started to chuckle when he uttered "Great Neck," after which he corrected himself (incorrectly) by saying "Great Bend." Then he finally got it right and said "Great Farms." (Great Neck and Great Bend are towns in New York.) "Great Neck might be closer for Westbrook kids to commute to than Great Farms!" quipped the next man to speak. Everyone in the audience giggled uneasily at this reminder that the process was being orchestrated by outside consultants more familiar with normative state figures than the particularities of place. This was underscored when one of the next speakers asked about the capacity numbers and the final report. Broder had started to explain the process, including when figures are sent to "Albany." (Albany is New York's state capital.) As several people blurted out "Trenton" (New Jersey's capital), Broder realized his mistake and corrected himself. I noticed people getting antsy, with a few trickling out. Perhaps it was the fact that it was getting late. Or maybe it was because Broder continued to drone on about *state* formulas that don't take into account the specificities of *their* community, and kept using wrong town names and even wrong states.

The conversation shifted gears for a moment to the lack of information about the new school. To explain his frustration with this, the next speaker used a metaphor from his job as a shirts salesman: it would be like him trying to sell a shirt without being able to answer for an interested buyer the size, the cost, the fabric, or the color. It was striking, he underscored, how little the district knew at this point in terms of what courses would be offered, what extracurriculars there would be. After another couple of comments, the man then looked around the room and asked, "Are there reporters here? I hope they'll make as big a headline that we're *not* racist with the same bold headlines that said we're racist." As he spoke, the one African-American family in the room got up and left. Perhaps they simply needed to get home like others who had left during the night. Or maybe it was in reaction to his comment, which, when juxtaposed with his shirt metaphor—particularly the need to know the "color"—was open to a wide range of interpretive possibilities. Their departure was particularly disquieting considering how Broder responded to the next woman's comments. As she shared in a calm voice, "It is very painful to be labeled racist. . . . It's an issue of community spirit," Broder nodded, and under his breath I thought I heard a quiet yes in agreement. His reaction was quite

striking in comparison to his lack of confirmation of concerns about segregation at the Mill meeting, not to mention the timing soon after the
African-American family had left amid loud sidebar conversations in
the audience as people talked with their neighbors in angry tones about
the article.

The intensity in the room escalated in the next speaker's comments.
She stated the name of the development in which she lived, which was one
of the first subdivisions built in Westbrook: "I've been involved in the
town, and this town is home to us. We want our kids to go here because
Westbrook is their home. We moved here thinking *parents* would commute, not *kids*. You just mention numbers and money and not the kids
and their emotions. And we never got answers. . . . You're up there as
scapegoats for the board. They're using you!" Her tone turned extremely
angry, and Broder responded in kind. "If you remember nothing [else]
from tonight, remember this: you can question our judgment, but we get
concerned when our integrity is questioned. *We're not pawns!*" he retorted
in a loud, frustrated tone. "I'm raising my voice now for a reason." He then
recommended that they address the redistricting issues, particularly since
there were many people who wanted to speak and time was running out.
The woman's face revealed extreme anger as she yelled that he'd been raising his voice all night whenever a woman spoke. "No we haven't," Broder
argued back.

One of the next speakers did focus on redistricting, though at first he
commented—half-joking, half-serious—that "people have behaved fairly
well here tonight!" He then said that he had been to and spoken at the
other meetings: "I have heard lots of opinions in different schools, and I
have come up with a possible option 6. Whether we like it or not, we're
part of a larger district and have to learn to work together. It's not just
Westbrook, but Danboro, Bowen . . . and other areas. . . . We're gonna
need some redistricting. [We] may not want to hear it, but we have to
work as a larger community or we'll have even bigger problems." There
was an awkward pause before he said "other areas." This might have been
because those areas, which include downtown Milldale, did not house the
overcrowded schools. Yet after explaining that it would be much cheaper
to add on to Great Farms High School, he shared ideas about how the
lines could be redrawn by commenting, "It doesn't make sense to move

[Westbrook kids] across Milldale Township and Danboro to Great Farms."
He noticeably failed to mention downtown Milldale, even though many of
the quickest routes from Westbrook to Great Farms take you right through
its downtown. Perhaps this was an instance of "tap-dancing" around the
Mill.

"Most are against redistricting," the next woman to speak began. "I
grew up in Brooklyn and had split sessions. If redistricting is just a Band-
Aid, split sessions would keep kids in their schools until construction is
done." Broder explained that option 4 would accommodate kids who
wanted to stay in their schools. Kelly then addressed the problem of split
sessions: "There's no question you can learn, but it's not the desirable way
to do it in terms of educational opportunity. . . . [You'll end up] doubling
class size. . . . In other places, as soon as pressure is felt, people jump on
the bandwagon." The woman nodded as he spoke, and then asked, "So
you're saying we should go with building?" As they nodded in agreement,
she asked why they couldn't have split sessions in the meantime. After all,
she went on to college and then graduate school after having gone to high
school with split sessions. With a coy smile and extra emphasis of her
Brooklyn accent, she declared, "It didn't do me no harm!" Several people
in the audience giggled at her playful, familiar post-Brooklyn pride.

Frustrations about the process resurfaced. "I heard that we should get
involved," said the next speaker. "Yet, we have a board that's hired to do
that. We shouldn't have to push them in their final hour. . . . I'm an
accountant. That's what I do. The board should be doing what they were
hired to do. . . . We've all seen the development in the area and knew it was
coming." Another man vented, "I've been to all these meetings, and I feel
like nothing's getting done. We go home upset because we receive no more
information. . . . What's gonna happen next year?! It seems like 1, 2, and 3
aren't options. You'd get a better response if people knew what the education and extracurriculars will be. My kid came home one day and told me
that she heard the best teachers from the district will go there. Kids might
go if we know. Is it really state-of-art?" The crowd got riled up by this
man's comments, with the applause growing increasingly louder with each
remark. "We're all frustrated. That's why people are walking out. I'm not
interested in 2002. I want to know about next year [i.e., 1999]. Tell us
about the new school and let my daughter decide. Stop insulting us with

saying 1, 2, and 3 are still options!" He continued to speak, adding a little humor as he described the scenario each night at his house when he got home from the meetings: "I keep going home to my wife, and she asks me what happens. I say, 'Nothing.'" Many people in the audience started to laugh, and he turned in their direction and said, "You're laughing because you agree with me!" He then turned back toward Broder, and Broder said to him in a warm, affectionate tone, "Tell your wife that you spoke in front of two of the most eminent educators—and they agreed with you." Whether this was genuine confidence or false confidence, Broder's concerns about their "integrity"—embarrassingly evident in this comment—were perhaps relieved when the next speaker laid blame for the muddled process and hostility in the room on the board: "We know they'll do what they want. Our fear is that this is all a show." A slight smile (perhaps of relief) appeared on Broder's face.

It was just about time for the meeting to end, and the second-to-last speaker began by saying that when he was looking to buy a house, he did a lot of research about SAT scores and other markers of a good school: "I bought into Westbrook—not the Milldale Regional High School system. I'd rather my kid be overcrowded for a bit while building." He then asked, "Will developers [of subdivisions] give money toward this? I know it's happened in the past." Broder confirmed that it had happened in some communities, but that he had not heard any plans. Returning to the man's comment about "not" buying into a regional district, Broder reminded him (and the audience) that although they were not going to recommend total redistricting, option 5 would be about proximity areas. To which the last speaker declared, "People here *want* proximity," after which someone from the audience yelled out angrily, "No we don't!" The speaker continued, saying that she was really hurt to hear that people at Bowen had said that they were scared to have their children go to the Mill. Her daughter attended the medical program there because it was the best program for her career path: "If they're going to go to college, then they have to deal." Another voice from the audience screamed out, "She did it *voluntarily*," after which another person loudly declared, "We don't want to!" And with that, the meeting was over, with not one disparaging comment about Danboro the entire night, and ending on the issue of "choice"—a key issue in the Danboro meeting the next night.

DANBORO HIGH SCHOOL: "ALL WE WANT IS *CHOICE, CHOICE, CHOICE!*"

As I approached Danboro High School, I saw flashing lights out front. I figured that there had been an accident. But as I got closer, I noticed a truck labeled "Traffic Safety Unit" beaming a spotlight onto the driveway leading to the school parking lot, and several cops and plainclothes officers with walkie-talkies near the entrance. At the other meetings, there had been policemen as well. I assumed they were there in part for security but also likely because they, too, had children in the district. But their presence on this night was quite significant. The whole scene felt like what one sees at a protest, when there is a fear that things could get out of hand. It reminded me of the comment that Broder made at the Bowen meeting when he joked that they might need an armored car to drive through Danboro. When I got inside the auditorium, the room was indeed packed. There must have been over four hundred people in attendance, and many more streamed in throughout the night, practically filling the auditorium. The crowd was almost as white as it was at the meeting the night before at Westbrook, though there was apparently a lot more wealth in the room— at least that which is suggested by leather coats and furs. As I walked down the aisle to find a seat, I briefly chatted with people in the audience whom I knew. Interestingly, this meeting was quite the opposite of what the consultants may have feared: the tone was largely cordial toward them, even if it at times heckling and cross-talk overwhelmed the conversation. In fact, there was an atmosphere of chumminess that could easily be read as class collusion. With rugged entitlement in full view, including neoliberal sentiments about choice, privatization, secession, and class privilege, the discussion resonated not only with Wendi's liberal reasoning about her SUV, but also the post-urban way of being middle-class in Danboro, with its particular articulation of class, race, and gender.

Broder and Kelly's opening remarks were clearer and more articulate than at any of the previous meetings. Broder began, "We're not representing anyone but [our firm]. . . . [We are not] prepared to risk our national reputation and give up our objectivity." He said that he wanted to map out what their "assigned responsibility is and isn't since it's been confused and has come up at the other meetings." He explained that it was their "charge" to fill the new school and relieve overcrowding at the three most over-crowded schools, though it quickly became clear that the problem required "[going] beyond what we were paid to do." He underscored, "We're not here to sell anything. We're here to hear you and to react to tell you where we stand." Kelly then took the floor, noting, "We're not doing the building survey, but we will recommend that in the final report." He then explained that within five years all of the schools would be at or over capacity, with the Mill at 95 percent. Broder then took time to explain the nature of the process, including sending the report to the board with their recommendations. While Broder was talking, an African-American couple from the meeting two nights before at the Mill walked in. It was the woman from the task force who had questioned Broder and Kelly's expertise, and her husband, who had wondered if they were presenting the information the same way each night. They sat down a few rows ahead of me, so I was able to see their reactions throughout the night.

Broder continued to explain how the first three options were con-structed to fill Great Farms High School, though after the January 7th meetings, they (i.e., the consultants) realized that first three options would not solve the long-term problem. So, he explained, they came up with option 4: "We have heard that this is something that you want, but we developed it ourselves. . . . In general, we tried to avoid involuntary redis-tricting." There was a loud round of applause from the audience, and peo-ple smiled and nodded in appreciation. Broder continued to talk about option 4, explaining that it involved "volunteers from the overcrowded schools: here, Westbrook, and Bowen. . . . We think it deserves to be an option." There was more clapping, after which Broder added, "Understand: option 4 is coupled with . . . construction. If you don't deal now, you may have to go into split sessions." There again was much cross-talk in the audience, during which he commented, "You have very fine representation on the board," and said that while he "didn't plan this," he asked the board members to please stand up for applause.

Broder and Kelly's clear explanations and preemptive caveats, com-bined with their introduction of the board members from Danboro, could be read as indicative of suspected behind-the-scenes maneuvering with Danboro parents, or, on the other hand, as attempts to align with those revealed to have the most power in the district. (Or benignly, they simply could have just hoped to avoid fueling contention with their opening remarks, as had occurred at previous meetings.) Regardless of their intentions, a generous tone emerged from the audience shortly into the public comments. The second man to speak thanked them for their job: "It's a pleasure to see how you're handling this. I've heard more in the last fifteen minutes than I have in the last six months!" Amid great applause from the audience, Broder smiled and acknowledged, "Others haven't been so nice." The man then remarked, "We don't want to be redistricted . . . and be bused away." Raising his voice as if on a soapbox at a political rally, he continued, "We're in the United States of America, and we have *choice!* Option 4 is the only one." He said there should be "no more nights of being out and deciding if we have to move. Some are thinking about private schools." He liked option 4 because it's *"voluntary."* "It seemed to work with the U.S. Army when they ditched the draft. They have plenty of volunteers!" He then said that, contrary to "ludicrous accusations and insults to everyone's intelligence," what it's been about is that "all we want is *choice, choice, choice!*" It's "not about race . . . or who they could or not be with," he underscored. The applause from the audience was deafening. He made no mention of the fact that most "volunteers" for the army come from working-class and poor communities, often of color, with limited other "choices" of employment, and that even in a middle-to-upper middle-class town like Danboro, many people cannot afford to "choose" a private school, like countless others in the district. As critical engagements with liberal democracy have long shown, not only is choice often a class privilege, but limiting individual choice in the interests of the greater good is *not* contrary to liberal democracy.[21] There likely would still be schools in the United States with official (and not just *de facto*) segregation had this not been the case, and as the president from the local NAACP chapter noted, the Milldale High School District would likely stay segregated if left to individual choice.

In an interesting discursive representation of this paradox of citizenship in a liberal democracy, the next speaker first asked about how the lines were drawn and then complained, "Why does it have to be *us?*" Broder explained that it had to do with who is closest to Great Farms High School. She pushed him: "Why should that mean *we're* stuck?" Broder reminded her that they were not the only ones in this situation: "We've been criticized about this in terms of the Westbrook kids as well." She then asked a couple of more questions about the amount of money the district had for addressing the problem, and then offered, "Since we are all equal citizens, why not put all five schools in a hat and decide [who goes to Great Farms] that way!" This recommendation had been offered at Bowen, Township, and the Mill as well, though in the spirit of equal sacrifice for the public good—and not as an attempt to find a way out of it.

"Everyone wants to stay in Danboro," the next woman stated. "If we need another high school, why not build it here?" She said it could be like in Great Neck, where there's Great Neck North High School and Great Neck South High School. (Broder smiled at her suggestion. I don't know if she was at the meeting the night before when Broder made his "Great Neck" slip.) If the solution wasn't something like this, she suggested, "then Danboro would secede." Lots of applause and cheers came from the audience, during which she continued, "We'll bring it up to the town and see if people would want to pay more taxes . . . and take a vote." If not, she worried, "it'll end up like an urban setting with thirty-plus kids in each classroom." In this "white flight" town, one cannot but wonder if it was simply the number of students in the classroom that she feared, or if her invocation of an "urban" setting also conjured the racial diversity of the urban schools they left behind. Broder responded by saying that they could consider this option if they wanted and "start a group" to explore the possibilities, though he reminded her that it was not just Danboro that was overcrowded. At previous meetings, when total redistricting was raised, Broder was adamant that it was a bad idea; he never recommended that people "start a group" to explore it. It is a very costly move to secede from a regional district. It is hard to know if Broder sought to avoid confrontation or if he did not consider this public form of neoliberal secession (versus the "private" form of going to a private school) a bad idea.

Broder's "bonding" with the audience took on a new texture as he began to schmooze the crowd in blatant and class-infused ways. The next man to speak, who explained that his kids were still many years away from high school, said that he "appreciated" the consultants' ability to "deal with a spirited crowd!" He then inquired about what option 4 would mean ten to fifteen years down the line: "Are we gonna need redistricting again, and so will there be no choice then?" Broder acknowledged that this was a huge and "dynamic" town and joked that he and the other consultants were constantly getting lost when driving around to look for a restaurant. He smiled and laughed in a comfortable way and asked the audience, "Can anyone recommend a good restaurant?!" A guy in the audience yelled out, "You can come over to my house. My wife will make you a good dinner!" There was boisterous laughter in the auditorium, during which the woman from the task force who had spoken at the Mill meeting had a look of shock on her face. If you bought the conspiracy theory that people from Danboro were orchestrating the process (or at least trying to), this moment of extreme chumminess could be your "proof." Or, it could be read as evidence of the consultants' attempt to woo those who they realized held much power.

The class-infused and gendered conviviality continued in Broder's banter with the next man, who asked if option 4 was realistic: "Are there volunteers from any polling you've done?" Broder acknowledged that they assumed that they would get volunteers, though it could not be guaranteed, and there was expectation that the school would open under capacity. Broder then said that figuring out these numbers was a lot like dealing with his bills at the end of each month: "I think I have enough money to pay my bills, but I don't how many times my wife will spend money without me knowing!" There were tons of laughs from the audience, including many of the women. This kind of humor was frequently heard in Danboro; it was a source of pride for many to be in a financial situation of unbridled spending and to have wives who did not have to work unless they wanted to. The woman from the task force was wriggling in her seat, looking around the room with an expression of disbelief on her face. The man who was speaking, though, did not let Broder's schmoozing go unchecked. He said that while he, too, liked the "option on the table because there's choice," he felt that it was not realistic "because we can't know." He distrustfully asked, "So [are you saying it's possible] just to end the meeting and give us a false hope?" Broder quickly replied, "It's not just a false hope. . . . It's now in the ball game, and the board *has* to consider the voluntary option."

After some more questions about the process with the board, the staff at the new school, and the curriculum that might be offered, during which some people started to trickle out, Broader noted, "Remember that option

4 means starting small," adding, "The superintendent will have discre-
tion." So if a freshman was on the varsity team at his school, he could
request a waiver to stay at his old school. "So, the *superstars* will get that?"
a woman asked in a displeased tone. There was a lot of cross-talk in the
audience, likely because this information was new. A few people quietly
mentioned that this was great news: there were loopholes that could be
maneuvered if their kid was redistricted. Broder then shifted to the new
school. "There will be open houses," he told them. "You can go, even if your
kids are not going. . . . You built it!"

The same woman continued to speak, asking, "What about a fifth option
with split sessions? I heard it came up at Westbrook." Kelly took the question and reminded the audience that the problems they were facing were
far too constraining. His tone turned sarcastic when he noted that split
sessions were "used in the city schools in the Middle Ages!" In a mocking
tone, with a cynical smile on his face—and with an accentuated outer-bor-
ough New York accent—he commented that the woman who brought it up
had said, "It didn't do me no harm!" As these words came out of his mouth,
the audience erupted into laughter—the kind that suggests knowing familiarity. Out of the corner of my eye, I could see that the woman from the
task force looked horrified as she turned toward her husband and looked
around the room. I wondered if she interpreted his comments—and the
laughter in the room—as a form of racialized collusion. The accent that
Kelly used to utter those words could have been heard as mimicry of an
African-American accent, though the woman who had said it at the meeting the night before was white. My sense was that this was an instance of
self-mockery in this largely post-Brooklyn crowd, with a hint of class judgment of those who would consider returning to the conditions they left
behind and risen above. And yet the slippery indexicality of the accent—
semiotically evoking both black and white urbanites—meant that Kelly's
utterance was open to a range of interpretations. Accents, like words, are
"overpopulated"—to draw on Bakhtin's language.[22] Barring a poll of those
in the room, we cannot know if the laughter was imbued with racial and
class-encoded disdain (akin to the undercurrent in the class-ranking
debates that residents from the Mill did not "value" education in the same
way), or if it was self-referential, class-encoded jabbing (or something in
between). Yet it is in part the post-Brooklyn nature of the town—the class

aspirations, white-flight fears, and urban anxieties—that helped shape the habitus in Danboro. Even if it was technically "wrong" for the task-force woman to assume that Kelly was referring to an African-American accent, the laughter in the room could still have arisen because people thought that Kelly was referring to someone from the Mill—a class if not also a racial other. She could have been "right."

When the laughter died down, Broder continued to address the woman who asked the question about split sessions: "We will say it's a bad idea." He then commented on something else that the consultants thought was a bad idea: "Some have said that we should have total redistricting, then carve it up to equal capacity. We have taken a position publicly and will repeat it: 'No.' We have done it elsewhere and it's worked, but here you don't have space, so we won't waste the board's or your time with it." Once again the task-force woman was on the edge of her seat. Even if total redistricting did not make sense for the immediate needs of the district, Broder did not make it clear—as he did at other meetings—that some redistricting would be necessary at some point once further construction was complete. In light of his acquiescent reaction to the woman who suggested that Danboro secede, it was clear that Broder was not going to recommend to this crowd that they come to terms with what it meant to be a part of a regional district.

The next set of remarks made this lacuna more evident. The first speaker started by saying that what he heard at this meeting was this: "We need two high schools more or major additions to the other six. We need to *yell* about building now—like we did against redistricting. This has snuck up on us. . . . It seems to me: don't mess with the district now when we'll have a bigger problem down the road." There was loud applause from the audience. Broder said that he agreed, pointing out, "Option 4 says that," after which he quickly added, "although we're not selling anything; we're not advocates." The same man continued to speak, with his fist in the air as he yelled in pep-rally fashion, "Build, build, build, baby, build!" The audience erupted into applause, and a few people let out emboldened hoots. "Can we have a straw poll to see if 4 is possible?" the next speaker asked. Broder responded by pointing out that everyone is "not yet fully informed," so it was not clear what a poll would provide. He cautioned her, "Never ask if you don't want to deal with the consequences. . . . If there are low numbers, the board can reject option 4." Broder knew that the result was likely to be low from the limited show the night before. Broder may have claimed that he was not an "advocate," but he was clearly trying to orchestrate a preferred outcome.

The collusive overtone of the meeting was briefly tempered as distrust of the process emerged in the next speaker's comments—and the heckles they inspired. "Most here have no faith in the board," he commented, to which loud clapping erupted from all over the room. "You're being hired to give us an option?! We don't have to hire you to know we have *choice*. The first three are garbage . . . negated by the board already. People are walking out of this meeting because they're exasperated. What's your purpose?" As Broder responded, it was the first time during the night that he had a defensive comportment, and it was somewhat hard to hear him over the cross-talk in the audience. He replied by reminding the man that option 4 was not the end, after which a woman sitting behind me yelled out, "We're in January!" The man who had been speaking picked up on her frustration. He asked acerbically, "Do we find out in August?" He then pointed out the key predicament as he saw it: the community needs communication from the consultants because they don't trust the board, and yet the board hired them. Broder quickly reminded the man, "We've been here two months. It usually takes eight." There was lots of chatter in the audience, during which one man yelled out, "We don't have [eight months]!" Another woman sitting behind me shouted in a mocking tone, "Just burn the [new] school!" People sitting around her started to laugh, and one woman leaned in toward her and sarcastically joked, "It's a good idea!"

After a few more comments, which included a suggestion that the board resign for "destroying our community, tearing it apart," affability toward the consultants returned when the next man who got up to speak thanked the consultants for "being more responsive than the board." Yet consideration of their request to limit cross-talk was no longer heeded, and it was unclear the extent to which anyone was still listening, including me. Shari had spotted me in the audience and came over to say hello. (Shari is the mother who kept hearing *projects* when I described for her my research project.) She sat down in an open seat next to me and started to tell me about Stephanie's new boyfriend. It seemed as if everyone was chitchatting at this point. There was a palpable feeling of confidence in all that sidebar conversation, as if there was no need to listen or participate since things were going their way, despite voiced concerns about the process itself. At one point, I looked toward the task-force woman and her husband. I figured that the look on her face would help me gauge the discussion. But shortly after Shari sat down, they must have left. Perhaps they, too, felt like the decision had already been made.

FINAL DECISIONS

On March 2nd, four and a half weeks later, during which the board reversed its decision to remove class ranking, the consultants presented their final report to the board. There was a little twist to what everyone at the meetings had expected. While they recommended that option 4 be considered seriously, they also put forth a newly designed option 5. Unlike option 4, with its focus on volunteers, the plan for option 5 recommended mandatory redistricting based on proximity: in addition to moving all Great Farms students out of Danboro High School to Great Farms High School, more Bowen students would be moved into Milldale Township High School, and a section of Westbrook would be redistricted to the Mill. This plan was publicized in a half-page advertisement in a local paper before the official presentation at the March 2nd meeting. But by the time the consultants presented the report at the meeting, it had been modified to open Great Farms High School at full capacity by also reassigning students from adjacent areas of Danboro and Milldale Township.

Not surprisingly, the audience was packed that night. There were almost one thousand people in attendance. Parents from Westbrook, in particular, were extremely vocal about the possibility of being redistricted to the Mill. The week before, someone had placed flyers in mailboxes in areas of Westbrook that were to be redistricted, calling the Mill an "inferior" school. When Broder began to describe the modified option 5 at the meeting, one person yelled out, "Over my dead body!" Others pleaded for an option 6, curious as to why their children were being reassigned to the Mill when Danboro was geographically closer. In an interview with a reporter following the meeting, a resident from Milldale Township observed, "People from Westbrook are starting to feel that noise from people from Danboro made a significant enough impression that they were not redistricted to the Mill."[23]

There were two more board of education meetings—on March 9th and March 16th—before the board had to make its final decision on March 23rd. These meetings did not include public participation; they were simply workshop discussions between the board, the administration, and members of the task force. The interim superintendent made it clear in statements to the local papers that while the public was welcome to attend, outbursts from the audience would not be tolerated. The audience was considerably smaller at these meetings, with no more than fifty people at the start. But sure enough, there were still outbursts, and at one of the meetings, a father from Westbrook was escorted out by the police.

The "noise" from Westbrook parents did appear to affect the process, however, for by the night of the final meeting on March 23rd, an option 6 had been developed. It continued to recommend that all Great Farms students be moved to Great Farms High School, and that students from Bowen be spread out among Bowen High School, Milldale Township High School, and Great Farms High School. But contrary to option 5, *volunteers* would be sought from Danboro and Westbrook for Great Farms High School. If there were not enough volunteers, only then there would be forced redistricting: Danboro students to Great Farms and Westbrook students to the Mill. At the close of the March 23rd meeting—at midnight, after four hours of debate in which public participation was allowed—the board voted to ask the federal court judge, who was still overseeing the district, to consider options 5 and 6, with a preference for option 6.

After three weeks of reviewing the options, the federal court judge issued his decision: a modified version of option 6. It was to be in effect solely for the 1998–99 school year, after which the board of education— once properly reinstated—would have the authority to make student-placement decisions for the district. In the modified version, Bowen students would still be spread out among three high schools. But Danboro and Westbrook students would not be forced to redistrict if there were not enough volunteers. In his twelve-page opinion, quoted in a local paper, he emphasized the importance of "bonds" that are formed between students—and between students and their municipality—which he said "are part of the human equation. They impact upon child development and must be respected. No involuntary transfer should be made."

Needless to say, many parents from Bowen were upset by the judge's decision, which undermined the very idea of a regional district and disregarded the fact that Bowen students had to involuntarily transfer. According to the man from Westbrook who had filed the suit that deemed the board unconstitutionally representative several months before, these complaints from Bowen parents were "a very unfortunate jealousy.... [T]hey were angry because Danboro and Westbrook parents had a *choice*." This same article suggested that parents from Bowen had been "largely silent" throughout the process about their frustrations with what they deemed "special treatment" of Danboro and Westbrook parents. Yet if you recall, there was an extraordinary amount of public discussion—from Bowen residents and from others around the district—underscoring the fact that "choice" is (or at least, should be) limited when the good of the district (as a whole) is at stake. Many parents also underscored on several occasions that the majority of students would not be "psychologically impaired" if forced to move schools, assuming proper orientation and support at home.

Foreshadowing the final plan, an article was published in a national newspaper the week before the judge handed down his decision. The author of the article also sidestepped district concerns in his encapsulation of the process: "School redistricting battles often hinge on such divisive issues as the racial makeup of student populations or the vastly different achievement levels at neighboring schools. While there have been hints of socioeconomic rivalry between towns in the Milldale district, with Danboro and Westbrook seen as a bit more affluent, the arguments have tended to focus more parochially on the issue of keeping children close to home." Yes, the arguments did tend to focus on the "issue of keeping children close to home." But as this chapter has underscored, claims about doing things "for the good of the children" or "community spirit" or "choice" are often codes for race and class desires, and have *effects* with classed and racialized implications. To no one's surprise, once the board was reinstated and was able to devise a plan for student placement for the 1999–2000 and 2000–2001 school years, students from Danboro and Westbrook continued to be districted for "their" schools, and a group of Danboro parents revisited the possibility of seceding from the district, though that was once again deemed too costly.

In the aftermath of these debates, I was talking with a woman from Westbrook about how people from Danboro and Westbrook are quite comfortable speaking their minds in front of an auditorium filled with hundreds of people. I told her that although it could easily be explained away by "ethnicizing" it—since many people in both towns are of Italian, Jewish, or Irish descent, I felt that there was so much more to the story. She told me that she believed it had something do with the feelings of impotence they had in Brooklyn when faced with the huge and daunting bureaucracy of the New York City public schools. People did not feel like their voice could be heard, and often were not even sure to whom they should be talking. Out here in New Jersey, she pointed out, the mayor could be your next-door neighbor, and members of the board of education probably have children on your kid's soccer team.

This woman made a powerful point. Part of what people in Danboro and Westbrook learned through their suburban move was the insidious way that class works. Whom you know—and having intimate access to them—enables significant power and authority. But like my concern about "ethnicizing" these redistricting debates, I am also hesitant to attribute the "noise" that people made simply to the Brooklyn residual. As this book has revealed, even with all of the privileges and newfound empowerment afforded people through their suburban move, many people still had a sense of powerlessness, as if they needed to continuously fight to maintain their class and race privilege. The effects of the changing class structure and diminishing state entitlements put increasing stress on local communities and individual citizens, throwing into relief subtle gradations within the middle class and among middle-class sensibilities. Heightened anxieties from these circumstances—compounded by nearsighted planning, limited local funds, fractured leadership, racial anxieties, and third-party involvement (both the consultants and the judge)—led many people in Danboro and Westbrook to work diligently to regulate their borders rather than to coalitionally come together with those in their (literal and metaphorical) district. With a state that ruled against a basic premise of regionalism, and with federal regulations that did not require addressing existing segregation, it is no surprise that efforts to promote an expansive notion of community and collective approaches to growing inequalities lost out to neoliberal entrenchment.

7 A Conclusion, or Rather, a Commencement

It was not quite spring yet. The March air contained a chill and a hint of the icy smell of winter. But it seemed like everyone in Danboro was all aflutter with planning for June's graduation festivities. Lauren, Erika, and their four closest friends—Nicole, Stacey, Shannon, and Beth—decided to go together on a dress-shopping trip to Short Hills, a town in northern New Jersey with an upscale mall. Lauren and Nicole's moms were coming along, which meant that there would not be enough room for everyone to fit in one car. So it was decided that the two moms should drive up together in a separate car. Lauren was thrilled with this arrangement, since it meant that her mom would have time alone with Nicole's mom. Nicole was one of her closest friends, and yet the two moms had met only once before.

Lauren's mom—like most of the parents of the girls in this close-knit group—had always been quite wary of Nicole's mom, Mary. It was because the girls spent *a lot* of time at Nicole's house. Often it was for innocuous gatherings, like group viewings of *Dawson's Creek* on Monday nights and *Beverly Hills 90210* on Wednesday nights—two of the most popular teen television shows at that time. But on most weekend nights, as all of the parents knew, the girls were over at the house partying with their guy friends, even while Mary was home. As Lauren once described it, the house was their "party central." I was at Nicole's house a couple of times, and it did feel a bit like a frat house. Kids were coming and going at all hours of the night. Although they all had cell phones or beepers, which they used to get in touch with each other, they usually just put aside those technologies in favor of driving past the house to see who was there.

From the outside, Nicole's house looked like all the other moderately sized colonial-style homes in her development, which was not too far from where the Sillens lived. But the minute you walked in the door, it had quite a different feel. There had clearly been little or no upkeep of the house. Several of the cabinet doors in the kitchen were falling off their hinges. The pool in the backyard was full of leaves, and the landscaping around it was in tatters. The couches in the den were frayed, and the stains on the rug looked like they had been there for years. Obviously, no one had to take their shoes off when they walked into this house. Of course, this was part of what the kids loved about hanging out there. They could just kick back.

It was on the drive to the Short Hills mall that Linda, Lauren's mom, finally had the chance to "bond" with Mary, as Lauren described it. Mary shared with her stories about the extremely difficult things that she and Nicole had gone through over the years, most of which were related to a messy divorce with Nicole's father, who had since moved back to Brooklyn. Even though it had been some time since things were particularly dire, and although they were doing quite well overall, Mary acknowledged to Linda that emotional and financial struggles still endured. As they were talking, Linda understood for the first time why Mary liked the fact that Nicole had friends around her all the time, and why her house was "falling apart"—as Lauren had often described it to her.

Mary and Linda continued to talk throughout the day, during which they came up with an idea that really excited them: rather than each family having its own graduation dinner, why not have a big graduation dinner and bring the whole group of girls and their families together? The girls had become so close during their high school years, in part through getting each other through these kinds of trials and tribulations—that is, struggles we typically envision when we think about middle-class youth being "at risk" (depression, drug use, eating disorders). It would be a truly fitting way to celebrate their graduation and their supportive friendships.

By the end of the day, Mary and Linda had devised a plan. Mary worked for one of the municipal services in town, so she knew of a public hall they would be able to rent cheaply. If they did it right, the whole party—including a catered dinner—would cost a fraction of the expense of individual family dinners out.

A few days after this shopping trip, I was hanging out with Lauren in a Starbucks attached to a mega–Barnes & Noble on Route 2, right across from the entrance to the mall. It was one of the few places that felt a bit like a "town center." Over coffee Frappucinos, Lauren told me how excited she was about the graduation-party idea. She was disappointed, though, because a couple of the parents did not want to do it. "They have to go to fancy restaurants," she vented. One of the two families who were not interested in the plan was Erika's family. (It was Erika's dad who had left his garage door open on prom night, leaving in view his Porsche.) Erika told Lauren that it was because her grandparents were coming into town, and the family needed to spend quality time together. Lauren was not convinced, since Erika's grandparents were sleeping over at their house. In a frustrated huff Lauren wondered, "So what would be the big deal about spending *two hours* with the rest of the group?" It was not because of her grandparents, Lauren explained to me. It was because "god forbid they should have their daughter's graduation dinner in a [municipal building]." Lauren was not surprised that Erika's family would not do it, she admitted, but she was still "bummed" about it. "But whatever," she remarked. "It will still be fun."

The group graduation dinner was, in fact, quite fun. As were the separate dinners that the other families had at "fancy restaurants." But as these girls celebrated their graduation and an end to their high school years, this rift—in its own intimate way—was another example of the increasing middle-class divide's effect on everyday life. Graduations are called *commencements*—a suggestive term that implies that they are as much beginnings as they are conclusions. For this group of girls, before geography had a chance to separate them when they went off to college, intraclass tensions infused their friendships and eroded their close-knit group.

Like other local articulations of shifts in the class structure explored in this book, this moment provides insight into emerging class configurations and social materialities in the late 1990s—the kind that would be thrown into relief during the economic crash of 2008 and with which we are still contending today. Nicole and Mary's house, in particular, foreshowed an image that has come to be iconic of the housing crisis: a decaying suburban home. The fact that their house appeared "normal" from the outside was a striking counterpoint in the late 1990s to the new "McMansions" that had meticulous facades and landscaping, and yet had rooms that echoed from lack of furniture. Like those new megahouses with their excessive interior space—a metaphorical material embodiment of the housing bubble and its disproportionate valuation—Nicole and Mary's crumbling home also was a reminder of the changes in the middle class and affecting the middle class, if only one had stepped inside to see.

I end this book with this particular story not only for how it foretells structural transformations under way, but also for how it typifies the kinds of moments that we need to keep in focus to appreciate the subtle ways that class matters. It would be easy to write off these events as having nothing to do with anxieties emerging from changing material and discursive conditions. People have long wanted upscale dresses to wear to graduations and to have dinners at "fancy restaurants" to celebrate significant occasions. Differing tastes and class desires have long lead to petty disputes and tensions between parents, children, and their friends. And parents have long been concerned about their kids hanging out at houses like Nicole and Mary's home and have tried to keep their kids (and themselves) away from people considered to be "bad parents," like Bonnie's concern about Sam playing with Gordon because of rumors about the ways that Sandy earned her money. But as I have illustrated in each chapter, these so-called "private" or "individual" or "community" habits, desires, and sentiments—while seemingly mundane and local, and at times familiar—have much broader significance when viewed through the lens of changes in the material conditions undergirding middle-class life. They matter differently.

The inability of some people to feel secure in their piece of the postwar suburban American dream during the late 1990s was caused, in part, by the fact that it did indeed become harder to maintain, even as others were successfully "keeping up with the Dow Jones." While much attention was paid to the stock-market boom, there was much less focus at the time on the major class shift under way and its role in creating volatile job markets, influencing community borders and boundaries, and affecting intimate desires and family dynamics. As people struggled to sustain their lifestyle within their means or to carry on living well above them, class insecurities grew even more intense. The feeling among many people in Danboro of being crowded (and potentially crowded *out*) was caused by far more than overdevelopment in the area, congestion on the roads, upscaled consumer desires, post-Brooklyn fears of racial encroachments, and personal problems like those facing Nicole and Mary. Given the increasing dominance of neoliberal logics and the widening abyss growing within the shrinking middle class, which began in the 1970s and was dramatically exacerbated during the economic boom years of the late 1990s, there was a lot more at stake in people's "concern for 'seeming'"[1] and anxieties about their children's futures.

The ethnographic moments unpacked in this book bring to life the ways that people were reorienting themselves—both consciously and unconsciously—to the discursive and material displacement of residual approaches to middle-class life in favor of newly dominant neoliberal sensibilities and practices. My analysis demonstrates the ways that memories of an ambivalent past and anxieties about an ominous future influence the experience of class in a particular historical moment. Each chapter reveals the ways that anxieties emerging from feelings of insecurity produced class-encoded habits, desires, and sentiments that shaped local conditions and the quality of everyday life, often making people (and their neighbors) less secure. The constellation of these ways of being, which I have termed *rugged entitlement,* is a product of this particular period in the everprotean nature of liberal ideology in the United States. Amid declining entitlements and safety nets and the blurring of lines between public and private, old strategies articulated with new tactics for appeasing class anxieties, including the predominance of ever larger SUVs, increasing square footage of people's homes, and the desire for gates in a place that had—until the 1990s—embodied the "shared lawn" liberal democratic ideal propagated by Olmsted a century before. As the suburban American dream amped up during its last hurrah, "wants" turned into "needs" that turned into ever more expansive (and expensive) needs, even as infrastructural essentials like school facilities became overburdened. The "cruel optimism"[2] of that time became all the more apparent as the American-dream ideal came crashing down in the new millennium.

RUGGED ENTITLEMENT IN THE NEW MILLENNIUM

This book has made a powerful case for keeping in view practices, sites, and strategies that we might consider typical of an earlier moment in time or simply not "new" to the time period with which we are concerned. The design of suburbs like Danboro and efforts to keep new carpet clean were surely not novel at the end of the twentieth century. Yet I have argued that to understand what is often characterized as the "neoliberal moment" (or any moment, for that matter), we need to appreciate more than just its new spaces, subjectivities, and modes of citizenship. Equally as represent-ative of a time period and as agentive in shaping it—and thus correspond-ingly as crucial when considering a historical moment to follow—are the dynamics produced when the residual interweaves with the dominant. As Raymond Williams has noted, "The complexity of a culture is to be found not only in its variable processes and their social definitions—traditions, institutions, and formations—but also in the dynamic interrelations, at every point in the process, of *historically* varied and variable elements."[3] As this book has shown, we cannot fully grasp the post-1970s, post-Fordist period without understanding postwar liberal sensibilities, just as we can-not truly appreciate the post-Brooklyn residents of Danboro without rec-ognizing the racialized urban lives that preceded their suburban move. As such, we limit our tools of analysis for grappling with the problems of today if we are not conscious of the aspects of rugged entitlement that continue to matter in striking ways. The monumental events that ushered in the new millennium—most notably 9/11, a decade of war in Iraq and Afghanistan, and the economic crash of 2008—can make it feel as if the end of the last century was a radically different historical moment. But "old" anxieties and concerns about security continue to infuse the "new."

There are many examples in the 2010s to which we can turn to see the rearticulation of rugged entitlement in the new millennium. Take, for example, the type of subjectivity that we saw produced in youth like Doug, who came of age in a moment of neoliberal governmentality in which entrepreneurial selves were developed through a variety of means, includ-ing busy after-school lives and active E*Trade accounts. Despite the stock-market collapse, ominous questions about the future of the U.S. economy, and ire over the crushing weight of college loans—or rather likely *because* of all three—the majority of students in the early 2010s, including those like Doug's little brother, Sam, continue to yearn for jobs in finance and college degrees in business and economics—unlike a few decades before, when history and English literature were all the rage. Times have changed, but the feeling among many students that they need to be exceedingly self-sufficient—including choosing a "practical" college education and careers with high incomes—has become entrenched.

The anxiety that middle-class youth and adults feel in the early twenty-first century makes sense. We live in a world with growing income inequality in which life is an economic tightrope for all but a privileged few. As Lauren Berlant has noted, it is "the end of an era of social obligation and belonging . . . : no longer is precarity delegated to the poor or the *sans-papiers*."[4] Despite movements such as Occupy Wall Street and Strike Debt that seek to challenge the status quo of class and debt in the market-driven economy, many more students are persistently driving after class. The structure of feeling of rugged entitlement continues to fuel the neoliberal common sense: that it is too risky to do anything but focus on one's own security or that of one's family or immediate community, even if that means putting aside concerns about the social good. Under this pressure, universities are increasingly becoming vehicles for rugged entitlement themselves, bowing to pressures to focus predominantly on producing a prepared workforce and not also a critical citizenry that can figure out how to change the current course. This is all the more troubling as it becomes increasingly clear that even when youth follow the so-called practical right path, which in many cases involves turning away from long-standing interests or other ways of contributing to the world because they feel that they cannot afford to do otherwise or were told by those around them that this was the case, it does not guarantee them economic security.

There has been lot of discussion since the economic crash of 2008 about the predatory nature of neoliberal capitalism, including these conditions facing college students. Particular attention has been paid to the problem of "too big to fail" banking systems, the freewheeling movement of capital in and out of real estate securities and derivatives, and a host of insufficiently-regulated-by-the-state practices, including predatory lending itself. There has been much less discussion about the conditions that have enabled people to become "prey" for these predatory practices—that is, to be susceptible to being taken advantage of by certain changing political-economic and sociocultural circumstances. In many ways, those who fell prey in the lead up to the crash were not just those who took on predatory loans. I would argue that even those whose homes did not end up in foreclosure when the bubble burst, such as the families in this book, also were prey—as were most Americans once the American dream itself had became predatory.

The postwar American dream continued to be promoted and sold long after it had transformed into something unattainably upscaled and had become a means for a small group of people and corporations—now referred to as the 1 percent—to cash out. People were ideologically encouraged to continue to drive after class amid largely unchallenged claims at the time about housing prices and stock-market surges, even if people had a sense that things were "off," and as was noted in the fine print. If there has been one thing that has long united a good portion of Americans—regardless of class, race, gender, religion, ethnic background, sexual orientation, political affiliation, or national origin—it has been the desire for the American dream and a comfortable middle-class (now upper-middle-class) lifestyle. Even though many of the material conditions for that dream have come crumbling down and many people have been forced to radically alter their lives, many of its affective structures, including rugged entitlement, live on. These durable dispositions do not change overnight just because we have entered a new historical moment—an important theoretical perspective to keep in mind as we think about how to change the current conditions.

DURABLE DISPOSITIONS:
HABITUS, HISTORY, AND CHANGE

The form of "critique" that runs throughout the book requires that we go beyond thinking about the ways that a political-economic moment is grounded in a particular location and in the specificities of people's lives. The relationship between class subjectivities and the political-economic order of things is dynamic. Habitus—our "durable dispositions"—do far more than reproduce class structures; they play a key role in producing structures of feeling and the common sense of a time. Like new regimes of accumulation and new modes of governance, classed subjectivities also are modes of capitalist regulation. Developed through the minutiae of the everyday, they make things possible but also limit; they shape longings for what is imagined and what is not yet imaginable; they are products of history and also are historical forces. They are part of what makes us susceptible prey, but they are also agents of social change.

These durable dispositions get their durability because of how deeply ingrained they are in our minds, bodies, and everyday ways of being: what kinds of restaurants we find appropriate for special family occasions; the referent that comes to mind when we hear a particular word like *projects;* the way we inflect our voices at a town hall hearing or a board of education meeting; what kind of car we think is suitable to drive. They are what make us feel like ourselves, what is comfortable, familiar, and known. Because of this—that intimate feeling of being who we are—we forget that habitus are products of historical forces. As Bourdieu explains, the dialectic between conditions and our habitus "transforms the distribution of capital, the balance-sheet of a power relation, into a system of perceived differences . . . whose objective truth is misrecognized."[5] We are not born with classed subjectivities; we become classed over the course of our lives. Our childhood years are extremely powerful moments for habit formation, but just as there are changes to the spaces through which we move and the discourses in our midst and the things that are possible and no longer possible, our durable dispositions, too, can change. They are durable but not unchangeable, even though habit-change is a demanding and complicated process.

The formation and transformation of habitus is thrown into relief during times when people, often nonchalantly, remark that they are "used to" to something or *have become* "used to" something, or when they say that something "doesn't bother" them anymore. We saw this in Linda's narrative about how she went from being "used to" apartment living in Brooklyn to having become "used to [the] style" of suburban strip malls and highway traffic. We saw this when little Sam said that he "just [had] to get used to" the disciplinary practices involved in keeping the carpet clean, and that it didn't "bother" him much anymore. We saw this when Julia said that having parents (or rather a mom) who worked long hours was what she was "used to." Even little Danielle, who at three years old constantly whined about getting into the car *again* when her family first moved from Brooklyn, had become used to living in a place geared toward (ever bigger forms of) automobility, driving around town on her seventeenth birthday in an SUV much like the one that Wendi drove. Even Lauren, who complained about Erika's family's choice to have their graduation dinner at a "fancy restaurant," was used to these kinds of classed tensions with Erika's family.

Everything that people in the United States have long been "used to" and have *become* "used to" are not only products of the cultural conditions of upbringing and daily dynamics in people's lives. These personal histories are themselves formed out of conditions that have been created through broader historical dynamics—of liberal democracy and racial formations, meritocracy and the myth of rugged individualism, global capitalism and middle-class formation, suburban development and the spatialization of inequality, automobility and public education, gender ideologies and neoliberal logics. All of these histories, many of which have been discussed throughout this book, are misrecognized when we think of our durable dispositions as simply personal preferences—and not also the products of state policies, corporate influence, institutional arrangements, and ideological claims. As we try to imagine ways of creating a more equitable and just economy, it is incumbent upon us not only to remember that which created who we are now, including aspects of rugged entitlement that endure, but to keep in mind that the decisions we make now, whether they are in regard to policy, governance, or spatial arrangements, will create the next generation's common sense.

TIME FOR A NEW COMMON SENSE ABOUT THE AMERICAN DREAM

The United States is notorious for its deep discomfort with the realities of class and the role of the state in undergirding not only people's everyday lives but also the workings of capitalism itself. In many other parts of the world, people in anxious times often question first the role of their state or international organizations in managing global economic conditions, as my experiences as a student in Zimbabwe in the early 1990s first revealed to me. In the United States, on the other hand, people's scope tends to be more local: what they themselves could have done differently, how they match up with their neighbors, what was happening in their job, their town, or their family. Yet even when the state is questioned, as we saw during the economic collapse and continue to see today, the debate tends to involve concerns about the role of the state *in general,* rather than what *kind* of state involvement is needed in particular moments in time in a liberal democracy. The long-standing ideological claim that "everyone is middle class"—and that they got there on their own volition—further muddies the waters; for even after the 2008 economic meltdown and repeated acknowledgements of the changing class structure and related social conditions, class analysis in the public discourse continued to invoke "the middle class" or income-bracket parts, with only sparse attention to the dominant common sense that had pushed residual logics to the margins. Now that it has become increasingly clear that a robust U.S. middle class is no longer needed and necessary for the global bourgeoisie, perhaps it is time that we start thinking of other ways to find "a little security in an insecure world." It is time for a new common sense about the American dream.

I began this book with a discussion of Gramsci's notion of "common sense"—the unconscious way of perceiving that we experience as an "instinct" but that is in fact "an elementary historical acquisition."[6] It is the fusion of class ideologies with long-standing belief systems and moral sensibilities. Gramsci longed for a time, such as the eighteenth century, when the common sense was revolutionary. But during his lifetime, as in the time period of this book, common sense was—for the most part—leading down a class-divisive path. The neoliberal common sense of rugged entitlement, which came sharply into view in the late 1990s, was a sensibility that not only entrenched the long-term common sense about the American dream as a primary means of becoming successful and having the proper family, home, and life. It also infused these desires and expectations with a post-seventies neoliberal governmentality that presumed a level of entrepreneurship and risk that was not part of the original postwar American dream. It was quite the opposite in the immediate postwar period: it was meant to be risk free for homeowners, with the federal government largely shouldering the risk. By the late 1990s, it was not just an amped-up American dream with bigger houses and bigger cars and added expenses for "stupid things." It was built on an economic bubble and unchecked faith in proclamations about a volatile boom economy that was rigged against the average American.

Amid contemporary efforts to overhaul these conditions, it is useful to recall progressive commonsense reactions and "unlikely coalitions" that emerged in Danboro before the crash in reaction to neoliberalization and the entrenchment of rugged entitlement. Just as there were warnings floating around during the late 1990s about bloated markets, problematic policy changes, and predatory lending, there was a sense of things being "off" in local communities and people's daily lives. The "bonding" that occurred between Mary and Linda during their drive to and from the Short Hills mall resonates quite profoundly with other such moments. At the Zoning Board of Adjustment meeting, descendants of old farming families found themselves joking and making snide remarks about the proposed six-foot-high ornamental security gate with families who were living in moderately sized colonial-style homes. Julia felt a great sense of relief and connection with her "down-to-earth" friends from Milldale Township High School, who were less concerned than her Danboro friends with having designer bags, fancy cars, and the latest clothes. Wendi, right after her accident, found that the family in the other Blazer was far nicer to her than the family in the Mercedes, who never even looked her way. And even though some families from Danboro and Westbrook worked together to ensure that their children would not be redistricted, many people from the other towns—and from Danboro and Westbrook, too—raised their voices in an effort to promote a regional sensibility. These alliances—no matter how brief—were clearly welcomed by those involved. They represent a desire to retreat from the pressures and influences of rugged entitlement. They also reveal an opening—a potentially fruitful unsettled ambivalence amid the hesitant resolve. No ideological project is ever fully complete or produces its ideal subjects, and neoliberalization is no exception.

Granted, much of what I have written about in this book demonstrates the ways that rugged entitlement "won out" in the late 1990s, as when Doug's curiosities about communism were quelled by his enthusiasm for E*Trade or when Wendi's discomfort in her Blazer proved to be no match for her essentialist faith in the (supposed) safety of SUVs. But those seeds of doubt can bloom at any time, and amid the economic meltdown a decade later, an increasing number of people began asking themselves versions of the question that Doug had been asking himself: was all that driving after class—particularly for the suburban American dream—worth it? Did those efforts succeed in making people more secure, or did anxieties lead to purchases, practices, and place making that provided a *feeling* of security without being truly secure? Do we want to continue down the path of becoming a nation of luxury SUVs, six-foot-high ornamental security gates, increasingly more segregated spaces, and a dwindling middle class, or do we want to rethink the common sense that has led us down this path?

It thus seems fitting to end this book by thinking about "commencements" rather than "conclusions," since in many ways this story is just beginning. With the political-economic mess that happened since the time of my fieldwork, the essentialist faith that many people used to have in the postwar American dream has given way to new anxieties about the future. The question now becomes, Can we develop a new American dream, and if so, what will it look like? Can we devise one that does not compound processes of neoliberalizing space already under way, but rather works instead to mend the spatialization of inequality that was created through the postwar American dream and exacerbated by gentrification?[7] Will we be able to creatively address the enduring effects and affects of the housing crisis and economic collapse in a way that does not "suck up the world's wealth"—to use the phrasing from my time in Zimbabwe? The fact that this challenge is a global one is all the more reason to change our understanding of who (or rather, what conditions) should be deemed "at risk" to a healthy social order.

There is an emerging body of work and innovation amid ongoing efforts to retrofit suburbia for a more sustainable future, challenging the idea that Americans will never give up their love of low-density living.[8] It already is becoming evident that little Sam's generation has become more interested in urban living and car-free lives than the generation before, and with the recent election of a new mayor in New York City who campaigned on a progressive platform, perhaps there will be a change soon to the spatialization of class inequality in the United States. All of this might seem like something that Americans will have a hard time getting "used to." But recall that residents in Bowen had become "used to" the idea of being part of regional district, and in fact were huge proponents of regionalization after having been redistricted for so long. And now, even people in Danboro and Westbrook are starting to come around, since their towns, too, have over the years been redistricted to other schools (Danboro to Great Farms; Westbrook to Milldale Township). History provides plenty of evidence of change that was needed for the greater good, which eventually created in people a sensibility they might not have initially "chosen." Like Gramsci, we cannot let the pessimism of our intellect erode the optimism of our will.[9]

Notes

CHAPTER 1

1. Heintz, Folbre, and the Center for Popular Economics 2000:170.

2. For documentation of my ethnographic observations, I wrote field notes when I got home at the end of each day or the following day. I did my best to capture not just what happened or what people said, but their comportment, the tone of their voice, and the context in which the ethnographic moments occurred. The interviews, which consisted of open-ended and focused questions, sought to understand the ways that parents, children, and public officials narrated the pressures and pleasures of their everyday lives, and to inquire specifically about ethnographic moments that emerged as key forms of evidence during my research. The interviews were all taped to enable close linguistic, discursive, semiotic, and dialogic forms of analysis, though I also wrote field notes at the end of the days of the interviews to capture people's comportment and the setting of the interview. The interview tapes were coded with numbers to ensure confidentiality. I did not conduct the interviews until the final three months of my research. I took great care to fold my ethnographic presence into everyday life, and I feared that this fluidity might be disrupted through introducing formal interviews early in the process. Since this project is predominantly ethnographic, I conducted these interviews (thirteen in total) solely for supplemental material.

3. The meetings were extensively documented and/or taped to enable the same type of close linguistic, discursive, semiotic, and dialogic forms of analysis as the interviews.

4. Ehrenreich 1989:15.

5. Bledstein and Johnson 2001; Blumin 1989; Ryan 1981.

6. My discussion in this paragraph is drawn largely from Ehrenreich and Ehrenreich 1979.

7. Ehrenreich and Ehrenreich 1979:21. Emphasis in the original.

8. In Erik Olin Wright's (1989:26) terms, "these new middle classes . . . constitute contradictory locations, or more precisely, contradictory locations within exploitation relations."

9. My discussion in this paragraph has been particularly influenced by Baxandall and Ewen 2000; Beauregard 2006; Cohen 2003; Colomina 2007; Colomina, Brennan, and Kim 2004; Coontz 1992; Harvey 1990; Jackson 1985; Rouse 1995; and Wright 1981.

10. Keynesianism is named after John Maynard Keynes, an economist whose theories advocated for government involvement in the generation of demand when it was not sufficiently primed by the private sphere.

11. Cited in Jackson 1985:208.

12. My discussion in this paragraph is heavily influenced by Hodgson 1976 and Ortner 1998b:423.

13. Hodgson 1976:81

14. On federal housing policies ("redlining," "slum clearance," "urban renewal"), public discourses ("urban decline"), and other discriminatory practices ("blockbusting") that worked in tandem to undermine cities and attempts by people of color to acquire asset wealth through home ownership in the postwar period, see, for example, Beauregard 2003; Caro 1975; Cohen 2003; Gregory 1998; Jackson 1985:219–30; and Lipsitz 1998:1–23.

15. My discussion in this paragraph and the paragraph that follows draws heavily from Rouse 1995, as well as Ferguson 2009; Harvey 1990, 2005; Ong 2006; N. Rose 1999; and B. Williams 2004.

16. T. Mitchell 2011.

17. The presence of *liberal* in the term *neoliberal* and the phrase below, *postwar liberal ideal*, should not be confused with the use of *liberal* to refer to left-leaning politics. Rather, my use of *liberal* throughout this book refers to liberal ideology, as based on the philosophical texts of eighteenth-century philosophers such as John Locke. Liberalism in this respect refers to a strong commitment to private property and to individual rights, but with those rights heavily biased toward the propertied class.

18. My use of this phrase to encapsulate Gramsci's (1971) discussion of "bourgeois-dominated coalitions" comes from Rouse 1995:362.

19. The median household income in Danboro in 2000 was $101,322. The entire breakdown from the 2000 U.S. Census is as follows: $200,000 or more (12.2 percent), $150,000-199,999 (14 percent), $100,000-149,999 (24.7 percent), $75,000-$99,999 (14.4 percent), $50,000-74,999 (14.3 percent), $35,000-$49,999 (7 percent), $25,000-$34,999 (4.7 percent), $15,000-$24,999 (4.1 percent), $10,000-$14,999 (2.1 percent), and less than $10,000 (2.4 percent).

20. Ortner 1998b:423.

21. Ehrenreich 1989.

22. Newman 1988.

23. Newman 1993. I have put *white* in parentheses here because Newman refers to the baby boom generation without analytically grappling with their whiteness.

24. Newman 1993:26. See also Frank 2007.

25. Ortner 1998b:423. See also, for example, Davidson 2011; C. Katz 2001; and Lacy 2007.

26. See, for example, de Koning 2009; Fehérváry 2012; Fernandes 2006; Schielke 2012; Srivastava 2012; and Zhang 2010. For an extensive bibliography of the anthropological literature on the global middle classes, see Heiman, Freeman, and Liechty 2012.

27. Liechty 2012; Thompson 1963; Wacquant 1991.

28. Massey 1994:120.

29. Raymond Williams (1977:121) refers to this problematic type of historical approach as "epochal" analysis, whereby a cultural process is reified as a cultural system with dominant, fixed features. This static notion ends up relegating all other cultural processes as "marginal" or "incidental" or "secondary" evidence of the dominant features of the cultural process in question. While I draw on Williams's theoretical discussion here, Giddens's (1979) "theory of structuration" also rejects any differentiation of synchrony and diachrony and of the static and the dynamic.

30. R. Williams 1977:121. Emphasis added. For other anthropological approaches to the historical variability of elements interrelated with neoliberalism, see, for example, Collier 2011, Freeman 2007, and von Schnitzler 2008. The anthropological literature has been particularly fruitful for thinking through the nature of neoliberalism, with an understanding that, like all dominant ideologies, it is never fully hegemonic, nor the same thing in each place or time period, nor necessarily resembling its full ideals in practice.

31. According to the 2000 U.S. Census, 55.14 percent of workers over age sixteen in Danboro were in "Management, Professional & Related Occupations." The remainder worked in "Sales & Office Occupations" (28.66 percent), "Service Occupations" (6.3 percent), "Production, Transportation & Material Moving Occupations" (5.72 percent), and "Construction, Extraction & Maintenance Occupations" (4.17 percent).

32. Tsing 2005.

33. R. Williams 1977:122.

34. According to the 2000 U.S. Census, Danboro was 83.8 percent White, 12.7 percent Asian (6.1 percent Chinese, 4.3 percent Indian, 0.9 percent Filipino, 0.7 percent Korean, 0.2 percent Vietnamese, and 0.4 percent Other Asian), 2.9 percent Hispanic or Latino, 2.1 percent Black or African-American, 0.04 percent American Indian or Alaskan Native, 0.01 percent Native Hawaiian or other Pacific Islander, 1.0 percent two or more races, and 0.5 percent some other race.

35. There has been much debate about what a suburb actually is and whether or not the post–World War II period was the time during which the suburbanization of the United States occurred, as is suggested by the periodizing in Jackson 1985, or whether it was actually a move away from the traditional suburb. Fishman (1987) argues the latter, with the post–World War II period ushering in the rise of the "technoburb" or "technocity"—a new kind of regional community that was largely self-sufficient and thus not sub-urban. See also Garreau 1991 on "edge cities" and Soja 1992 on "exopolis." See also Sharpe and Wallock 1994, as well as the reply articles, for commentary on these debates. Danboro, though, is sub-urban in the sense that 30.8 percent of the workers in town, according to the 2000 U.S. Census, make a daily commute to a central city for work. However, residents do not rely on the city for the majority of their other commercial needs, and many work in office parks in New Jersey.

36. Jackson 1985.

37. West 1998.

38. Brenner 2004.

39. Ferguson 2009:172. See also Brash 2011.

40. N. Rose 1999.

41. Ho 2009:26.

42. "IPO" stands for "initial public offering." An IPO occurs when a private company first offers shares for public purchase in the form of stocks.

43. Since the 1990s, there has been a surge of anthropological attention to the spatialization of political-economic shifts. See, for example, Appadurai 1996; Brash 2011; Caldeira 2000; Chesluk 2004; Collier 2011; de Koning 2009; Ferguson and Gupta 2002; Gregory 1998; Guano 2002; Low 1996; Ong 2006; Moore 1998; Tilton 2010; Watts 1992; Zaloom 2006; and Zhang 2010.

44. On gentrification, see, for example, Hartigan 1999; Peréz 2004; Tilton 2010; and B. Williams 1988. On public–private partnerships, see Chesluk 2004.

45. On a New Urbanist-like community, see A. Ross 1999. On gated communities, see Low 2003.

46. My focus here is on ethnographic studies. Of course towns like Danboro were very present in the policy and planning literature among theorists of the "metropolitan" grappling with the political, economic, and environmental

futures of metropolitan regions. See, for example, Fishman 1990; B. Katz and Bradley 1999; and Orfield 1997.

47. Blakely and Snyder 1999.

48. Blakely and Snyder 1999:1.

49. I use the word *regulative* here because of the influence of regulation theory on my thinking. Seeking to revive a more dynamic sense of the workings of capitalism and to step out of a deterministic understanding of structures, Regulation School theorists revisit the sense of history best encapsulated in Gramsci's (1971) analysis of Taylorism and Fordism. It is, as Lipietz (1993:99) points out, a conception of history as "a fabric of contradictory relations, *autonomous* in relation to one another, although overdetermining rather than 'reflecting' one another." Yet most regulation theorists (e.g., Harvey 1990) appreciate this dynamism solely in the realm of political economy, viewing cultural productions (whether public or intimate) as mere reflections of those "contradictory" relations rather than as agentive forces in shaping them. They tend to leave out a key piece of the puzzle for Gramsci: that the "new man" produced is part of the regulative dynamic. Gramsci's writings remind us that if we want to fully grasp the workings of capitalism, we must go beyond Marx's emphasis on the means and relations production. The ways that people are being and becoming consumers, citizens, and reproducers are just as crucial to the regulation of capitalism as are new ways of being workers, new means of production, and new regimes of accumulation. See also Althusser 1969.

50. I thank Roger Rouse for directing my attention to the productive resonances between Gramsci's (1971) "new man" and Foucault's (1979) "docile bodies."

51. For a discussion on the problems with the categories of "base" and "superstructure," see R. Williams 1977:75–82.

52. Gramsci 1971:199.

53. This messiness frustrated Gramsci, for his own time had a common sense that he found conservative and unproductive, which is why he pushed for "organic" intellectuals to create a grand narrative and assemblage to create a counter–common sense. Yet Gramsci is often misread in this regard, as if he suggested that common sense is *necessarily* problematic, as if all cultural logics and traditional values are politically limiting. On the contrary, his writings make it clear that there have been time periods, such as the eighteenth century, in which the common sense was close to his ideal.

54. Bourdieu 1977:72.

55. Bourdieu 1977:72.

56. Quoted in Colapietro 1989:80–83.

57. Bourdieu 1984:172. For a historical anthropology of the "forgotten" history that created the modern middle-class habitus in Sweden, see Frykman and Löfgren 1987.

58. Foucault 1972:28.

59. K. Stewart 2007.

60. Sapir 1949.

61. Stoler 1996.

62. Finn 1998:16.

63. Although Bourdieu's writings on habitus are often viewed as not providing a theory of change, his understanding of habitus is productive for thinking about how subtle reorientations in one moment can lead to new habitus in the next.

64. Daniel 1996.

65. Lipietz 1993:126.

66. R. Williams 1977:113.

67. Mills 1951:xv.

68. R. Williams 1977:131.

69. R. Williams 1977:132.

70. R. Williams 1977:134. Emphasis added.

71. R. Williams 1977:131.

72. See D. Ross 1984.

73. Poulantzas 1978.

74. Lustig 1986.

75. Coontz 1992:69. Emphasis added.

76. Coontz 1992:71.

77. Hoover 1989:36. Emphasis added.

78. Beard 1931:6–7.

79. Coontz 1992:80.

80. Newman 1993:2. Keep in mind, however, that Newman's discussion—like much analysis of the middle class in the United States—relies heavily on the experiences of baby boomers who grew up comfortably in the suburban middle class. (See, for example, Pfeil 1990.)

81. Berlant 2011.

82. N. Rose 1996b.

83. For uses of *late capitalism* at the time, see, for example, Jameson 1991 and Stephens 1995. For uses of *postmodern*, see Harvey 1990 and Jameson 1991. For uses of *post-Fordist*, see Steinmetz 1994. For uses of *globalization*, see Appadurai 1996. On the shift to *transnationalism*, see Basch, Glick Schiller, and Szanton Blanc 1993; and Rouse 1995. On *advanced liberalism*, see N. Rose 1996a.

84. See, for example, Bourgois 2003 [1996]; Comaroff and Comaroff 1999; Nash 1994; Ong 1988; and Scheper-Hughes 1993.

85. See, for example, Ong 1999.

86. Heiman, Liechty, and Freeman 2012:20.

87. The families in my study are not only those whom I knew through the camp. Others I came to know through them or from simply living in the area and meeting people through other means.

88. Bergmann 2009; Finn 2001; Finn and Nybell 2001; Nybell 2001; Nybell, Shook, and Finn 2009; Stephens 1995; Tilton 2010.

89. Ethnographic studies of youth growing upon in low-income neighborhoods demonstrate that peaceful social change requires much more than the empowerment of youth in disadvantaged positions. They, too, often run up against an unforgiving structure of people, policies, and practices that keeps them out. See, for example, Bergmann 2009; Bourgois 2003 [1996]; Chin 2001; Davidson 2011; Lareau 2003; MacLeod 1995; Pérez 2009; and Tilton 2010.

90. That is, unless that drive is deemed too intense.

91. Finn 2001; C. Katz 2012. There has been much discussion about the fact that there are no longer "children at risk" and "risky children" teetering on the edge of "normal" development. Practically all children have become suspect and pathologized, each in their own way. As Sharon Stephens has underscored, "the very notion of a 'healthy adolescence' is becoming an oxymoron . . . adolescence is pathology and is marketed as such across class, race, ethnic and gender lines—though, of course, not transcending these lines" (quoted in Finn and Nybell 2001:41).

92. Finn 2001. For a broader discussion of this "conflation of care and control" in regard to the younger members of our society, see Finn and Nybell 2001.

93. Heiman 2001.

94. C. Katz 2008.

95. I say "relatively privileged" because they are not of the bourgeoisie. Until recently, critical youth studies produced little research on those who "conform in many ways to social expectations" (Valentine, Skelton, and Chambers 1998:24). As such, most youth studies concerned with class had focused on youth who were working-class or otherwise marginalized. See, for example, Fine 1991; Foley 1990; Gaines 1990; Hebdige 1979; MacLeod 1995; McLaren 1989; McRobbie 1991; T. Rose 1994; and Willis 1977. Yet there has been a growing literature that has brought middle-class youth to the fore. See, for example, Davidson 2011; de Koning 2009; Eckert 1989; C. Katz 2001, 2008, 2012; Kenny 2000; Lareau 2003; Liechty 2003; Ortner 1998b; and Schielke 2012.

96. Critical youth studies also had a long history of studies that focused exclusively on youth, with little attention to what might be gleaned by bringing the daily lives of youth and adults into the same analytical framework.

97. Foucault 1984a:50. Emphasis added. Foucault, like Gramsci, is but one of many theorists to engage with and expound upon the Kantian philosophy of critique. Nicely capturing this understanding of the critic (as opposed to one who offers criticism) is Arendt's (1968:4–5) discussion of Benjamin's approach to being a literary critic. For a discussion on the tradition of cultural critique within the discipline of anthropology, see Marcus and Fisher 1986.

98. There has been much written on this problem with liberal ideology, particularly because of its embeddedness in Christian theology. As Nietzsche (1982:499–500) pointed out, the concept of "free will" was "essentially for the

purpose of punishment." That is, "Men were considered 'free' so that they might be judged and punished—so that they might become *guilty:* consequently, every act had to be considered as willed, and the origin of every act had to be considered as lying within the consciousness." This creates the political paradox explored by Connolly (1991), Mehta (1990), and others, whereby the locus of responsibility and blame is located within individuals rather than in their conditions of emergence and being.

99. Jay MacLeod (1995:270–302) writes about a similar discomfort. Incidentally, he, too, was a summer camp counselor among those with whom he eventually entered a research relationship.

100. There is a long history in the social sciences of using particular towns and the people living within them as sites and subjects for studies that seek to understand broader historical change and widespread emerging ways of being. The classics include Robert S. Lynd and Helen Merrell Lynd's *Middletown: A Study in Modern American Culture* (1929), William H. Whyte's *The Organization Man* (1956), and Herbert J. Gans's *Levittowners: Ways of Life and Politics in a New Suburban Community* (1967).

CHAPTER 2

1. Douglas 1975:111. See Turner 1969 for an ethnographic illustration of and philosophical musing on the ways that ritual joking taps into the complexities of ontological struggles.

2. The Verrazano Bridge connects southwestern Brooklyn to the eastern end of Staten Island. The Outerbridge Crossing connects the western end of Staten Island to central New Jersey. Profound regional shifts occurred once both bridges were complete, for they enabled a more direct flow of people and goods to central New Jersey.

3. I use double prepositions—such as "out to Danboro"—throughout the book in order to best represent how people talked about their movement between locations. This colloquial language is indicative of the sentiment that the move "to" Danboro was also about getting "out" of Brooklyn.

4. There is an extensive literature on the "urban renewal" policies of the postwar period and their effects. See, for example, Beauregard 2003; Caro 1975; Fullilove 2004; Gregory 1998; Jackson 1985:190–230; and Jacobs 1961.

5. Rieder 1985:79.

6. For a perspective on the ebbs and flows of migration within and in and out of Brooklyn, see Suarez 1999:98–121. By the 2010s, of course, white migration *to* Brooklyn had become so extensive, in large part through gentrification, that according to the 2010 U.S. Census, whites had become the largest racial group in Brooklyn.

7. The term *post-urban* is used largely in regard to cities like Detroit, which are no longer urban in the way that they used to be. While towns like Danboro are clearly not post-urban in this regard, the people who largely make up Danboro left New York City during a time when people feared that the city was en route to becoming post-urban. I thus use this term not in regard to architectural landscape, but rather in regard to a sensibility. My use of *post-urban* also should not be confused with the term *exurban*, which traditionally refers to communities located in rural areas beyond the suburbs, largely made up of wealthy people who intentionally relocated far enough out of the city to make daily commutes back to it unfeasible. For a witty portrayal of "exurbanites" and their struggles to maintain a sense of cosmopolitanism amid the pastoral, see Spectorsky 1955.

8. On racial politics of class formation in the United States, see Roediger 1991 on the working class and Brodkin 1998 on the middle class.

9. Jews, Italians, and Irish continue to move to Danboro from Brooklyn, though in smaller numbers than in years past. According to the ancestry figures in the 2000 U.S. Census, those who make up 10 percent or more of the population in Danboro are: Italian (20.14 percent), Russian (10.75 percent), Irish (10.64 percent), and Polish (10.56 percent). There are no census figures for religious identifications, even ones like "Jewish" that are often viewed as an ancestral marker; there is therefore no way to assess the exact numbers of Jews in Danboro. One can assume, however, that the majority of those of Polish descent are Jewish; the Russian number, however, is more difficult to assess since many Russians moving into Danboro in recent years are not Jewish. But if the Russian percentage is adjusted down to account for recent non-Jewish arrivals, and the Polish figured is added along with a percentage or two from ancestries (all under 1 percent) that are likely to include Jews (e.g., Austrian, Eastern European, German, Hungarian, Israeli, Syrian, etc.), the percentage of Jews in Danboro is perhaps somewhere around 20 percent.

10. I also decided not to include ethnic markers because, as Sherry Ortner (1998a:4) notes, when ethnic categories are introduced in the United States, "[t] hey tend to swamp everything else." That is, "The [ethnicity] of the group becomes the dominant fact and the explanatory principle, whether the author wishes it or not" (1998a:6). Granted, some researchers of class find that they have no choice but to include ethnicity as a central analytical category. Ortner confronted this while conducting research for her 2003 book, *New Jersey Dreaming: Capital, Culture, and the Class of '58*. During her interviews, which were largely among Jews, she found that when she tried to ask about class (even when she made no mention of Jewishness), "the centrality of Jewishness to these people's lives and talk was overwhelming" (1998a:6). My project is a different project, in part because class *identity* was not a central question. I sought to understand how class is *lived* in people's everyday lives, so I did not ask directly about class. Yet there was a category of identity that was "overwhelming" during my

fieldwork: being post-Brooklyn. In some ways, the fact that I have placed ethnicity in the background follows in the footsteps of scholars, such as di Leonardo 1984, Gans 1962, Steinberg 1981, and Wilson 1978, who have argued that the material and ideological conditions of people's lives undergird much of what is often referred to as their "ethnicity" or "race."

11. R. Williams 1977:122.

12. R. Williams 1977:123.

13. R. Williams 1977:123.

14. On the Peircean notion of "collateral experience," or the observations and experiences that enable us to interpret the signs that we encounter, see Shapiro 1983:36–37.

15. Geertz 1993.

16. Foucault 1972:28.

17. As Bakhtin (1981:259) notably comments, "verbal art" is informative not only through the content that is uttered; linguistic forms of speech acts and events also are inextricable aspects of the means through which thoughts, perspectives, and affective states are revealed.

18. I had heard many people in town refer to those whom they followed out to Danboro as "pioneers." Of course, a "pioneer" from the perspective of a kid from Brooklyn is one who lives among farms on land that used to be a farm, rather than one who lives on farmland that used to be communal Native American land.

19. R. Williams 1973.

20. For a discussion of the ways that the city in eighteenth-century London came to be seen as an enemy of the newly forming nuclear bourgeois family, thus creating the cultural climate for the origins of the Anglo-American suburb, see Fishman 1987:18–38.

21. New Jersey Transit buses are geared toward travel to neighboring towns or to New York City, rather than within Danboro itself.

22. For a reevaluation of the planning traditions in the United States, see Fishman 2000.

23. There has been a growing literature on the increasing diversity of the suburbs. See, for example, Baxandall and Ewen 2000:239–50; Fong 1994; and Kalita 2003. At the same time, there has been a growth of historical studies on suburbia that demonstrate that the suburbs have long been more diverse along the lines of race and class than previously represented. See, for example, Nicolaides 2002 and Wiese 2004.

24. Berger 1972:8–9. Emphasis added.

25. Milldale was hit hard by the loss of local manufacturing industries in the 1960s and 1970s. In the years that followed, its downtown commercial business was greatly diminished by the influx of strip malls and large regional malls. See Cohen 2003:257–89 and Jackson 1985:257–61 for discussions on the effects of

shopping centers on central business districts. These suburban downtowns, however, began to gentrify during the late 1990s, increasingly drawing suburbanites back to suburban downtowns.

26. Nader 1969:292.

27. See Babcock and Bosselman 1973; Cohen 2003; Danielson 1976; Davidoff and Brooks 1976; Kirp, Dwyer, and Rosenthal 1995; Perin 1977; and Toll 1969.

28. See Kirp, Dwyer, and Rosenthal 1995 for a discussion on the battles for fair housing legislation in New Jersey, particularly the Mount Laurel cases.

29. See Blakely and Snyder 1999; and Low 2001, 2003.

30. Brodkin 1998:165.

31. According to the 2000 U.S. Census, of the 36,398 people in Danboro, there were 752 (or just over 2 percent) who were "Black or African American Alone" and 354 (or just under 1 percent) who were "Two or More Races."

32. There were always jokes made among groups of friends about people who were black or Mexican. One afternoon during prom season, I was sitting in the sun with a bunch of girls. They were in the grade below Lauren. One of the girls decided that she wanted to go to an Italian ices stand in downtown Milldale. As we all got up to get ready to leave, one of the girls suggested that we put shirts on over our bathing suits since there are so many "Sexicans" in downtown Milldale.

33. On nostalgia and longing, see Coontz 1992; Ivy 1995; Jameson 1991; K. Stewart 1988; and S. Stewart 1984.

34. Seremetakis 1994.

35. Bourdieu 1984:200.

36. Veblen 1967 [1899].

37. For Hegel's discussion on the dialectic of "lordship and bondage," see Hegel 1977:111–19.

38. It is important to note here that buying a house in which one cannot yet afford to furnish all the rooms is not uncommon among young families who hope to grow into their home financially over the years. What Nancy and Linda are referring to here are families whose concerns about the display of class appearances are the primary force driving their desires for their home and for how they take care of it.

39. Here Nancy was referring to the lyrics from the theme song of the 1970s TV show *The Jeffersons*. It is revealing that her free association in that moment brought to mind a show about the racial politics of class from the perspective of upwardly mobile blacks.

40. Gaines 1990:98.

41. On "panopticism," see Foucault 1979:195–228. Foucault's discussion on the Panopticon addresses that which is orchestrated on the part of a state, designed *intentionally* to create power that is both "visible and unverifiable." The dynamics that I discuss in this book are largely unintended, despite the fact that they are extraordinarily powerful and are productive disciplinary modes of capitalist

regulation. See also Whyte 1956 on the "practiced eye" in a suburban community in which consumption was supposed to be "inconspicuous."

CHAPTER 3

1. For an article that uses a variety of terms for these houses somewhat interchangeably, including *tract mansions,* see Harden 2002. See also Hayden 2003:190–91.

2. Incidentally, the land on which Tarragon Hills was being built was right next to the development that Stu and Linda fell in love with (but could not afford) when they were first looking at houses in Danboro during the late 1970s.

3. For people who played their cards right in Danboro and did not take out more than one other mortgage on their home, the increasing property values in town enabled them to be in the extraordinary position during the late 1990s of paying around three hundred dollars per month in mortgage payments for a four-bedroom home. This kind of situation is one of the great financial equalizers in towns like Danboro.

4. We often think of gentrification as a process that takes place when those with capital (developers or individuals) optimize their profit on land that had been previously devalorized. Yet Neil Smith (1996:68) notes that the rent gap required for gentrification and its displacements also can occur on land that had not been previously devalorized, such as when states loosen policies in regard to land use or when there is, for other reasons, "rapid and sustained inflation." The latter was the case in Danboro during the housing bubble.

5. The social, political, and economic effects of these architectural shifts in suburbia have yet to acquire a name that encapsulates the complexities of the transformation. Perhaps we could call this dynamic *pageantrification.* Drawing on *pageantry* as the root, this term highlights the pomp and elaborate class presentation that are intimately bound up in the architecture of this type of housing.

6. Danboro Township Code, Land Use Development (1999), §84–58.A: "Fences hereafter erected, altered or reconstructed in any zone in the Township of Danboro shall be open fences not to exceed three (3) feet in height above ground level when located in a front yard area." In the code, gates are subsumed within the term *fences.*

7. The Zoning Board of Adjustment is made up of citizens from the township who are appointed by the township's council. The zoning board hears requests on the part of individual homeowners and commercial applicants who want permission for a variance or exception to (or an interpretation of) the Danboro Township Land Use Development Code. Individual homeowners can come before the zoning board without legal representation, but commercial applicants

must have legal counsel. Since this couple was still in the process of purchasing the property, the property was still under the ownership of the developer of Tarragon Hills.

8. The county of which Danboro is a part, and New Jersey in general, do not tend to hail gates and gated communities as treasures of their municipalities, unlike what you see in Los Angeles or São Paulo, for example.

9. Perin 1977:179.

10. On the invention of the American lawn by Olmsted, see Pollan (1991:58–61). For a discussion of Olmsted's efforts to limit the height of fences during the early years of restrictive covenants, see Fogelson (2005:92).

11. Caldeira 2000:291–96.

12. Danboro Township Zoning Board of Adjustment, Regular Meeting, March 24, 1999.

13. My semiotic approach draws heavily on the writings of C. S. Peirce, particularly his attention to the iconic quality of signs and their relationship to subjectivity (Peirce 1955; Colapietro 1989). My analysis here, as in my analysis of other objects through the book, resonates with Latour's (2005) and Bennett's (2010) approaches to things.

14. Gramsci 1971:198–99.

15. Hanson 2007.

16. Bakhtin 1981:282.

17. Bakhtin 1981:276.

18. What I am addressing here is what Bakhtin calls "heteroglossia," or the determination of meaning within the matrix of social and historical conditions at play. See Andrea L. Smith (2004) on the resonance between heteroglossia and Gramsci's notion of common sense. The dynamic that I am addressing here also resonates with Warner's (2002) discussion on publics, particularly the way that people can "know"—even if not consciously—the moment in which they are no longer part of a "dominant public"; this type of momentary emergence of a counterpublic, even if in existence only for a brief time—as was the case during the zoning board debate—can still be quite agentive. See also Yeh (2012) on classes and publics.

19. Pollan 1991:58–61.

20. Anderson 1983.

21. Fogelson 2005:92.

22. There is a great likeness between restrictive covenants of the nineteenth century and contemporary public land-use zoning codes, because the latter were built on the tradition of the former. Property owners in the nineteenth century were on a "quest for [the] permanence" (Fogelson 2005) of property values at a time of volatile markets, industrial urbanism, land speculation, and the rise of "new money," and so developed covenants and deed restrictions modeled on those in England from the eighteenth and nineteenth centuries amid the breakup

of the commons (McKenzie 1994). Because mid-nineteenth-century subdivisions in the United States were prohibitive in cost to all but the elite, the main concern was the actions of one's class peers.

23. Blakely and Snyder 1999; Low 2003.

24. Peck and Tickell 2002.

25. On gentrification, see, for example, N. Smith 1996; N. Smith and Williams 1986; B. Williams 1988; and Zukin 1987. On the expansion of private homeowner associations, McKenzie 1994 and A. Ross 1999. On the militarization of urban space, M. Davis 1992. On the incursion of public-private partnerships into public domains of governance, Chesluk 2004 and Lipsitz 2006.

26. McKenzie 1994.

27. The continued importance of public governance is recognized in research on gentrification in urban cores, where city halls continue to be viewed as fundamental sites of struggle, even as public-private partnerships proliferate. While beyond the scope of the discussion here, it is also likely that comparable concerns about physical and discursive displacement will be (or already are) taking place within private homeowner associations, thus making homeowner association meetings an equally compelling ethnographic site for exploring these issues. For a classic ethnography of the ways that broader forces of social change are struggled over in the context of municipal law, see Greenhouse, Yngvesson, and Engel 1994.

28. Aside from a few anthropologists who have done work on zoning, such as Constance Perin's (1977) work on suburban land use in the 1970s and Edward LiPuma and Sarah Keene Meltzoff's (1997) study of land-use planning in South Florida in the 1980s and early 1990s, the analysis of zoning has largely been the domain of planners, historians, geographers, and policy makers. Yet with anthropology's increasing attention to technologies of space making as neoliberal strategies, zoning technologies have come to the fore as a key site of inquiry (Ong 2006).

29. Frug 1999:144.

30. There is an extensive literature on exclusionary zoning. My discussion in this section draws largely on Babcock 1966; Babcock and Bosselman 1973; Cohen 2003; Davidoff and Brooks 1976; Kirp, Dwyer, and Rosenthal 1995; Perin 1977; and Toll 1969.

31. Babcock and Bosselman 1973:28–30.

32. Quoted in Kirp, Dwyer, and Rosenthal 1995:65.

33. Kirp, Dwyer, and Rosenthal 1995:66.

34. Kirp, Dwyer, and Rosenthal 1995:61.

35. Babcock 1966.

36. Mehta 1990.

37. For a discussion of the Mount Laurel cases, which are viewed as being "the *Roe v. Wade* of fair housing, the *Brown v. Board of Education* of exclusionary zoning," see Kirp, Dwyer, and Rosenthal 1995. For a discussion of the persistence

of snob zoning because of the prevalence of "home rule," see Duncan and Duncan 1997.

38. Locke 1980 [1690]:52. Emphasis in original.

39. Frug 1999:145. The fact that reining in property owners is a fundamental aspect of liberal ideology is not often highlighted in public discourse in the United States. Hoover, who popularized the notion of American individualism, also vigorously promoted the idea of zoning ordinances under local control. By the mid-1920s—largely on account of his doing—the United States was proudly proclaiming itself a land of rugged individualists, even though half the states had adopted zoning laws based on Hoover's federal model, many of which served the interests of property owners. This was not seen as an ideological contradiction since support for citywide ordinances was largely articulated as being in the interest of advancing "general welfare," a catchphrase of the Progressive Era.

40. Dobriner 1963.

41. See Hayden (2003:188–89) for a discussion of other reluctant suburbs in the "rural fringe."

42. All of the people described in this chapter have been given pseudonyms, despite the fact they are public figures and/or were speaking at a public event, in order to enable town anonymity.

43. A flag lot is a piece of property with a narrow piece of land (the pole) that leads back to a rectangular-shaped section of the property (the flag). Such parcels also are referred to as "pork chop lots," a phrase suggestive of the process of carving up farmland into lots that look like pork chops. See Hayden 2004:78.

44. Danboro Township Code, Land Use Development (1999), §84–8B(2)(c). Emphasis added.

45. Danboro Township Code, Land Use Development (1999), §84–8B(1). Emphasis added. This language in the code reflects the majority opinions written for two key United States Supreme Court decisions at the dawn of municipal zoning. The first, *Village of Euclid, Ohio v. Ambler Realty Co.* in 1926, established the constitutionality of zoning vis-à-vis the Fourteenth Amendment right to due process of the law in regard to the "taking" of property, as long as "general welfare" was at stake and the enforcement of the law did not create "practical difficulty or unnecessary hardship" for property owners. The second, *Nectow v. City of Cambridge* in 1928, reigned in governmental powers that were arbitrary in their use of zoning regulations that did not "bear a substantial relation to the public health, safety, morals, or general welfare." Together, these two decisions granted local municipalities constitutional power to zone, and their zoning boards the authority to determine the fine line between "general welfare" and "unnecessary hardship."

46. Lawyers do not have to be sworn in to legal proceedings since they are considered officers of the court. Developers like Jay, on the other hand, need to go through the process of being sworn in like any other nonlawyer at a legal proceeding.

47. The wetlands requirements are part of the North American Wetlands Conservation Act. Wetlands are swamps or floodplains that developers in the past used to fill in to build residential and commercial properties. The conservation act made it illegal to do so, for environmental reasons (Rome 2001). Developers often create unusual parcels, like this flag lot, in order to maximize the development of their land. Although other aspects of the optimization of this property proved controversial, it is noteworthy that the developers were never questioned about the framing of the "hardship" as owing to environmental regulations—and not to their own desire to optimize the land.

48. Danboro Township Code, Land Use Development (1999), §84–1I.

49. Danboro Township Code, Land Use Development (1999), §84–2F.

50. Take for example, the following moment with Stu. In the previous chapter, I discussed a part of an interview with him in which he described the ethnic makeup of the people at the different stops that his bus to work makes as it heads to New York City. He was comfortable pointing out the towns that had a lot of "Orientals" and "Indians." But when it came time to refer to people at the stop in Milldale, he simply referred to them as "people from Milldale." I wanted him explicitly to say what he meant by this coded language, so I asked him, "And what are they?" He looked at me with a friendly smirk. Smiling as he refused to give in, he steadfastly and slowly reiterated, "They are people from Milldale." Eventually, later on in our discussion, he referred to them as "blacks."

51. Bakhtin 1981:276.

52. Bakhtin 1981:294. See also Derrida (1988:18) on our inability to "govern the entire scene and system of an utterance." While my discussion here focuses on coded language, *all* utterances have the potential for alternative interpretations. The intentionality driving our speech acts can never fully determine their effects. For a similar claim, see Foucault 1984b.

53. Kirp, Dwyer, and Rosenthal 1995:66

54. On various "techniques of optimization," see Ong 2006.

55. Warner 2002:103.

56. Giddens 1979:72.

57. Goffman 1981:134.

58. Their brief connection could be the start of what Rouse (1995:361) calls "contingent coalitions," or "hybrid vehicles of collective agency that, while often dominated by segments of a single class, link people from a variety of positions."

59. Daniel 1996:189–92.

60. Lefebvre 1991 [1974].

61. Despite suggestions that the economic crisis that began in 2008 could bring the end to neoliberalism and neoliberal space making and usher in a new New Deal or a neo-Keynesian era, the coming years likely will continue to witness the presence of neoliberal policies and practices alongside postwar liberal logics. All scales of government—federal, state, and local—will continue to pro-

vide fruitful sites in which to unearth microprocesses of meaning making and to theorize how anxieties, aesthetics, and moral logics shape the built form of everyday life.

CHAPTER 4

1. Bourdieu 1984:170. Emphasis added.

2. Sacks 1989:542.

3. On the everyday performance of social identity, see Goffman 1959.

4. Wrigley 1995.

5. Bourdieu 1984:200.

6. See Rollins 1985 and Brodkin 1998:18. There is an extensive academic scholarship on maids, servants, nannies, and other forms of domestic "help" that explores the experiences and implications of these intimate employer–employee relationships. See also, for example, Dill 1994; Goldstein 2003; Hansen 1989; Hondagneu-Sotelo 2001; Parreñas 2001; Romero 1992; Stoler 1995, 1996; and Stoler and Strassler 2000. For a comparable perspective in luxury service work, see Sherman 2007.

7. Ironically, many of these domestic service workers lived in neighborhoods in Brooklyn that families in Danboro had left behind in the late 1970s and early 1980s. One family I knew, whose ailing grandfather was living in their home, hired a Haitian health-care worker who they later found out lived on the same block in Brooklyn where one of their cousins had grown up.

8. I deal with the question of whether or not SUVs are actually "safe" in chapter 5.

9. See Schor 1998, 2004. See also Quart 2003 for a journalistic account of the marketing industry's intense focus on teens and tweens in the late 1990s and early 2000s.

10. A large portion of what Sam and I talked about during our afternoons together related to Nintendo games. Doug, too, said that most of what he talked about with Sam was video games. Since Sam was such a little kid, it was a way to relate to his brother. When Doug wanted to do something nice for Sam, he would rent him a video game.

11. Jacobson 1999.

12. Jacobson 1999.

13. For a more extensive discussion of this historical shift, see Jacobson 2004.

14. On the centrality of consumer goods in children's longings to belong, see Pugh 2009.

15. Douglas 1966:136.

16. Rabinow 1984:11.

17. de Certeau 1984.

18. Bourdieu 1977:90. For a more detailed discussion on the home and how "the meaning objectified in things or parts of space is fully yielded only through practices structured according to the same schemes that are organized in relation to them (and vice versa)," see Bahloul 1996 and Bourdieu 1990. For an excellent edited collection on the relationship between adult concerns and children's spaces, both inside and outside of the home, see Gutman and de Coninck-Smith 2008.

19. For a discussion of Heidegger's notion of "being-in-the-world," see Dreyfus 1991.

20. See, for example, Davidson 2011 and Lareau 2003. For a broader discussion of the problem of busyness, see the special "Busyness" issue of *Social Research* (Mack 2005).

21. The *Wall Street Journal* began using the tagline "Adventures in Capitalism" in a series of ads in the spring of 1999.

22. Quoted in Jackson 1985:231.

23. C. Katz 2012:178–79. See also C. Katz 2008.

24. For a linguistic anthropology discussion of racial remarks that are uttered subtextually through "inferences that the literal content of a text or an utterance invites," see Hill 2008:33.

25. According to the 2000 U.S. Census, the median household income in Danboro was $101,322; in Milldale Township, it was $77,185.

26. Bettie 2003.

27. On the details of the case of the "Morristown Madam," see "Madam of Bordello in Mansion Is Given Probation," *New York Times*, 12 May 1999, 4(B).

28. White 2000:64. Here, White is drawing on Foucault's (1978) thinking on "technologies of speaking."

29. White 2000:72.

30. White 2000:83.

31. Gluckman 1963:313.

32. Simmel 1950:405.

33. As Simmel (1950:406) elaborates, "The stranger is close to us, in so far as we feel between him and ourselves common features of a national, social, occupational, or generally human, nature. He is far from us, insofar as these common features extend beyond him and us, and connect us only because they connect a great many people."

34. Wrigley 1995.

35. Daniel 1996:191.

CHAPTER 5

1. Bradsher 1998.

2. Bradsher 2002:132–33.

3. Gramsci 1971.

4. See, for example, the following editorials: "Catching Up with SUVs" 1998; "Toward Cleaner SUVs" 1999; and "Cleaning Up the Big Cars" 1999; as well as the following articles and books: Barbanel 2000; Bradsher 1999a, 1999b, 1999c, 1999d, 2000a, 2000b, 2002; Cobb 1999; and Gladwell 2004.

5. C. Katz 2001:55 on nanny cams. For a comparable perspective on gates and gated communities, see, for example, Blakely and Snyder 1999; Caldeira 2000; and Low 2003.

6. See, for example, Fernandez 1991; Lakoff and Johnson 1980; and Martin 1987. This work builds on the long tradition in anthropology of cultural analysis of "dominant symbols" (Turner 1967) or "key symbols" (Ortner 1973).

7. Daniel 1996:102.

8. Daniel 1996:102.

9. Quoted in Haley 1993:98.

10. For a discussion of Stephen Pepper's concept of a "root metaphor," see Ortner 1973 and Turner 1974. For an example of the use of SUV-as-metaphor, now quite common, see D. Mitchell 2005.

11. Bradsher 2002:ix.

12. The culmination of Bradsher's years of investigative reporting on these issues was published in a 2002 book, entitled *High and Mighty: SUVs—The World's Most Dangerous Vehicles and How They Got That Way*. The majority of my discussions in this section starting with the fourth paragraph are drawn from this book.

13. On the development of car culture in the United States, see, for example, Flink 1975 and Jackson 1985:157–71, 246–71. For classic critiques of increasing dependence on automobility, see Keats 1958 and Mumford 1953:234–46. For ethnographic and cultural studies perspectives on car cultures, see Best 2006; Lutz and Lutz Fernandez 2010; and Miller 2001. For critical geography perspectives on automobility, see Featherstone 2004 and Urry 2004. For a discussion of the legal machinations that enabled cars to avoid the label of "dangerous instrumentality," thus setting some of the conditions for the uphill battle discussed here on the part of regulators and politicians, see Jain 2004.

14. On Fordism, see Gramsci 1971:279–318 and Harvey 1990:125–40.

15. See Hand 1997 for a discussion of the problems and pleasures that New Jersey teenagers faced in the early years of suburban development based on automobility. The fact that the automobile is the lynchpin for communities like Danboro means that teenagers are dependent upon other people to get them around until they are old enough to drive and have access to a car. It is this dynamic that has created the conditions for the sense of euphoria that teens like Stephanie and Wendi feel when they are finally able to drive themselves around town.

16. Jackson 1985:164.

17. Jackson 1985:164.

18. Jackson 1985:248.

19. Quoted in Jackson 1985:249.

20. Bradsher 2002:23.

21. Quoted in Bradsher 2002:25.

22. Bradsher 2002:28–29.

23. Bradsher 2002:xiv.

24. Quoted in Bradsher 2002:27.

25. Quoted in Bradsher 2002:34.

26. Bradsher 2002:81.

27. Bradsher 2002:123.

28. Quoted in Bradsher 2002:97.

29. For a discussion of the ways that mobility is constituted through new technologies and movements through space, including that of SUVs, see Jain 2002.

30. Bradsher 2002:xix.

31. The other unpredicted offshoot of a rugged image that implies freedom and protection has been the popularity of SUVs among the hip-hop community. Bradsher does not address this issue, but I would add that this not only has helped the sales of SUVs. It also expanded the flexible semiotic power of these vehicles to index lifestyles beyond escape from domestic embeddedness. They also can evoke other racial-spatial locations, like urban neighborhoods. The irony of course is that many suburban youth enjoy this indexicality of "ghetto" bravado while driving around listening to rap, blaring out an iconic reminder of what their parents left behind in their old Brooklyn neighborhoods. On the notion of "wiggers" (i.e., white emulators of black hip-hop culture), see Roediger 1998.

32. When Bradsher (2002:351) was at a retirement lunch with reporters at Henry Ford's Fair Lane estate, the outgoing vice president for safety and environment and her successor both said that the best vehicle for teens was a compact car like the Ford Tempo or a midsize sedan. This is what the outgoing vice president bought for her own child.

33. Wendi's use of *truck* may be a bit confusing here. Sport-utility vehicles are often called "trucks" in everyday speech, in part because they are technically categorized under "light trucks."

34. Bradsher 2002:345.

35. Gillespie and Rockland 1989:191.

36. Ehrenreich 1989:15.

37. Allport 1954:22.

38. Medin 1989:1477.

39. Allport 1954:23.

40. Medin 1989:1476. My thinking on essentialism here has been particularly influenced by Hirschfeld 1996.

41. Another avenue for exploring this paradox is through a framework that focuses on the social production of "risk," as exemplified in Douglas 1985 and Douglas and Wildavsky 1982.

42. See Colapietro 1989 and Peirce 1955 for a discussion of the subtle developmental production of habits and their relationship to subjectivities.

43. See Gramsci 1971:279–318.

44. For Gramsci's discussion of Ford's strategy of providing his workers with high wages so that they could afford to buy Ford vehicles, which in turn enabled the Ford company and the capitalist system as a whole to once again flourish, see Gramsci 1971:310–13. See also Debord 1995 [1967] on the transformation of workers into consumers.

45. Daniel 1996:190.

46. On consumption and citizenship, see, for example, Cahn 2008; Cohen 2003; Comaroff and Comaroff 2000; Fernandes 2006; Lipsitz 2006; Lomnitz 2003; O'Dougherty 2002; Patico 2008; Rouse 1995; and Zaloom 2009.

47. "Marge Simpson in 'Screaming Yellow Honkers.'" 1999. Chrysler commissioned a secret study in early 1998 out of concern that people might not buy SUVs because of the harm that they inflict on others. Their survey found that owners of the most menacing SUVs models (particularly the Dodge Durango) actually expressed very little concern about the harm that their vehicle could wreak on others (Bradsher 2002:446n2). Admittedly, though, as Bradsher (2002:108) notes, it has been difficult for researchers to truly tap into "the amount of thought Americans give to the people they hit during collisions."

48. See Mehta 1990 for a discussion of the core theoretical underpinnings of liberal ideology, which he contends are at the root of the exclusionary nature of liberalism.

49. Ehrenreich 1989:15.

50. Bradsher 2002:xix.

51. A. Davis 1997:322. See also Lowe and Lloyd's (1997:25–26) discussion of Davis's work.

CHAPTER 6

1. According to the 2000 U.S. Census, the following were the median household incomes in the towns in the district: Great Farms ($109,190), Danboro ($101,322), Westbrook ($83,575), Milldale Township ($77,185), Bowen ($68,069), Ellenville ($57,557), Lenape Crossing ($48,889), and Milldale Borough ($48,654).

2. Brenner 2004.

3. N. Rose 1996b.

4. Particularly influential in my thinking on shifts in power and authority through language practices is Goffman's notion of "footing," or the "change in the alignment that we take up to ourselves and . . . others . . . in the way we manage the production or reception of an utterance" (Goffman 1981:128).

5. Hill 2008:41.

6. Hill 2008:33. See also Hartigan 1999 and 2010.

7. For a discussion of the intersection of racial sentiments, middle-class anxieties, and public school education amid neoliberal reforms in Buenos Aires at this same time (the late 1990s), see Guano 2003.

8. For an excellent discussion of the ways that practices and subject positions are racialized, see Frankenberg 1993.

9. Danboro is the most northern town in the district, thereby providing the shortest commute to New York City, which is why suburbanization in the district blossomed there first.

10. Danboro, Westbrook, and Milldale Borough were the only towns in the late 1990s in which all students from the town attended the high school that bore their town's name (i.e., unless they chose to attend one of the special programs located in another high school, as Julia had done). In other towns, teenagers were sent to a variety of schools. Many students in Bowen were zoned for Milldale Township High School—geographically the closest other school in the district. Students living in Milldale Township on the border of Milldale Borough were zoned for Milldale High School. All students in Great Farms attended Danboro High School. Students from the little town of Ellenville all attended Westbrook High School, and all students from the other little town, Lenape Crossing, attended either Bowen High School or Milldale Township High School.

11. Gramsci 1971:377.

12. According to the 2000 U.S. Census, the populations of the towns in the district were as follows: Bowen (48,903), Danboro (36,398), Westbrook (33,423), Milldale Township (31,537), Great Farms (12,331), Milldale Borough (10,976), Ellenville (1,764), and Lenape Crossing (1,587).

13. The Milldale Regional High School District did receive some funding relief after the fact. For a discussion of a lawsuit against the state of New Jersey during this time, which sought to redress the burden of property taxes, see Kladko 1998.

14. The attendance at these meetings was much smaller (by at least half) than at the public forums held by the consultants: Bowen High School (144), Milldale Township High School (76), Milldale High School (125), Westbrook High School (215), Danboro High School (374). At these meetings, flyers were handed out for people to provide further feedback. These forms were also (supposedly) mailed to people in the district, although I never received one, nor did many people.

15. The dates for the meetings were as follows: Bowen High School on January 21, 1998; Milldale Township High School on January 22, 1998; Milldale High School ("the Mill") on January 26, 1998; Westbrook High School on January 27, 1998; and Danboro High School on January 28, 1998.

16. These meetings took place near the start of my fieldwork, and unfortunately I did not yet have the proper technology for recording in a vast space. I instead took careful notes, which I elaborated on each night when I got home.

The direct quotes from these meetings are therefore from my notes, and so they are as "direct" as quotes can be under those circumstances.

17. Chiles 1997.

18. For a discussion of the racial implications of the use of *you people* during the Mount Laurel zoning cases in New Jersey that led to fair-housing laws, see Kirp, Dwyer, and Rosenthal 1995:65–69.

19. My use of *framing* here is particularly influenced by Bateson's use of the analogy of the picture frame, wherein the "message intended to order or organize the perception of the viewer says, 'Attend to what is within and do not attend to what is outside'" (Bateson 1972:187).

20. Students were eventually provided representation on the task force.

21. Aggarwal 2013.

22. Bakhtin 1981:294.

23. In order to maintain the anonymity of the towns, I have not included citations for the newspaper articles quoted in this section.

CHAPTER 7

1. Bourdieu 1984:200.

2. Berlant 2011.

3. R. Williams 1977:121. Emphasis added.

4. Berlant 2011:19.

5. Bourdieu 1984:172.

6. Gramsci 1971:199.

7. Heiman 2007.

8. See, for example, Dunham-Jones and Williamson 2009 and Williamson 2013.

9. For Gramsci's discussion on the political thought that inspired him to use the programmatic slogan "Pessimism of the intelligence, optimism of the will," see Gramsci 1971:173–75.

References

Aggarwal, Ujju. 2013. *Public Education in the United States: The Production of a Normative Cultural Logic of Inequality through Choice*. PhD dissertation. Graduate Faculty in Anthropology, City University of New York.

Allport, Gordon W. 1954. *The Nature of Prejudice*. New York: Doubleday Anchor Books.

Althusser, Louis. 1969. "Contradiction and Overdetermination." In *For Marx*, pp. 89–128. New York: Vintage Books.

Anderson, Benedict. 1983. *Imagined Communities: Reflections on the Origins and Spread of Nationalism*. London: Verso.

Appadurai, Arjun. 1996. *Modernity at Large: Cultural Dimensions of Globalization*. Minneapolis: University of Minnesota Press.

Arendt, Hannah. 1968. "Introduction: Walter Benjamin, 1892–1940." In *Illuminations: Walter Benjamin*, edited by Hannah Arendt, pp. 1–55. New York: Schocken Books.

Babcock, Richard. 1966. *The Zoning Game: Municipal Practices and Policies*. Madison: University of Wisconsin Press.

Babcock, Richard, and Fred Bosselman. 1973. *Exclusionary Zoning: Land Use Regulation and Housing in the 1970s*. New York: Praeger.

Bahloul, Joëlle. 1996. *The Architecture of Memory: A Jewish-Muslim Household in Colonial Algeria, 1937–1962*. Cambridge: Cambridge University Press.

Bakhtin, Mikhail M. 1981. *The Dialogic Imagination: Four Essays by M.M. Bakhtin*, edited by M. Holquist; translated by C. Emerson and M. Holquist. Austin: University of Texas Press.

Barnabel, Josh. 2000. "Fatal Explorer Accidents Involving Bad Tires Soared in '99." *New York Times*, 19 September, pp. C1, C16.

Basch, Linda, Nina Glick Schiller, and Cristina Szanton Blanc. 1993. *Nations Unbound: Transnational Projects, Postcolonial Predicaments, and Deterritorialized States*. New York: Gordon and Breach.

Bateson, Gregory. 1972. "A Theory of Play and Fantasy." In *Steps to an Ecology of Mind*, pp. 177–93. New York: Ballantine Books.

Baxandall, Rosalyn, and Elizabeth Ewen. 2000. *Picture Windows: How the Suburbs Happened*. New York: Basic Books.

Beard, Charles A. 1931. *The Myth of Rugged American Individualism*. New York: John Day Company.

Beauregard, Robert. 2003. *Voices of Decline: The Postwar Fate of U.S. Cities*. New York: Routledge.

———. 2006. *When America Became Suburban*. Minneapolis: University of Minnesota Press.

Bennett, Jane. 2010. *Vibrant Matter: A Political Ecology of Things*. Durham, NC: Duke University Press.

Berger, John. 1972. *Ways of Seeing*. London: British Broadcasting Corporation and Penguin Books.

Bergmann, Luke. 2009. *Getting Ghost: Two Young Lives and the Struggle for the Soul of an American City*. New York: New Press.

Berlant, Lauren. 2011. *Cruel Optimism*. Durham, NC: Duke University Press.

Best, Amy L. 2006. *Fast Cars, Cool Rides: The Accelerating World of Youth and Their Cars*. New York: NYU Press.

Bettie, Julie. 2003. *Women without Class: Girls, Race, and Identity*. Berkeley: University of California Press.

Blakely, Edward J., and Mary Gail Snyder. 1999. *Fortress America: Gated Communities in the United States*. Washington, DC: Brookings Institution Press.

Bledstein, Burton J., and Robert D. Johnson, eds. 2001. *The Middling Sorts: Exploration in the History of the American Middle Class*. New York: Routledge.

Blumin, Stuart Mack. 1989. *The Emergence of the Middle Class: Social Experience in the American City, 1760–1900*. Cambridge: Cambridge University Press.

Bourdieu, Pierre. 1977. *Outline of a Theory of Practice*. Translated by Richard Nice. New York: Cambridge University Press.

———. 1984. *Distinction: A Social Critique of the Judgement of Taste*. Translated by Richard Nice. Cambridge, MA: Harvard University Press.

———. 1990. "Appendix: The Kabyle House or the World Reversed." In *The Logic of Practice*, translated by Richard Nice, pp. 271–83. Palo Alto: Stanford University Press.

Bourgois, Philippe. 2003 [1996]. *In Search of Respect: Selling Crack in El Barrio*. Cambridge: Cambridge University Press.

Bradsher, Keith. 1998. "Automakers Seek to Make Light Trucks Safer in Crashes." *New York Times*, 22 March, pp. D1, D4.

———. 1999a. "Ford Adds Bars to Make a Large Sport Vehicle Safer." *New York Times*, 27 February, p. A8.

———. 1999b. "Study Cites Fatal Design of Sport Utility Vehicles." *New York Times*, 2 March, p. A12.

———. 1999c. "Some Worry Sport Utilities Are Too Much for New York." *New York Times*, 2 July, pp. A1, B6.

———. 1999d. "With Sport Utility Vehicles More Popular, Overall Automobile Fuel Economy Continues to Fall." *New York Times*, 5 October, p. A22.

———. 2000a. "Heavy Traffic: No Wonder S.U.V.'s Are Called Light Trucks." *New York Times*, 16 January, p. A4.

———. 2000b. "Auto Industry May Ease Safety-Ratings Stance: Opposition to Rollover Rankings at Issue." *New York Times*, 19 September, p. C16.

———. 2002. *High and Mighty: SUVs—The World's Most Dangerous Vehicles and How They Got That Way*. New York: Public Affairs.

Brash, Julian. 2011. *Bloomberg's New York: Class and Governance in the Luxury City*. Athens: University of Georgia Press.

Brenner, Neil. 2004. "Urban Governance and the Production of New State Spaces in Western Europe, 1960–2000." *Review of International Political Economy* 11 (3): 447–88.

Brodkin, Karen. 1998. *How Jews Became White Folks and What That Says about Race in America*. New Brunswick, NJ: Rutgers University Press.

Cahn, Peter S. 2008. "Consuming Class: Multilevel Marketers in Neoliberal Mexico." *Cultural Anthropology* 23 (3): 429–52.

Caldeira, Teresa P. R. 2000. *City of Walls: Crime, Segregation, and Citizenship in São Paulo*. Berkeley: University of California Press.

Caro, Robert A. 1975. *The Power Broker: Robert Moses and the Fall of New York*. New York: Random House.

"Catching Up With S.U.V.'s." 1998. *New York Times*, 17 November, p. A24.

Chesluk, Benjamin. 2004. "'Visible Signs of a City Out of Control': Community Policing in New York City." *Cultural Anthropology* 19 (2): 250–75.

Chiles, Nick. 1997. "Jersey Schools Lack Diversity from the Top." *Star-Ledger* (Newark, NJ), 16 March, p. A1.

Chin, Elizabeth. 2001. *Purchasing Power: Black Kids and American Consumer Culture*. Minneapolis: University of Minnesota Press.

"Cleaning Up the Big Cars." 1999. *New York Times*, 7 May, p. A26

Cobb, James. 1999. "When Two Would Be a Crowd: The Case of the Missing S.U.V." *New York Times,* 2 April, p. F1.

Cohen, Lizabeth. 2003. *A Consumer's Republic: The Politics of Mass Consumption in Postwar America.* New York: Vintage Books.

Colapietro, Vincent M. 1989. *Peirce's Approach to the Self: A Semiotic Perspective on Human Subjectivity.* Albany: State University of New York Press.

Collier, Stephen J. 2011. *Post-Soviet Social: Neoliberalism, Social Modernity, Biopolitics.* Princeton, NJ: Princeton University Press.

Colomina, Beatriz. 2007. *Domesticity at War.* Cambridge, MA: MIT Press.

Colomina, Beatriz, AnnMarie Brennan, and Jeannie Kim, eds. 2004. *Cold War Hothouses: Inventing Postwar Culture from Cockpit to Playboy.* New York: Princeton Architectural Press.

Comaroff, Jean, and John L. Comaroff. 1999. "Occult Economies and the Violence of Abstraction: Notes from the South African Postcolony." *American Ethnologist* 26 (2): 279–303.

———. 2000. "Millennial Capitalism: First Thoughts on a Second Coming." *Public Culture* 12 (2): 291–343.

Connolly, William E. 1991. *Identity/Difference: Democratic Negotiations of Political Paradox.* Ithaca, NY: Cornell University Press.

Coontz, Stephanie. 1992. *The Way We Never Were: American Families and the Nostalgia Trap.* New York: Basic Books.

Daniel, E. Valentine. 1996. *Charred Lullabies: Chapters in an Anthropology of Violence.* Princeton, NJ: Princeton University Press.

Danielson, Michael N. 1976. *The Politics of Exclusion.* New York: Columbia University Press.

Davidoff, Paul, and Mary E. Brooks. 1976. "Zoning Out the Poor." In *Suburbia: The American Dream and Dilemma,* edited by Philip Dolce, pp. 135–66. New York: Anchor Books.

Davidson, Elsa. 2008. "Marketing the Self: The Politics of Aspiration among Middle-Class Silicon Valley Youth." *Environment and Planning A* 40 (12): 2814–30.

———. 2011. *The Burdens of Aspiration: Schools, Youth, and Success in the Divided Socials Worlds of Silicon Valley.* New York: NYU Press.

Davis, Angela. 1997. "Angela Davis: Reflections on Race, Class, and Gender in the USA." Interview by Lisa Lowe. In *The Politics of Culture in the Shadow of Capital,* edited by L. Lowe and D. Lloyd, pp. 303–23. Durham, NC: Duke University Press.

Davis, Mike. 1992. "Fortress Los Angeles: The Militarization of Urban Space." In *Variations on a Theme Park: The New American City and the End of Public Space,* edited by Michael Sorkin, pp. 154–80. New York: Hill and Yang.

Debord, Guy. 1995 [1967]. *The Society of the Spectacle.* New York: Zone Books.

de Certeau, Michel. 1984. *The Practice of Everyday Life*. Berkeley: University of California Press.

de Koning, Anouk. 2009. *Global Dreams: Class, Gender, and Public Space in Cosmopolitan Cairo*. Cairo: American University in Cairo Press.

Derrida, Jacques. 1988. "Signature Event Context." In *Limited Inc.*, pp. 1–23. Evanston, IL: Northwestern University Press.

di Leonardo, Micaela. 1984. *The Varieties of Ethnic Experience: Kinship, Class, and Gender among California Italian-Americans*. Ithaca, NY: Cornell University Press.

Dill, Bonnie Thornton. 1994. *Across the Boundaries of Race and Class: An Exploration of Work and Family among Black Female Domestic Servants*. New York: Garland Publishing.

Dobriner, William Mann. 1963. *Class in Suburbia*. Englewood Cliffs, NJ: Prentice-Hall.

Douglas, Mary. 1966. *Purity and Danger: An Analysis of the Concepts of Pollution and Taboo*. London: Routledge.

———. 1975. "Jokes." In *Implicit Meanings: Essays in Anthropology*, pp. 90–114. London: Routledge & Kegan Paul.

———. 1985. *Risk and Acceptability according to the Social Sciences*. New York: Russell Sage Foundation.

Douglas, Mary, and Aaron Wildavsky. 1982. *Risk and Culture: An Essay on the Selection of Technical and Environmental Dangers*. Berkeley: University of California Press.

Duncan, Nancy G., and James S. Duncan. 1997. "Deep Suburban Irony: The Perils of Democracy in Westchester County, New York." In *Visions of Suburbia*, edited by Roger Silverstone, pp. 161–79. New York: Routledge.

Dunham-Jones, Ellen, and June Williamson. 2009. *Retrofitting Suburbia: Urban Design Solutions for Redesigning Suburbs*. Hoboken, NJ: John Wiley & Sons.

Dreyfus, Hubert L. 1991. *Being-in-the-World: A Commentary on Heidegger's Being and Time. Division I*. Cambridge, MA: MIT Press.

Eckert, Penelope. 1989. *Jocks & Burnouts: Social Categories and Identity in the High School*. New York: Teachers College Press.

Ehrenreich, Barbara. 1989. *Fear of Falling: The Inner Life of the Middle Class*. New York: HarperPerennial.

Ehrenreich, Barbara, and John Ehrenreich. 1979. "The Professional-Managerial Class." In *Between Labor and Capital*, edited by Pat Walker, pp. 5–45. Boston: South End Press.

Featherstone, Mike. 2004. "Automobilities: An Introduction." *Theory, Culture & Society* 21 (4/5): 1–24.

Fehérváry, Krisztina. 2012. "The Postsocialist Middle Classes and the New 'Family House' in Hungary." In *The Global Middle Classes: Theorizing through Ethnography,* edited by Rachel Heiman, Carla Freeman, and Mark Liechty, pp. 117–44. Santa Fe, NM: School for Advanced Research Press.

Ferguson, James. 2009. "The Uses of Neoliberalism." *Antipode* 41 (1): 166–84.

Ferguson, James, and Akhil Gupta. 2002. "Spatializing States: Toward an Ethnography of Neoliberal Governmentality." *American Ethnologist* 29 (4): 981–1002.

Fernandes, Leela. 2006. *India's New Middle Class: Democratic Politics in an Era of Economic Reform.* Minneapolis: University of Minnesota Press.

Fernandez, James W., ed. 1991. *Beyond Metaphor: The Theory of Tropes in Anthropology.* Stanford, CA: Stanford University Press.

Fine, Michelle. 1991. *Framing Dropouts: Notes on the Politics of an Urban Public High School.* Albany, NY: SUNY Press.

Finn, Janet. 1998. *Tracing the Veins: Of Copper, Culture, and Community from Butte to Chuquicamata.* Berkeley: University of California Press.

———. 2001. "Text and Turbulence: Representing Adolescence as Pathology in the Human Services." *Childhood* 8 (May): 167–91.

Finn, Janet, and Lynn Nybell. 2001. "Introduction: Capitalizing on Concern: The Making of Troubled Children and Troubling Youth in Late Capitalism." *Childhood* 8 (May): 139–45.

Fishman, Robert. 1987. *Bourgeois Utopias: The Rise and Fall of Suburbia.* New York: Basic Books.

———. 1990. "Megalopolis Unbound." *Wilson Quarterly* 14 (Winter): 25–48.

———, ed. 2000. *The American Planning Tradition: Culture and Policy.* Washington, DC: Woodrow Wilson Center Press.

Flink, James. J. 1975. *The Car Culture.* Cambridge, MA: MIT Press.

Fogelson, Robert M. 2005. *Bourgeois Nightmares: Suburbia, 1870–1930.* New Haven, CT: Yale University Press.

Foley, Douglas E. 1990. *Capitalist Culture: Deep in the Heart of Tejas.* Philadelphia: University of Pennsylvania Press.

Fong, Timothy P. 1994. *The First Suburban Chinatown: The Remaking of Monterey Park, California.* Philadelphia, PA: Temple University Press.

Foucault, Michel. 1972. *The Archaeology of Knowledge & The Discourse on Language.* New York: Pantheon Books.

———. 1978. *The History of Sexuality.* Vol. 1, *An Introduction.* New York: Vintage Books.

———. 1979. *Discipline and Punish: The Birth of the Prison.* New York: Vintage Books.

———. 1984a. "What Is Enlightenment?" In *The Foucault Reader,* edited by Paul Rabinow, pp. 32–50. New York: Pantheon.

———. 1984b. "What Is an Author?" In *The Foucault Reader,* edited by Paul Rabinow, pp. 101–20. New York: Pantheon.

Frank, Robert H. 2007. *Falling Behind: How Rising Inequality Harms the Middle Class.* Berkeley: University of California Press.

Frankenberg, Ruth. 1993. *White Women, Race Matters: The Social Construction of Whiteness.* Minneapolis: University of Minnesota Press.

Freeman, Carla. 2007. "The 'Reputation' of Neoliberalism." *American Ethnologist* 34 (2): 252–67.

Frug, Gerald E. 1999. *City Making: Building Communities without Building Walls.* Princeton, NJ: Princeton University Press.

Frykman, Jonas, and Orvar Löfgren. 1987. *Culture Builders: A Historical Anthropology of Middle-Class Life.* New Brunswick, NJ: Rutgers University Press.

Fullilove, Mindy Thompson. 2004. *Root Shock: How Tearing Up City Neighborhoods Hurts America, and What We Can Do about It.* New York: Ballantine Books.

Gaines, Donna. 1990. *Teenage Wasteland: Suburbia's Dead End Kids.* Chicago: University of Chicago Press.

Gans, Herbert J. 1962. *The Urban Villagers: Group and Class in the Life of Italian-Americans.* New York: Free Press.

———. 1967. *The Levittowners: Ways of Life and Politics in a New Suburban Community.* New York: Columbia University Press.

Garreau, Joel. 1991. *Edge City: Life on the New Frontier.* New York: Doubleday.

Geertz, Clifford. 1993. "Thick Description: Toward an Interpretive Theory of Culture." In *The Interpretation of Cultures,* pp. 3–30. New York: Basic Books.

Giddens, Anthony. 1979. *Central Problems in Social Theory: Action, Structure and Contradiction in Social Analysis.* Berkeley: University of California Press.

Gillespie, Angus Kress, and Michael Aaron Rockland. 1989. *Looking for America on the New Jersey Turnpike.* New Brunswick, NJ: Rutgers University Press.

Gladwell, Malcolm. 2004. "Big and Bad: How the S.U.V. Ran Over Automotive Safety." *New Yorker* 79 (42): 28–33.

Gluckman, Max. 1963. "Gossip and Scandal." *Current Anthropology* 4 (June): 307–16.

Goffman, Erving. 1959. *The Presentation of Self in Everyday Life.* New York: Anchor Books.

———. 1981. *Forms of Talk.* Philadelphia: University of Pennsylvania Press.

Goldstein, Donna M. 2003. *Laughter Out of Place: Race, Class, Violence, and Sexuality in a Rio Shantytown.* Berkeley: University of California Press.

Gramsci, Antonio. 1971. *Selections from the Prison Notebooks,* edited and translated by Quintin Hoare and Geoffrey Nowell Smith. New York: International Publishers.

Greenhouse, Carol J., Barbara Yngvesson, and David M. Engel. 1994. *Law and Community in Three American Towns.* Ithaca, NY: Cornell University Press.

Gregory, Steven. 1998. *Black Corona: Race and the Politics of Place in an Urban Community*. Princeton, NJ: Princeton University Press.

Guano, Emanuela. 2002. "Spectacles of Modernity: Transnational Imagination and Local Hegemonies in Neoliberal Buenos Aires." *Cultural Anthropology* 17 (2): 181–209.

———. 2003. "A Color for the Modern Nation: The Discourse on Class, Race and Education in the *Porteño* Middle Class." *Journal of Latin American Anthropology* 8 (1): 148–71.

Gutman, Marta, and Ning de Coninck-Smith, eds. 2008. *Designing Modern Childhoods: History, Space, and the Material Culture of Children*. New Brunswick, NJ: Rutgers University Press.

Haley, Michael C. 1993. "A Peircian 'Play of Musement': Pablo Picasso's Bull's Head as Poetic Metaphor." In *The Peirce Seminar Papers: An Annual of Semiotic Analysis*, edited by Michael Shapiro, vol. 1, pp. 97–123. Providence, RI: Berg Publishers.

Hand, Susanne. 1997. "Making the Suburban State: Teenagers, Design, and Communities in New Jersey." In *Teenage New Jersey, 1941–1975*, edited by Kathryn Grover, pp. 13–36. Newark: New Jersey Historical Society.

Hansen, Karen Tranberg. 1989. *Distant Companions: Servants and Employers in Zambia, 1900–1985*. Ithaca, NY: Cornell University Press.

Hanson, Paul W. 2007. "Governmentality, Language Ideology, and the Production of Needs in Malagasy Conservation and Development." *Cultural Anthropology* 22 (2): 244–84.

Harden, Blaine. 2002. "Big, Bigger, Biggest: The Supersize Suburb . . . ." *New York Times*, 20 June, pp. F1, F12.

Hartigan, John, Jr. 1999. *Racial Situations: Class Predicaments of Whiteness in Detroit*. Princeton, NJ: Princeton University Press.

———. 2010. *What Can You Say?: America's National Conversation on Race*. Stanford, CA: Stanford University Press.

Harvey, David. 1990. *The Condition of Postmodernity*. Cambridge, MA: Blackwell.

———. 2005. *A Brief History of Neoliberalism*. New York: Oxford University Press.

Hayden, Dolores. 2003. *Building Suburbia: Green Fields and Urban Growth, 1820–2000*. New York: Vintage Books.

———. 2004. *A Field Guide to Sprawl*. New York: W. W. Norton.

Hebdige, Dick. 1979. *Subculture: The Meaning of Style*. New York: Routledge.

Hegel, G. W. F. 1977. *Phenomenology of Spirit*. Translated by A. V. Miller. Oxford: Oxford University Press.

Heiman, Rachel. 2001. "The Ironic Contradictions in the Discourse on Generation X, or How 'Slackers' Are Saving Capitalism." *Childhood* 8 (May): 274–92.

———. 2007. "The Last Days of Low-Density Living: Suburbs and the End of Oil." *Built Environment* 33 (2): 213–26.

Heiman, Rachel, Carla Freeman, and Mark Liechty, eds. 2012. *The Global Middle Classes: Theorizing through Ethnography*. Santa Fe, NM: School for Advanced Research Press.

Heiman, Rachel, Mark Liechty, and Carla Freeman. 2012. "Introduction: Charting an Anthropology of the Middle Classes." In *The Global Middle Classes: Theorizing through Ethnography*, edited by Rachel Heiman, Carla Freeman, and Mark Liechty, pp. 3–29. Santa Fe, NM: School for Advanced Research Press.

Heintz, James, Nancy Folbre, and the Center for Popular Economics. 2000. *The Ultimate Field Guide to the U.S. Economy: A Compact and Irreverent Guide to Economic Life in America*. New York: New Press.

Hill, Jane. 2008. *The Everyday Language of White Racism*. West Sussex, UK: Wiley-Blackwell.

Hirschfeld, Lawrence A. 1996. *Race in the Making: Cognition, Culture, and the Child's Construction of Human Kinds*. Cambridge, MA: MIT Press.

Ho, Karen. 2009. *Liquidated: An Ethnography of Wall Street*. Durham, NC: Duke University Press.

Hodgson, Godfrey. 1976. "The Ideology of the Liberal Consensus." In *America in Our Time: From World War II to Nixon—What Happened and Why*, pp. 67–98. New York: Doubleday.

Hondagneu-Sotelo, Pierret. 2001. *Doméstica: Immigrant Workers Cleaning and Caring in the Shadows of Affluence*. Berkeley: University of California Press.

Hoover, Herbert. 1989. *American Individualism: The Challenge to Liberty*. West Branch, IA: Herbert Hoover Library Association.

Ivy, Marilyn. 1995. *Discourses of the Vanishing: Modernity, Phantasm, Japan*. Chicago: University of Chicago Press.

Jackson, Kenneth T. 1985. *Crabgrass Frontier: The Suburbanization of the United States*. New York: Oxford University Press.

Jacobs, Jane. 1961. *The Death and Life of Great American Cities*. New York: Vintage Books.

Jacobson, Lisa. 1999. "Crossing the Boundaries of Dependency: Child Consumers and Mass Marketing, 1910–1940." Paper presented at the American Studies Association Annual Meeting, Montreal, 28 October.

———. 2004. *Raising Consumers: Children and the American Mass Market in the Early Twentieth Century*. New York: Columbia University Press.

Jain, Sarah S. Lochlann. 2002. "Urban Errands: The Means of Mobility." *Journal of Consumer Culture* 2 (3): 419–38.

———. 2004. "Dangerous Instrumentality: The Bystander as Subject in Automobility." *Cultural Anthropology* 19 (1): 61–94.

Jameson, Fredric. 1991. *Postmodernism, or The Cultural Logic of Late Capitalism*. Durham, NC: Duke University Press.

Kalita, S. Mitra. 2003. *Suburban Sahibs: Three Immigrant Families and Their Passage from India to America*. New Brunswick, NJ: Rutgers University Press.

Katz, Bruce, and Jennifer Bradley. 1999. "Divided We Sprawl." *Atlantic Monthly* 284 (December): 26, 28, 30, 38–42.

Katz, Cindi. 2001. "The State Goes Home: Local Hypervigilance and the Global Retreat from Social Reproduction." *Social Justice* 28 (3): 47–56.

———. 2008. "Childhood as Spectacle: Relays of Anxiety and the Reconfiguration of the Child." *Cultural Geographies* 15:5–17.

———. 2012. "Just Managing: American Parenthood in Insecure Times." In *The Global Middle Classes: Theorizing through Ethnography*, edited by Rachel Heiman, Carla Freeman, and Mark Liechty, pp. 169–87. Santa Fe, NM: School for Advanced Research Press.

Keats, John. 1958. *The Insolent Chariots*. Philadelphia: J. B. Lippincott Company.

Kenny, Lorraine Delia. 2000. *Daughters of Suburbia: Growing Up White, Middle Class, and Female*. New Brunswick, NJ: Rutgers University Press.

Kirp, David L., John P. Dwyer, and Larry A. Rosenthal. 1995. *Our Town: Race, Housing, and the Soul of Suburbia*. New Brunswick, NJ: Rutgers University Press.

Kladko, Brian. 1998. "25 School Districts Sue State; Middle-Class Towns Claim Property Tax Rates Are Too High; They Want More Aid." *Asbury Park (NJ) Press*, 21 April, pp. A1, A8.

Lacy, Karyn R. 2007. *Blue-Chip Black: Race, Class, and Status in the New Black Middle Class*. Berkeley: University of California Press.

Lakoff, George, and Mark Johnson. 1980. *Metaphors We Live By*. Chicago: University of Chicago Press.

Lareau, Annette. 2003. *Unequal Childhoods: Class, Race, and Family Life*. Berkeley: University of California Press.

Latour, Bruno. 2005. *Reassembling the Social: An Introduction to Actor-Network-Theory*. Oxford: Oxford University Press.

Lefebvre, Henri. 1991 [1974]. *The Production of Space*. Oxford: Blackwell.

Liechty, Mark. 2003. *Suitably Modern: Making Middle-Class Culture in a New Consumer Society*. Princeton, NJ: Princeton University Press.

———. 2012. "Middle-Class Déjà Vu: Conditions of Possibility, from Victorian England to Contemporary Katmandu." In *The Global Middle Classes: Theorizing through Ethnography*, edited by Rachel Heiman, Carla Freeman, and Mark Liechty, pp. 271–99. Santa Fe, NM: School for Advanced Research Press.

Lipietz, Alain. 1993. "From Althusserianism to 'Regulation Theory.'" In *The Althusserian Legacy*, edited by E. Ann Kaplan and Michael Sprinker, pp. 99–138. New York: Verso.

Lipsitz, George. 1998. *The Possessive Investment in Whiteness: How White People Profit from Identity Politics.* Philadelphia: Temple University Press.

———. 2006. "Learning from New Orleans: The Social Warrant of Hostile Privatism and Competitive Consumer Citizenship." *Cultural Anthropology* 21 (3): 451–68.

LiPuma, Edward, and Sarah Keene Meltzoff. 1997. "The Crosscurrents of Ethnicity and Class in the Construction of Public Policy." *American Ethnologist* 24 (1): 114–31.

Locke, John. 1980 [1690]. *Second Treatise of Government,* edited by C.B. Macpherson. Indianapolis: Hackett Publishing Company.

Lomnitz, Claudio. 2003. "Times of Crisis: Historicity, Sacrifice, and the Spectacle of Debacle in Mexico City." *Public Culture* 15 (1): 127–47.

Low, Setha. 1996. "Spatializing Culture: The Social Production and Social Construction of Public Space in Costa Rica." *American Ethnologist* 23 (4): 861–79.

———. 2001. "The Edge and the Center: Gated Communities and the Discourse of Urban Fear." *American Anthropologist* 103 (March): 45–58.

———. 2003. *Behind the Gates: Life, Security, and the Pursuit of Happiness in Fortress America.* New York: Routledge.

Lowe, Lisa, and David Lloyd. 1997. "Introduction." In *The Politics of Culture in the Shadow of Capital,* edited by Lisa Lowe and David Lloyd, pp. 1–32. Durham, NC: Duke University Press.

Lustig, R. Jeffrey. 1986. *Corporate Liberalism: The Origins of Modern American Political Theory, 1890–1920.* Berkeley: University of California Press.

Lutz, Catherine, and Anne Lutz Fernandez. 2010. *Carjacked: The Culture of the Automobile & Its Effects on Our Lives.* New York: Palgrave Macmillan.

Lynd Robert S., and Helen Merrell Lynd. 1929. *Middletown: A Study in Modern American Culture.* New York: Harcourt, Brace & World, Inc.

Mack, Arien, ed. 2005. "Busyness." Special issue, *Social Research* 72, no. 2 (Summer).

MacLeod, Jay. 1995. *Ain't No Makin' It: Aspirations and Attainment in a Low-Income Neighborhood.* Boulder, CO: Westview Press.

"Madam of Bordello in Mansion Is Given Probation." 1999. *New York Times,* 12 May, p. B4.

Marcus, George E., and Michael M.J. Fisher. 1986. *Anthropology as Cultural Critique: An Experimental Moment in the Human Sciences.* Chicago: University of Chicago Press.

"Marge Simpson in 'Screaming Yellow Honkers.'" 1999. *The Simpsons,* Episode no. 218, Code AABF10, 21 February.

Martin, Emily. 1987. *The Woman in the Body: A Cultural Analysis of Reproduction.* Boston: Beacon Press.

Massey, Doreen. 1994. *Space, Place, and Gender*. Minneapolis: University of Minnesota Press.

McKenzie, Evan. 1994. *Privatopia: Homeowner Associations and the Rise of Residential Private Government*. New Haven, CT: Yale University Press.

McLaren, Peter. 1989. *Life in Schools: An Introduction to Critical Pedagogy*. New York: Longman.

McRobbie, Angela. 1991. *Feminism and Youth Culture: From "Jackie" to "Just Seventeen."* Boston: Unwin Hyman.

Medin, Doug L. 1989. "Concepts and Conceptual Structure." *American Psychologist* 44 (December): 1469–81.

Mehta, Uday. 1990. "Liberal Strategies of Exclusion." *Politics and Society* 18:427–54.

Miller, Daniel, ed. 2001. *Car Cultures*. Oxford: Berg.

Mills, C. Wright. 1951. *White Collar: The American Middle Classes*. Oxford: Oxford University Press.

Mitchell, Don. 2005. "The S.U.V. Model of Citizenship: Floating Bubbles, Buffer Zones, and the Rise of the 'Purely Atomic' Individual." *Political Geography* 24 (1): 77–100.

Mitchell, Timothy. 2011. *Carbon Democracy: Political Power in the Age of Oil*. New York: Verso.

Moore, Donald S. 1998. "Subaltern Struggles and the Politics of Place: Remapping Resistance in Zimbabwe's Eastern Highlands." *Cultural Anthropology* 13 (3): 344–81.

Mumford, Lewis. 1953. *The Highway and the City*. New York: Harcourt, Brace & World.

Nader, Laura. 1969. "Up the Anthropologist—Perspectives Gained from Studying Up." In *Reinventing Anthropology*, edited by Dell Hymes, pp. 284–311. Ann Arbor: University of Michigan Press.

Nash, June. 1994. "Global Integration and Subsistence Insecurity." *American Anthropologist* 96 (1): 7–30.

Newman, Katherine S. 1988. *Falling from Grace: The Experience of Downward Mobility in the American Middle Class*. New York: Vintage Books.

———. 1993. *Declining Fortunes: The Withering of the American Dream*. New York: Basic Books.

Nicolaides, Becky M. 2002. *My Blue Heaven: Life and Politics in the Working-Class Suburbs of Los Angeles, 1920–1965*. Chicago: University of Chicago Press.

Nietzsche, Friedrich. 1982. "Twilight of the Idols." In *The Portable Nietzsche*, edited and translated by Walter Kaufmann. New York: Penguin Books.

Nybell, Lynn. 2001. "Meltdowns and Containments: Constructions of Children at Risk as Complex Systems." *Childhood* 8 (May): 213–50.

Nybell, Lynn M., Jeffrey J. Shook, and Janet L. Finn, eds. 2009. *Childhood, Youth, and Social Work in Transformation*. New York: Columbia University Press.

O'Dougherty, Maureen. 2002. *Consumption Intensified: The Politics of Middle-Class Daily Life in Brazil*. Durham, NC: Duke University Press.

Ong, Aihwa. 1988. "The Production of Possession: Spirits and the Multinational Corporation in Malaysia." *American Ethnologist* 15 (1): 28–42.

———. 1999. *Flexible Citizenship: The Cultural Logics of Transnationality*. Durham, NC: Duke University Press.

———. 2006. *Neoliberalism as Exception: Mutations in Citizenship and Sovereignty*. Durham, NC: Duke University Press.

Orfield, Myron. 1997. *Metropolitics: A Regional Agenda for Community and Stability*. Washington, DC: Brookings Institution Press.

Ortner, Sherry B. 1973. "On Key Symbols." *American Anthropologist*, 75 (October): 1338–46.

———. 1998a. "Identities: The Hidden Life of Class." *Journal of Anthropological Research* 54 (Spring): 1–17.

———. 1998b "Generation X: Anthropology in a Media-Saturated World." *Cultural Anthropology* 13 (August): 414–46.

———. 2003. *New Jersey Dreaming: Capital, Culture, and the Class of '58*. Durham, NC: Duke University Press.

Parreñas, Rhacel Salazar. 2001. *Servants of Globalization: Women, Migration, and Domestic Work*. Stanford, CA: Stanford University Press.

Patico, Jennifer. 2008. *Consumption and Social Change in a Post-Soviet Middle Class*. Stanford, CA: Stanford University Press.

Peck, Jamie, and Adam Tickell. 2002. "Neoliberalizing Space." *Antipode* 34 (3): 380–404.

Peirce, Charles Sanders. 1955. *Philosophical Writings of Peirce*, edited by Justus Buchler. New York: Dover Publications.

Peréz, Gina. 2004. *The Near Northwest Side Story: Migration, Displacement, & Puerto Rican Families*. Berkeley: University of California Press.

———. 2009. "JROTC and Latino/a Youth in Neoliberal Cities." In *Rethinking America: The Imperial Homeland in the 21st Century*, edited by Jeff Maskovsky and Ida Susser, pp. 31–48. Boulder, CO: Paradigm Publishers.

Perin, Constance. 1977. *Everything in Its Place: Social Order and Land Use in America*. Princeton, NJ: Princeton University Press.

Pfeil, Fred. 1990. "'Makin' Flippy-Floppy': Postmodernism and the Baby-Boom PMC." In *Another Tale to Tell: Politics and Narrative in Postmodern Culture*, pp. 97–123. London: Verso.

Pollan, Michael. 1991. "Why Mow?" In *Second Nature: A Gardener's Education*, pp. 54–65. New York: Dell Publishing.

Poulantzas, Nicos. 1978. *Class in Contemporary Society*. London: Verso.

Pugh, Allison J. 2009. *Longing and Belonging: Parents, Children, and Consumer Culture*. Berkeley: University of California Press.

Quart, Alissa. 2003. *Branded: The Buying and Selling of Teenagers*. New York: Perseus Publishing.

Rabinow, Paul. 1984. "Introduction." In *The Foucault Reader,* edited by Paul Rabinow, pp. 3–29. New York: Pantheon.

Rieder, Jonathan. 1985. *Canarsie: The Jews and Italians of Brooklyn against Liberalism*. Cambridge, MA: Harvard University Press.

Roediger, David R. 1991. *The Wages of Whiteness: Race and the Making of the American Working Class*. New York: Verso.

———. 1998. "What to Make of *Wiggers:* A Work in Progress." In *Generations of Youth: Youth Cultures and History in Twentieth-Century America,* edited by Joe Austin and Michael Nevin Willard, pp. 358–66. New York: NYU Press.

Rollins, Judith. 1985. *Between Women: Domestics and Their Employers*. Philadelphia: Temple University Press.

Rome, Adam. 2001. *The Bulldozer in the Countryside: Suburban Sprawl and the Rise of American Environmentalism*. Cambridge: Cambridge University Press.

Romero, Mary. 1992. *Maid in the U.S.A.* New York: Routledge.

Rose, Nikolas. 1996a. "Governing 'Advanced' Liberal Democracies." In *Foucault and Political Reason: Liberalism, Neo-Liberalism and Rationalities of Government,* edited by Andrew Barry, Thomas Osborn, and Nikolas Rose, pp. 37–65. Chicago: University of Chicago Press.

———. 1996b. "The Death of the Social? Refiguring the Territory of Government." *Economy and Society* 25 (3): 327–56.

———. 1999. *Powers of Freedom: Reframing Political Thought*. Cambridge: Cambridge University Press.

Rose, Tricia. 1994. *Black Noise: Rap Music and Black Culture in Contemporary America*. Middletown, CT: Wesleyan University Press.

Ross, Andrew. 1999. *The Celebration Chronicles: Life, Liberty, and the Pursuit of Property Value in Disney's New Town*. New York: Ballantine Books.

Ross, Dorothy. 1984. "Liberalism." In *Encyclopedia of American Political History,* edited by Jack P. Greene, pp. 750–63. New York: Scribners.

Rouse, Roger. 1995. "Thinking through Transnationalism: Notes on the Cultural Politics of Class Relations in the Contemporary United States." *Public Culture* 7 (Spring): 353–402.

Ryan, Mary. 1981. *Cradle of the Middle Class: The Family in Oneida County, New York, 1790–1865*. Cambridge: Cambridge University Press.

Sacks, Karen Brodkin. 1989. "Toward a Unified Theory of Class, Race, and Gender." *American Ethnologist* 16 (August): 534–50.

Sapir, Edward. 1949. "The Unconscious Patterning of Society." In *Selected Writings of Edward Sapir*, edited by David Mandelbaum, pp. 544–59. Berkeley: University of California Press.

Scheper-Hughes, Nancy. 1993. *Death without Weeping: The Violence of Everyday Life in Brazil*. Berkeley: University of California Press.

Schielke, Samuli. 2012. "Living in the Future Tense: Aspiring for World and Class in Provincial Egypt." In *The Global Middle Classes: Theorizing through Ethnography*, edited by Rachel Heiman, Carla Freeman, and Mark Liechty, pp. 31–56. Santa Fe, NM: School for Advanced Research Press.

Schor, Juliet B. 1998. *The Overspent American: Upscaling, Downshifting, and the New Consumer*. New York: Basic Books.

———. 2004. *Born to Buy: The Commercialized Child and the New Commercial Culture*. New York: Scribner.

Seremetakis, C. Nadia, ed. 1994. *The Senses Still: Perception and Memory as Material Culture in Modernity*. Boulder, CO: Westview Press.

Shapiro, Michael. 1983. "Peirce's Semeiotic." In *The Sense of Grammar: Language as Semeiotic*, pp. 25–72. Bloomington: Indiana University Press.

Sharpe, William, and Leonard Wallock. 1994. "Bold New City or Built Up 'Burb?: Redefining Contemporary Suburbia." *American Quarterly* 46 (March): 1–30.

Sherman, Rachel. 2007. *Class Acts: Service and Inequality in Luxury Hotels*. Berkeley: University of California Press.

Simmel, Georg. 1950. "The Stranger." In *The Sociology of Georg Simmel*, edited and translated by Kurt H. Wolff, pp. 402–8. New York: Free Press.

Smith, Andrea L. 2004. "Heteroglossia, 'Common Sense,' and Social Memory." *American Ethnologist* 31 (2): 251–69.

Smith, Neil. 1996. *The New Urban Frontier: Gentrification and the Revanchist City*. New York: Routledge.

Smith, Neil, and Peter Williams, eds. 1986. *Gentrification of the* City. Boston: Allen and Unwin.

Soja, Edward. 1992. "Inside Exopolis: Scenes from Orange County." In *Variations on a Theme Park: The New American City and the End of Public Space*, edited by Michael Sorkin, pp. 94–122. New York: Hill and Wang.

Spectorsky, A. C. 1955. *The Exurbanites*. New York: J. P. Lippincott Company.

Srivastava, Sanjay. 2012. "National Identity, Bedrooms, and Kitchens: Gated Communities and New Narratives of Space in India." In *The Global Middle Classes: Theorizing through Ethnography*, edited by Rachel Heiman, Carla Freeman, and Mark Liechty, pp. 57–84. Santa Fe, NM: School for Advanced Research Press.

Steinberg, Stephen. 1981. *The Ethnic Myth: Race, Ethnicity, and Class in America*. Boston: Beacon Press.

Steinmetz, George. 1994. "Regulation Theory, Post-Marxism, and the New Social Movements." *Comparative Study of Society and History* 36 (January): 176–212.

Stephens, Sharon. 1995. "Introduction: Children and the Politics of Culture in 'Late Capitalism.'" In *Children and the Politics of Culture*, edited by Sharon Stephens, pp. 3–48. Princeton, NJ: Princeton University Press.

Stewart, Kathleen. 1988. "Nostalgia—A Polemic." *Cultural Anthropology* 3 (August): 227–41.

———. 2007. *Ordinary Affects*. Durham, NC: Duke University Press.

Stewart, Susan. 1984. *On Longing: Narratives of the Miniature, the Gigantic, the Souvenir, the Collection*. Baltimore: Johns Hopkins University Press.

Stoler, Ann Laura. 1995. "Domestic Subversions and Children's Sexuality." In *Race and the Education of Desire: Foucault's History of Sexuality and the Colonial Order of Things*. Durham, NC: Duke University Press.

———. 1996. "A Sentimental Education: European Children and Native Servants in the Netherlands Indies." In *Fantasizing the Feminine: Sex and Death in Indonesia*, edited by Laurie Sears, pp.71–91. Durham, NC: Duke University Press.

Stoler, Ann Laura, and Karen Strassler. 2000. "Castings for the Colonial: Memory Work in 'New Order' Java." *Comparative Study of Society and History* 14 (January): 4–48.

Suarez, Ray. 1999. *The Old Neighborhood: What We Lost in the Great Suburban Migration, 1966–1999*. New York: Free Press.

Thompson, E. P. 1963. *The Making of the English Working Class*. London: Gollancz.

Tilton, Jennifer. 2010. *Dangerous or Endangered?: Race and the Politics of Youth in Urban America*. New York: New York University Press.

Toll, Seymour. 1969. *Zoned American*. New York: Grossman Publishers.

"Toward Cleaner S.U.V.s." 1999. *New York Times*, 20 February, p. A14.

Tsing, Anna Lowenhaupt. 2005. *Friction: An Ethnography of Global Connection*. Princeton, NJ: Princeton University Press.

Turner, Victor. 1967. *The Forest of Symbols: Aspects of Ndembu Ritual*. Ithaca, NY: Cornell University Press.

———. 1969. *Chihamba, the White Spirit: A Ritual Drama of the Ndembu*. Manchester, UK: Manchester University Press.

———. 1974. *Dramas, Fields, and Metaphors: Symbolic Action in Human Society*. Ithaca, NY: Cornell University Press.

Urry, John. 2004. "The 'System' of Automobility." *Theory, Culture & Society* 21 (4/5): 25–39.

Valentine, Gill, Tracey Skelton, and Deborah Chambers. 1998. "Cool Places: An Introduction to Youth and Youth Cultures." In *Cool Places: Geographies of*

Youth Culture, edited by Tracey Skelton and Gill Valentine, pp. 1–32. New York: Routledge.

Veblen, Thorstein. 1967 [1899]. *The Theory of the Leisure Class.* New York: Penguin Books.

von Schnitzler, Antina. 2008. "Citizenship Prepaid: Water, Calculability, and Techno-Politics in South Africa." *Journal of Southern African Studies* 34 (4): 899–917.

Wacquant, Löic J. D. 1991. "Making Class: The Middle Class(es) in Social Theory and Social Structure." In *Bringing Class Back In: Contemporary and Historical Perspectives,* edited by Scott G. McNall, Rhonda F. Levine, and Rick Fantasia, pp. 39–64. Boulder, CO: Westview Press.

Warner, Michael. 2002. *Publics and Counterpublics.* New York: Zone Books.

Watts, Michael J. 1992. "Space for Everything (A Commentary)." *Cultural Anthropology* 7 (1): 115–29.

West, Debra. 1998. "Suburbs' Mass-Market Mansions; Baby Boom Luxury: Huge Home, Often on a Tiny Lot." *New York Times,* 18 March, pp. B1, B6.

White, Luise. 2000. "Historicizing Rumor and Gossip." In *Speaking with Vampires: Rumor and History in Africa,* pp. 56–86. Berkeley: University of California Press.

Whyte, William H. 1956. *The Organization Man.* Philadelphia: University of Pennsylvania Press.

Wiese, Andrew. 2004. *Places of Their Own: African American Suburbanization in the Twentieth Century.* Chicago: University of Chicago Press.

Williams, Brett. 1988. *Upscaling Downtown: Stalled Gentrification in Washington, D.C.* Ithaca, NY: Cornell University Press.

———. 2004. *Debt for Sale: A Social History of the Credit Trap.* Philadelphia: University of Pennsylvania Press.

Williams, Raymond. 1973. *The Country and the City.* New York: Oxford University Press.

———. 1977. *Marxism and Literature.* New York: Oxford University Press.

Williamson, June. 2013. *Designing Suburban Futures: New Models from Build a Better Burb.* Washington, DC: Island Press.

Willis, Paul. 1977. *Learning to Labor: How Working Class Kids Get Working Class Jobs.* New York: Columbia University Press.

Wilson, William Julius. 1978. *The Declining Significance of Race.* Chicago: University of Chicago Press.

Wright, Erik Olin. 1989. "A General Framework for the Analysis of Class Structure." In *The Debate on Classes,* edited by Erik Olin Wright, pp. 3–43. New York: Verso.

Wright, Gwendolyn. 1981. *Building the Dream: A Social History of Housing in America.* Cambridge, MA: MIT Press.

Wrigley, Julia. 1995. *Other People's Children.* New York: Basic Books.

Yeh, Rihan. 2012. "A Middle-Class Public at Mexico's Northern Border." In *The Global Middle Classes: Theorizing through Ethnography,* edited by Rachel Heiman, Carla Freeman, and Mark Liechty, pp. 189–212. Santa Fe, NM: School for Advanced Research Press.

Zaloom, Caitlin. 2006. *Out of the Pits: Traders and Technology from Chicago to London.* Chicago: University of Chicago Press.

———. 2009. "The Spectacle of Wealth and Its Costs." *Social Psychology Quarterly* 72 (3): 203–5.

Zhang, Li. 2010. *In Search of Paradise: Middle-Class Living in a Chinese Metropolis.* Ithaca, NY: Cornell University Press.

Zukin, Sharon. 1987. "Gentrification: Culture and Capital in the Urban Core." *Annual Review of Sociology* 13 (August): 129–47.

Index